Contradictory Lives

Contradictory Lives

BAUL WOMEN IN INDIA AND BANGLADESH

Lisa I. Knight

OXFORD
UNIVERSITY PRESS

OXFORD
UNIVERSITY PRESS

Oxford University Press is a department of the University of Oxford.
It furthers the University's objective of excellence in research, scholarship,
and education by publishing worldwide.

Oxford   New York
Auckland   Cape Town   Dar es Salaam   Hong Kong   Karachi
Kuala Lumpur   Madrid   Melbourne   Mexico City   Nairobi
New Delhi   Shanghai   Taipei   Toronto

With offices in
Argentina   Austria   Brazil   Chile   Czech Republic   France   Greece
Guatemala   Hungary   Italy   Japan   Poland   Portugal   Singapore
South Korea   Switzerland   Thailand   Turkey   Ukraine   Vietnam

Oxford is a registered trade mark of Oxford University Press
in the UK and certain other countries.

Published in the United States of America by
Oxford University Press
198 Madison Avenue, New York, NY 10016

Library of Congress Cataloging-in-Publication Data
Knight, Lisa I.
Contradictory lives : Baul women in India and Bangladesh / Lisa I. Knight.
p.   cm.
Includes bibliographical references and index.
ISBN 978-0-19-977354-1 (hardcover); 978-0-19-939684-9 (paperback)
1. Baul women—Religious life—India—West Bengal.   2. West Bengal (India)—
Religious life and customs.   3. Baul women—Religious life—Bangladesh.
4. Bangladesh—Religious life and customs.   5. Identity (Psychology)—
Religious aspects—Bauls.   I. Title.
BL1284.832.W4K65 2011
204'.22082095414—dc22   2010041717

To Ed and Stefan,
for sharing in the journey

ACKNOWLEDGMENTS

This book could not have been completed without the generous support of certain institutions, teachers, family, and friends. I am particularly indebted to the many women and men who patiently answered my endless and wandering questions and were willing to share a bit of themselves. Some of their names are in the pages of this book, but there are others who are unnamed who have also contributed immensely. Although my aim has been to have this book be driven by their concerns and perspectives, I bear complete responsibility for the final result.

The research on which this book is based was funded by Fulbright in 1998–99 and in 2000 for fieldwork in India and by the American Institute of Bangladesh Studies during 1999 and again in 2000 for fieldwork in Bangladesh. Fulbright personnel gave me many kinds of assistance at various points in my research. In Kolkata (Calcutta), Uma Das Gupta of the Fulbright Foundation provided me with helpful conversations and valuable contacts in Santiniketan early in my work. Fulbright also established my affiliation with Visva-Bharati University in Santiniketan, which provided me with a large network of scholars who kindly assisted me in numerous ways, both academic and personal. My fieldwork in Bangladesh was diffused over a large area of the country, and the personnel of the American Institute of Bangladesh Studies in Dhaka assisted greatly in making my numerous travels more comfortable. I am especially indebted to Mizanur Rahman Shelley, who always seemed to provide me with ideal contacts in each new region I explored.

I would like to thank Furman University for the financial support and sabbatical that allowed me to return to India and write a chapter on songs. For the support and encouragement I have received from my colleagues in the Religion Department and the Asian Studies Department at Furman I am very grateful. I wish to also thank Suresh Muthukrishnan for his work in creating a map for this book.

My academic life was fostered at Syracuse University, and I owe many people my sincere appreciation for sharing their knowledge and advice with me, several of whom encouraged me in ways more profound than just academic. I can find no words to describe my gratitude to my advisor, Susan S. Wadley, who was with me on many of my most uncertain moments in this journey. She read through several drafts and offered me critical suggestions and encouragement. Her advice and her caring nature have been remarkable. Ann Grodzins Gold has given very close and critical readings of my work and has posed invaluable questions and pushed my analysis further. John Burdick gave me many words of encouragement throughout my time at Syracuse and thoughtfully and eloquently proposed several avenues for future thought. I am grateful also to Sudipta Sen, whose sharp wit and keen insight offered many valuable topics to think about. Tazim Kassam gave a close and immensely helpful reading of my work. Hans Buechler posed thoughtful and engaging questions early on as I was working through my research proposal.

In India and Bangladesh, several professionals, colleagues, and friends contributed to helping my project and making my life there much more comfortable. I am indebted to Ashim Kumar Adhikary of Visva-Bharati, who offered many interesting insights and words of encouragement as I carried out my research. Sasanka Sekhar Pal, who with his family opened up his home to me during my first visit to Santiniketan in 1997, also contributed greatly to my understanding of Bauls and Baul women in the area. My gratitude goes to both these professors and their families for their help and warm hospitality. I am also grateful for the help and friendship of Kirsty Milward, Rahul Bose, Jeanne Openshaw, Hita Brata (Bachoo-da) Roy, H. K. S. Arefeen, Amin Hasan Kazi, Sonia Nishat Amin, Soumyo Chakrabarty, Kumkum and Ranjit Bhattacharya, Rachel McDermott, Donna Wulff, Gerry Forbes, Mandira Bhaduri, Hena Basu, Trina Purahit Roy, Dilip Ghosh and family, Manila Chowdhury, Feroz Ahmad, Mohammed Tanjul Ahmad, Rafiq Miya, Munibor Sarkar, Mujib Sarkar, and Lolan Mohammed. I extend a special thank you to Parvathy Baul and Ravi Gopalan Nair who created the woodcut that appears on the book cover. There are many others who contributed in great and small ways; all of them are significant, and I am grateful.

Other members of the academic community contributed in important ways to this project. Kalyani Menon was always willing to read whatever I sent her and consistently gave helpful comments and encouragement; Manan Ahmed kindly shared his expertise; Laura Ring pointed me in some helpful directions; Sandra Comstock helped me brainstorm during the regular work strikes or *hartāl*s in Bangladesh (and, with Hugo Moreno, made life in Dhaka enjoyable). I wish to thank Cynthia Read and Lisbeth Redfield of Oxford University Press for all their help along this path of publication. My anonymous readers for Oxford gave me valuable and very encouraging feedback, and I appreciate the time they took to carefully read my work. I would also like to thank Meena Khandelwal, Sondra Hausner, Joyce Flueckiger, and Martha Selby for their many insightful suggestions. An earlier version of chapter 6 appeared as "Renouncing Expectations: Single Baul Women Renouncers and the Value of Being a Wife," in Women's Renunciation in South Asia: Nuns, Yoginis, Saints, and Singers, edited by Meena Khandelwal, Sondra L. Hausner, and Ann Grodzins Gold, copyright 2006 Palgrave Macmillan and reproduced with kind permission of Palgrave Macmillan. Outside the academic community, I wish to mention Heidi MacKinnon, who left us much too early. Her infectious excitement and curiosity pushed my analysis further, as she kept asking me to explain to her what these Baul women renouncers, who appeared so similar to householders, were actually renouncing. Chapter 6 emerged as an attempt to answer her question.

Finally, my deepest gratitude goes to my family, whose constant support throughout this intermittently rocky journey has meant the world to me. It is from them that I gained my inspiration, perseverance, and desire to learn. My father, Douglas Knight, taught me to question, to learn about others, and to try to make sense of the world. I could always rely on him for a close and careful reading of anything I sent him, and for that I am immensely grateful. My mother, Evelyn McDaniel, has been a constant source of encouragement, eagerly reading drafts and sharing in the journey. Without her loving attention to her grandson, some sections would not have been completed when they were. Whenever I felt discouraged with my progress, Catherine Snow kindly reminded me of the many times I had returned home from school as a child to announce that this time I had surely failed my assignment. Gary McDaniel offered much support and many needed breaks. My son Stefan has been the most joyful of distractions, returning with me to India in 2007 and reminding me that even though work is fun there are other important things in life too. Without a doubt, this book would not have taken the shape it did without the help of my husband, Ed Yazijian. It is from Ed's record collection, which we eventually came to share, that I first heard the heartfelt Baul songs that gripped my attention. Ed literally shared a number of my journeys, sometimes willingly, at other times reluctantly; his valuable assistance and presence in the field and upon our return have sustained me. With such deep appreciation for members of my family, I have a good understanding of why Baul women, even when eagerly pursuing otherworldly goals, rarely abandon their familial ties.

CONTENTS

NOTE ON DIACRITICS, TRANSLITERATION, AND NAMES

Diacritics have been used for Bengali words following the convention of the Library of Congress. Some exceptions have been applied, however, particularly where certain diacritics would suggest to the non-Bengali specialist reader a pronunciation that strays significantly from the Bengali (for instance, I write *saṅginī* instead of *saṅinī*). In Bengali, the letter "a" is often pronounced more like a short "o" (so that *baishṇab* would be pronounced *boishnob*), but I have chosen to transliterate the short "a" in this case as "a" to differentiate it from the longer sounding "o." Also, in Bengali, the final inherent "a" is usually not pronounced, so I have omitted it in most cases (such as *sannyās* instead of *sannyāsa*). Regional differences in pronunciation need to be kept in mind: when quoting someone, I generally retain their pronunciation and wording, supplying, if needed for understanding, in brackets words that are implied by the larger context but not necessarily obvious in the particular quote. While the Bengali language has regional variations in pronunciation and spelling, I have followed spellings offered by the *Sahitya Samsad* dictionaries for words frequently used within this book. Many of the Islamic words that come from Arabic or Persian are modified in the Bengali language (such as Shari'at and *nāmāj* in Bengali). The *Perso-Arabic Elements in Bengali* has been consulted for Islamic terms.

Names of individuals (human and deity), place-names, and sectarian groups are generally written without use of diacritics and are presented in their anglicized versions or have been modified for easier pronunciation in English.

Deciding whether or not to use pseudonyms for those I worked with has been particularly difficult. After much debate and many conversations, I have decided on the following unsatisfactory approach. In cases when I discuss a fairly well-known individual or a person who has expressed a particular desire to be known or is the composer of songs I discuss, I have kept their original names. In the few cases where I felt I was disclosing views or information that could, in one way or another, be sensitive, I have used pseudonyms. For many of the women I met, being a Baul was something they had to negotiate alongside local expectations of appropriate ways of behaving and worshipping. My primary concern was not to subject women to unnecessary criticism, and so I have made, as best I could while still aiming to demonstrate well-founded arguments, choices about what information to include and exclude and what changes to make to their identities. I believe these women deserve to have their voices heard. Given the kind of visibility attained by Bauls, I have not always been convinced that their identity should also be known.

MAP AND FIGURES

PART I

Multiple Sites

1

Finding Baul Women

Mosammat Saiyedunanessa Khanum was the mother of two male Baul performers I came to know in Sylhet, a northeastern district of Bangaldesh. Her sons, Munibor and Mujib, told stories about their childhood and their father, Ali Hosen Sarkar, a famous Baul *śilpī* (artist) and *sādhak* (ritual practitioner) from Netrakona in north-central Bangladesh. Mujib fondly called his father carefree (*udāsi*), a common description of Bauls. Many Hindu and some Sufi holy people are called *udāsi* when they are so completely focused on spiritual matters that they have lost all attachment to worldly possessions and achievements. People described as *udāsi* are unencumbered by societal expectations and responsibilities, and they tend to live in the moment rather than plan ahead. As if highlighting his father's *udāsi* behavior, Mujib told stories of how their father would invite guests to their home and feed them so generously that there would be little or no food left for himself or his family. In addition to being too carefree to tend to his family, Ali Sarkar was often itinerant, traveling to sing at programs and to visit other Bauls. Munibor somberly added that their father was also addicted to opium and that he died early. Listening to these stories, I became interested in meeting the wife of this Baul who was so driven by his spiritual and musical (and narcotic) preoccupations that, according to his sons, he often forgot to tend to his wife and children. I was curious to hear how she balanced the Baul life with raising a family and whether or not she shared Ali Sarkar's *udāsi* ways.

As was typical of my work with Bauls, I spent a long time looking for her. Her sons sent us to her conjugal village, but we finally found her living with her daughter and son-in-law outside of Dhaka. As I expected, Mosammat acknowledged that family life was difficult and that raising children within the economic uncertainty of their household consumed most of her thoughts at the time. But rather than bemoan the economic hardships of that time, she emphasized her own creative work and desires. Although her husband had been the famous Baul artist of the house, she explained that she also had written hundreds of songs. Sitting in a cot in a room with her daughter and son-in-law, Mosammat told me how she began writing songs.

> MOSAMMAT SAIYEDUNANESSA KHANUM: I began writing songs when I was nine years old. After writing some, my *murśid* [spiritual guide; guru] forbade me. "Don't write any more" [he told me]. "If one makes people cry, one [also] has to cry. When people hear your ghazals, they'll cry, and in your life there will be sadness and difficulty. Don't cry.... [Because of your writing] you will have to suffer; you will be sad. Don't write." Even so, there's no stopping writing. Writing had begun. [After my *murśid*'s instruction, it was] through this girl [daughter Ruby] that my writing continued. [But] I don't take up the pen anymore [myself].
>
> HER SON-IN-LAW: When something comes to mind, she says to my wife: "Write!" My wife then picks up the notebook and pen. She's following exactly *murśid*'s order.
>
> MSK: I don't touch a pen.

This anecdote, celebrated by her family as a sign of her cleverness, reveals Mosammat's passion for creating songs and her determination to follow her own trajectory. It also alludes to the difficulties and sadness encountered on that path. In the context of her own life, Mosammat's writing has brought her both little recognition and lots of disappointment.

Mosammat did not get support for her writing from her *murśid*, and, for very different reasons, she also did not get it from her husband. When their sons were still young, Mosammat submitted 25 of her own songs to the radio station in order to be registered as a songwriter. By being registered, her songs would be eligible to be chosen and sung by radio artists, and as a result Mosammat would receive remuneration and recognition for her talent. Mosammat asked her husband, who had regular contact with the radio station, to inquire about her registration. But when he repeatedly failed to do so, Mosammat torched three of her diaries in a moment of anger and defiance, destroying some 75 songs. Even despite Mosammat's creativity and defiant streak, it was much easier for her husband and sons to perform and gain recognition as Baul *śilpīs*. Although Mosammat is included in a book on Netrakona Bauls (Rahmān 1994) in a section devoted primarily to her husband and his songs, she is also the unacknowledged author of some famous songs performed and recorded by other Bangladeshi artists. Mosammat's own efforts to make her songs available to the public were hindered both by societal expectations that privileged men's visibility and by the negligence of her carefree husband. While Mosammat describes herself as *udāsi* and as a *pāgli* (mad woman) who had her mind always on otherworldly concerns ("Who is the Creator?" she recalls asking herself as a nine-year-old girl), as a wife and mother her own aspirations took a back seat. Although probably not an intended meaning in her *murśid*'s warning, trying to transcend social roles and defying the expectations of others can lead to difficulties.

Baul Women as Encumbered Actors

Bauls[1] of West Bengal (India) and Bangladesh[2] are a religious group most typically characterized as men who carry a one-stringed instrument (*ektārā*), wear ocher-colored clothes, and wander the countryside singing and performing their passionate music. Although their roots may extend deeper, they have existed for at least a century.[3] In practice and belief, they have been influenced by local traditions of the more orthodox Gauriya (Bengali) Vaishnavism, which cultivates ties to a larger and even more orthodox Vaishnava community, the unorthodox Tantric-influenced Sahajiyas,[4] and Sufism (the mystical path in Islam). Like Sufis, Bauls believe there are two types of religious teachings: one focused on the exoteric, followed by the general public (as the Shari'at in Islam) and typically criticized by Bauls as misguided and dependent on hearsay; the other focused on the esoteric (referred to by Sufis as the Ma'rifat, or, mystical knowledge). Like many other South Asian mystical traditions that follow an esoteric path, Bauls present an alternative to conventional society, and membership is attained through initiation by a guru or *murśid*. However, unlike many other religious groups, Bauls intentionally reverse a number of orthodox practices. They are fiercely opposed to the caste system, sectarianism, and the discrimination of women and regularly cross religious and caste boundaries as they speak, sing, practice, and live their lives. Bauls tend to come from the villages and low castes, though some are high caste and/or urban. While most overturn the caste system by disputing its relevance, a few do so by positioning themselves as Brahmins.

Bauls come from Hindu and Muslim backgrounds and communities and after initiation continue to live as minorities within those communities. While they tend to retain aspects of those religious identities to varying degrees, Baul teachings aim to deconstruct what is viewed as problematic about those normative religions. Most Bauls continue to use the Hindu or Muslim terminology of the dominant society, but gradually some of those terms take on new meanings that reflect decidedly Baul perspectives. Where there is regular interaction among Hindu and Muslim Bauls, the concepts of the other's religion are sometimes used to critique one's own previous religious orientation.[5] Like other Tantric-influenced groups, such as the Naths and the Sahajiyas, Baul beliefs and practices put them at odds with normative society. This is especially true of their Tantric-influenced perspective that the body is a microcosm of the universe and should be the locus of their spiritual work. Criticizing aspects of normative Hindu and Muslim society, Bauls argue that truth cannot be found in texts, such as the Vedas or the Qur'an, in empty rituals, or in buildings, such as temples or mosques. Instead, Bauls focus their spiritual lives on realizing the Divine, which they believe resides within the human body, and uniting the male and female principles through sexo-yogic practices.[6] Unlike most other Tantric traditions, Bauls focus on realizing love through their practices, and in this way they resemble Sufis, who long for experiential knowledge of God, as well as the Gauriya Vaishnavas and Sahajiyas, who seek to imitate the love experienced by

Radha for her lord Krishna. In philosophy, song, and ritual practice (*sādhanā*), Bauls view women as embodiments of an overflowing *śakti* (power or energy, conceptualized as feminine), as worthy of respect, and as gurus to their male partner.

At least in terms of ideology if not always in practice, women are elevated to high status among Bauls. Yet, even more than their male peers, Baul women are positioned in a landscape of various discourses[7] that place multiple and often conflicting expectations on them. Baul discourses on gender highlight women's spiritual contributions, and often Baul men also advocate societal respect for women. However, *bhadralok* (Bengali elite) discourses of Bauls, echoed in most scholarship, emphasize an idealized view of Bauls that is more congruent with the behavior of male *sādhu*s or *sannyāsī*s (holy men who have renounced their previous social identity and responsibilities) in its emphasis on itinerancy and a lack of concern for material security.[8] *Bhadralok* and other potential patrons of Baul music tend to seek Bauls who not only sing well but also display evidence of a carefree, unencumbered life, free from societal restraints and expectations; they seek Bauls who are *pāgal*, or, mad with love for the Divine. In stark contrast, non-Baul neighbors stress a discourse of patriarchy that places women in the home, requires modesty before men, and certainly discourages them from performing music in front of strangers or wandering from village to village. In significant ways, these various popular and scholarly discourses of Bauls marginalize women participants, with some Bengalis denying altogether the existence of women Bauls. This book takes the view that Baul women, like the Baul men who constitute the subject of many books on Baul songs and philosophy, are worth listening to.

I begin this work with the above anecdote in order to suggest that Baul women are encumbered actors. Unlike their male peers, they are never completely carefree and unencumbered by societal restraints and expectations. Mosammat was encumbered by her responsibilities as a mother and wife, married to a husband who was too carefree to meet basic domestic needs. More broadly speaking, Mosammat was encumbered by a patriarchy that legitimizes Baul men's performance and itinerancy and devalues women's public contributions. As highlighted in the quoted passage above, Mosammat was also encumbered by her relationship to a *murśid* who attempted to prohibit her from writing.

The Baul women I met faced many different types of obstacles, stemming from areas such as patriarchy, tradition, family, gurus, and patrons. The discursive landscape of Baul and gendered identity, as articulated by Bauls, *bhadralok*, non-Baul neighbors, and many others, is a veritable field of conflicting expectations and pitfalls. Yet despite the constraints they feel, Baul women actively create a meaningful life for themselves, often challenging the status quo along the way. Indeed, some of the women I met deliberately aim to transform society. Utilizing songs, everyday speech, and example, they proselytize aspects of Baul ideology, seeking to create a more enlightened and egalitarian society.

Many, like Mosammat, are quite clever and defiant in their attempts to direct the course of their lives. Mosammat, told not to write by her *murśid*, knew very well that she was going against her *murśid*'s wishes by composing songs, whether she wrote them down with her own hand or not. Rather than stop creating songs, she defied her *murśid*'s instructions yet in the anecdote claimed she was still following his order not to "write." By choosing to assert a literal interpretation of this prohibition, she exerts her own will and draws on her own capacity to act. Mosammat exercises agency in the way she interprets her *murśid*'s wishes, and the result has been a long life of composing numerous songs. The anecdote shows that Mosammat's writing did not merely happen, but was achieved deliberately and consciously when challenged.

The message of resistance is central to Mosammat's story, and many other Baul women in these pages can be seen as defying the social structures that circumscribe their lives. However, in discussions with other Baul women it is not so clear. Whereas Baul ideology extols women, it is perhaps surprising how frequently Baul women seem to succumb to pressures to behave in ways upheld by normative society as appropriate for their gender. How do we make sense of Baul women's acquiescence to normative society, when it occurs? Should we conclude that these women are so encumbered that they have no agency or that they choose not to act upon the agency available to them as Bauls?

Although we might wish to celebrate clear moments of rebellion and self-actualization, agency is not always manifested in obvious ways or with clear results. Sometimes it emerges more subtly in words: in stories, in re-creations of one's life, in reinterpretations of others' words, or in criticisms or gossip about others. I agree with many scholars who argue that language is a form of social action (for instance, Ahearn 2001; Butler 1997, 2004; Duranti 1997; Lamb 2001).[9] Mosammat's act of telling her story is thus in itself a meaningful act. Her reinterpretation of her *murśid*'s words is acknowledged openly by her and her family as an important part of Mosammat's history; it is celebrated. As her daughter and son-in-law chuckle while listening, they emphasize the cleverness and righteousness of her action by pointing out that she never *really* defied her *murśid*. The story, whether or not it reflects an "actual" event, is infused with the meaning of its telling. Telling one's story should be viewed as an act of agency in which individuals not only reflect on their lives and situations but also assert their own identity and make claims about their own situation and the actions of others. Talking—whether telling one's story or participating in a dialogue—can create reality. It can re-create one's past or assert one's present identity. Thus, although Mosammat's life is colored by disappointment over the lack of recognition for her own poetic contributions, she repositions herself squarely in the center of a story about clever defiance against obstacles.

For encumbered Baul women, resistance and defiance are not always the most useful or feasible ways to respond. Sometimes the most *effective* response is to give the appearance of upholding norms. In fact, challenging the status quo can create a very difficult life, a reality that should not be overlooked. Therefore, trying to determine how much agency a person has cannot always be done by observing their actions—and the results of their actions—since sometimes their choice *not* to act is not merely passivity. In this book, I focus primarily on what I see as intentional acts (Ortner 2006)—whether physical or linguistic—and whether or not their meanings are overt or hidden (Scott 1990). In the diverse ways in which Baul women respond to discourses that seek to define their identity and behavior, Baul women are indeed quite conscious and deliberate about their actions, positioned as they are amid conflicting expectations.

When there are discrepancies between what one says and what one does, as is sometimes the case with Baul women, we are likely to find important sites of struggle. Work on women's folklore and personal narratives in South Asia (as well as elsewhere) has demonstrated that women, despite their outward actions that appear to conform to gendered expectations, may actually, in the face of dominant ideologies, harbor different perspectives, which they disseminate through stories, songs, and rituals (Raheja and Gold 1994; Flueckiger 1996; Egnor 1989; Ramanujan 1991). Conversely, sometimes women appear to maintain the status quo through their words while challenging it through their actions. We can look at moments of contradiction for what they might reveal about discourses that are debated rather than merely accepted.

Although resistance is one reading of Mosammat's anecdote, it is not the only reading. Lila Abu-Lughod, taking a cue from Foucault that "Where there is power, there is resistance," suggests that one could also look at resistance in order to find and analyze forms of power: "We could continue to look for and consider nontrivial all sorts of resistance, but instead of taking these as signs of human freedom we will use them strategically to tell us more about forms of power and how people are caught up in them" (Abu-Lughod 1990:42). Resistance should be considered in the context in which it is meaningful, the constraints and limitations on people that give rise to it. For instance, also suggested in the anecdote is the importance of following a *murśid*'s orders. *Murśid*s or gurus provide their disciples not only guidance in the realm of spiritual matters but also instruction on basic day-to-day activities and social as well as personal decisions. Although one can find plenty of examples of individuals who decide that their *murśid* is not really compatible or helpful (in which case another one may be sought), the role of the *murśid* is generally taken very seriously. The seriousness of this hierarchical relationship between *murśid*/guru and disciple is suggested in Mosammat's anecdote by the importance placed on both the *murśid*'s instruction to Mosammat and the way she (re)interprets that instruction. Without consideration of the power a *murśid* has, Mosammat's story would have little cultural significance and would not be marked as noteworthy by her family. Thus Mosammat's story not only reveals her commitment to composing songs and her own defiance of her *murśid*'s wishes; it also highlights the importance of the *murśid*–disciple relationship and the power a *murśid* has over the lives of disciples. In addition to other forms of hierarchy in South Asia (such as caste, gender, and class), the guru–disciple relationship constitutes an important one for many.

Women's experiences thus need to be situated in the contexts of their relationships with men and within a larger social context in order to understand both why their voices matter and why they are frequently ignored (e.g., Abu-Lughod 1990; Gal 1991; MacLeod 1991, 1992; Raheja and Gold 1994). In this book, I consider Baul women's lives in the context of power structures in which they can to some extent act and are to some extent restrained. I examine the ways in which women construct their lives, in both the telling and the living. I focus particularly on discourses concerning ideal or "real" Bauls and appropriate behavior for Bengali women, as these two discourses emerged as important to the Baul women I met. It is these discourses that cause women to feel particularly encumbered, but these discourses also open up the possibility for alternative behaviors and life choices. As will become very evident, these discourses about "real" or "good" Bauls and "good" Bengali women are often in conflict with one another, and the ways in which Baul women negotiate simultaneously their Baul and gendered identities highlight both their agency and the ideologies of authority. Furthermore, as the women in this book discuss traveling to programs, singing songs, and taking formal vows of renunciation, we see that they draw on these discourses in some very different ways in order to fulfill their own particular hopes and needs. In short, although Baul women are encumbered, they draw on the very tools of their encumbering in order to create a better life and society.

Parameters and Blunderings

This project did not begin as a study on Baul identity. When I first arrived in Santiniketan in 1997 to do some preliminary fieldwork and test the feasibility of a research project on gender and agency among Bauls in Bengal, I already had an idea, based largely on inconsistencies and contradictions in the literature on Bauls as well as my own general skepticism, that the boundaries around Bauls were more fluid than most scholars I had read claimed. This hunch was supported by conversations I had with Jeanne Openshaw, an anthropologist who had recently completed her doctoral degree at the University of London based on fieldwork with Bauls spanning a period of over nine years. In her own work she examines the vast literature on Bauls dating from the first sources that make any reference to Bauls. She argues that *bāul* did not begin to be used to refer to a group of people until the late 1800s, the meaning perhaps solidifying as such around the turn of the century. But the term was used more by *bhadralok* (Bengali elite) than by the so-called Bauls (as a result, Openshaw opts for *bartamān-panthī*,[10] which is used more frequently than *bāul* among the people she researched). Although conversations with Openshaw reassured me that I did not have to be too concerned with trying to grasp local definitions of Baul, I still found that I could not get away from trying to understand what my interviewees meant when, and if, they called themselves Bauls. This was particularly the case for Baul women, for whom the label seemed especially tenuous. Although Openshaw's own dissertation,[11] which I read upon my return to Syracuse in 1998, helped me understand *bhadralok* views on Bauls, I still found I had to tackle the problem of Baul identity and authenticity with regard to women. I had to understand why, for instance, many *bhadralok* I met dismissed Baul women. Further complicating conceptions of Baul identity, my experience in parts of Bangladesh, most notably in Sylhet, showed me that *bāul* can have very different meanings. Whenever women were called Baul, or denied that identification, I was challenged to question just what was meant by that term.

One of my biggest difficulties in implementing the project was that I had no clear solution for how to define the boundaries around my subject matter. I knew that I was going to work with Baul women, but I also knew that some of them called themselves Bauls while others did not; that some learned songs and were performers, whereas others were not; that some practiced Baul rituals but others did not. I was interested also in the situation of women who were married to Bauls but did not consider themselves Bauls: Why not? Were they able to live seemingly normal lives, or were they somehow stigmatized by being married to a Baul? What role, if any, did they play in *sādhanā* (ritual practice)? I had concluded early on that I could not—or rather, would not—decide on a definition of Baul, based either on previous scholarly literature or from my own making, and then work with only so-defined Bauls. I knew that by doing so I would inadvertently create another category of "real Baul," a shortcoming I had found in most earlier studies. Furthermore, and this was very important, I believed I would be hindered from learning what it means to be a woman within the Baul community as well as the larger society if I did not try to understand the very diverse responses—denial, avoidance, acceptance, embracing—that Baul women had to that identity and way of life.

On a more practical level of day-to-day fieldwork, however, I had to figure out just whom I was going to interview and with whom I would follow up in greater depth. Asking local people to supply me with the names of Baul women in the area only confirmed that they, as a group, were as confused as I. If one person told me that someone was a Baul, most likely someone else would insist that that individual was *not* a real Baul. Initial fieldwork showed, then, that just as the scholarship is contradictory, there also is no indigenous consensus about what makes someone a Baul. Yet somehow, something—however fluid and contextually fluctuating—unites this very diverse group. And even if some women in the study knew less about Baul beliefs and practices than did many more of the men, they nonetheless knew enough to decide whether or not they wanted to be considered a Baul.

Despite and because of this ambiguity about how to define and identify Bauls, I chose to embrace the entire awkward package and interview any and all women who were associated with Bauls, through marriage or their own choosing, whether or not they personally called themselves Bauls. I did not seek out daughters of Bauls for interviews unless they were married or of marriageable age. The main reason for this is that in the Baul families I knew, teenage daughters were generally not around, most having already been married off, usually to men from low-caste poor families, often *jāt baishṇabs*.[12] I asked mothers with young children if they hoped their son or daughter would become a Baul. Their answers gave me a good indication of how much they valued Baul life, their responses sometimes contradicting initial positive portrayals. With the exception of young, unmarried daughters, I was interested in talking with a wide range of other women—housewives, performers, widows, women whose husbands had left them, ritual practitioners, gurus. I even listened attentively when upper-middle-class women from Kolkata (Calcutta) said they too were Bauls. My justification for such a cumbersome approach was that I wanted to understand both what it means for women to be Bauls and how Baul women live their lives. In order to do so, I needed to listen to them all.

That is not to say, however, that I always did listen. Despite my own decision not to judge the authenticity of Bauls I met, I did at times find myself saying "now she seems like a real Baul because..." while dismissing others for what I perceived as an opportunistic association with Baul identity or a lack of knowledge. Questions about the nature of my own choices about whom I would interview further emerged when I contemplated, often too late, why I was not interested in interviewing someone again. Looking back, I now realize there were many people I could have learned from but did not because, at the time I met them, I did not recognize what they would be able to show me. Fortunately this was not always the case. I recall travelling with two Baul women early in my fieldwork to a village a few hours away by bus to watch them perform at an all-night harvest celebration. Walking between the rice paddy fields to the village as the sun was starting to set, one woman told me that another foreign woman had interviewed her a few times and had then disappeared without a trace. In the village I saw their hosts welcome them, give them a spare room in which they and their small group of Bauls could change from their ordinary clothes to bright ocher-colored (*geruyā*) clothes, beads (*mālā*), and scarves and apply sectarian markings (*tilak*) of sandalwood paste on their forehead and body. After an all-night performance, I returned home with them the next morning and did not visit them again for many months. It was not until much later, and when I had begun to spend more time with one of the women, that I realized I had dismissed these women as ordinary housewives who had seized on the popularity of Bauls to make a living. I had left them in search of other more "real" Bauls. Despite my intentions, I was still hoping to find people for whom being a Baul was *more* than a way to earn a living. I hoped to find individuals for whom being a Baul involved embracing certain philosophy and rituals. I also hoped that the Bauls I would find were not already interviewed by other foreigners, as if that somehow tainted my data or my relationship with them. I feared that, depending on their experience with other foreigners, they would have expectations of me that I did not want to deal with.

Most foreigners in the Santiniketan area who sought out Bauls were not trained researchers. Instead, many of them were looking for Bauls to bring to foreign programs or to make recordings, or they were interested in learning Baul songs or ritual practices. From my observations, many of these foreigners, like the *bhadralok* I discuss in detail in the following chapter, have their own exotic imaginings of

Bauls. Bauls were interesting because of their carefree behavior, their passionate singing, their colorful dress, and their knowledge of Tantric-based rituals. I was wary of being pigeonholed by Bauls I met as another foreign woman who wanted to learn either songs or sexo-yogic rituals. I also feared that they would have expectations of me based on the behavior of other foreigners. Some of my early experiences confirmed these fears and influenced many of my later actions.

One of my first interviews was arranged by a Muslim rickshaw driver who helped me make some initial contacts with Bauls he knew. That first day was an exercise in frustration. He picked me up early in the morning and took me some distance to another village to meet a couple I had, as it turned out, already met closer to home. Disappointed that I was not meeting anyone new that day, I decided to go ahead and do a semi-formal interview with a tape recorder. The Baul man said he wanted us to go somewhere private to talk, as there are many Baul matters that should be kept secret, and he waved away my guide. He directed us over to an empty schoolhouse where the Baul couple and I sat to talk.

After only about five minutes, however, I realized that the tape recorder was not working properly, so I cut the interview short, suggesting we resume another time, and we talked casually for a little longer. When I asked them about other Bauls I met, they told me not to waste my time because those other Bauls were not "real" Bauls; they were only singers (*śilpī bāul*). The man claimed that not only had he and his wife been singing Baul songs their entire lives but that they, unlike almost all other Bauls in the area, also practiced *sādhanā* (in their case, sexo-yogic rituals). In their claim of authenticity was also a not-so-subtle suggestion that I learn about *sādhanā* from them.

For many reasons (including their presumption that it was the "secret" Baul *sādhanā* I was interested in), I did not see them again for over a month. When I did, it was at the home of the Baul man's parents, whom I visited occasionally. As we were sitting alone in the courtyard, the young Baul began demanding with increasing hostility that I pay him a large sum of money (5,000 rupees or about 140 U.S. dollars at that time) for our previous "interview." I was dumbfounded.

That experience taught me to set clear parameters for my research as I wanted at all costs to avoid miscommunicating my intentions. For this reason I decided to tell new Bauls I met that I was not interested in learning Baul songs or Baul *sādhanā*. Instead I stated that I was researching women and wanted to know about their lives and life stories, and I made a point of emphasizing that I wanted to talk primarily to women. Although I was also interested in the views of Baul men, I never had to state that I wanted to hear from them. Conversations with men happened whether I sought them out or not, but the same was not true with women. For instance, whenever I arrived at the home of a Baul family and explained that I was researching Baul women, it was not unusual for the man of the house to sit down with me and tell me to go ahead and ask *him* all the questions I had about Baul women.

While I believe this approach helped me get through my fieldwork with Bauls, as well as remain focused on the work, it did create some limitations. There is much to learn about Baul women in rituals and songs, as many Baul songs focus on women and the role of women in Baul rituals. Interesting questions remain on the nature of women's roles in *sādhanā*, on their own understandings of the rituals involved and what they hope to gain from them, questions typically answered only from the male point of view.[13] I barely scratched the surface on these subjects, approaching them only through Bauls I believed were unlikely to misunderstand my intentions or when, as in Bangladesh, I was with my husband (that too proved problematic, for many of the same reasons as it might have in the Santiniketan area). In the fall of 2007, however, I returned to West Bengal to visit some of my Baul friends with the intention of pursuing one of the topics I originally glossed over: Baul songs. I already had some songs and commentaries recorded from my previous fieldwork, but during the 2007 trip I increased my collection of songs by women. While many women sing songs composed by Baul men, I also collected songs composed by three women. These songs, discussed in chapter 5, reflect women's views about their lives as Bauls.

The research for this book is based on nearly two years of fieldwork conducted between 1997 and 2000 and then again in 2007. Although there are some parameters around my research and some questions that still remain to be answered, my intention for this book is to provide a more complex view, grounded in ethnographic research, of what being *bāul* means for women.

Itinerancy and Fixed Places: On Researching Baul Women

I prepared a questionnaire for initial interviews, which I usually tape-recorded, and interviews were open-ended and conducted by myself in Bengali. On a few occasions in both West Bengal and Bangladesh I took a Bengali woman as an assistant to participate in the interview. In Bangladesh, however, I was accompanied by my husband, Ed Yazijian, whose Bengali language skills helped me particularly in areas with regional Bangladeshi dialects that were impenetrable to me. He often also participated in interviews, asking some of the questions I had prepared in advance as well as a few of his own. All of the interviews during my time in West Bengal, however, were conducted by me and not in Ed's presence. I employed qualitative research methods, and my questions evolved throughout the course of my research. In Bangladesh, I had several spells of illness, and between sick days and regular strikes (*hartāl*s) there were many slow days. The (only) benefit to this was that it gave me time to reflect on what I had learned thus far and to revise my own questions. In both West Bengal and Bangladesh, especially when speaking to those I visited frequently, interviews often turned into conversations. At those times I rarely used a tape recorder, relying instead on my memory and taking brief notes soon thereafter, typing them into my computer whenever I could.

The fieldwork for this book was conducted in multiple conceptual and physical sites. Understandings of "Baul women" are found not only in the locales in which they live but also in discourses, in life stories, and in reported or observed experiences. Literature on multisited ethnography (Marcus 1995) and the challenges that a current heightened awareness of globalization poses to a bounded concept of culture (Appadurai 1990; Gupta and Ferguson 1997a, 1997b; Metcalf 2001) have suggested that physical boundaries around our subjects are considerably more fluid than many had assumed. As Akhil Gupta and James Ferguson argue, "The idea that 'a culture' is naturally the property of a spatially localized people and that the way to study such a culture is to go 'there' ('among the so-and-so') has long been part of the unremarked common sense of anthropological practice" (1997b:3). Culture was probably never localized and bounded in place; migration, trade routes, and commerce have long connected people in seemingly disparate locales. Although current perceptions of accelerated globalization seem to make those connections more obvious, it is doubtful that cultures were ever discrete units.

Although it is common still to think of Bauls as rooted in the soil of Bengali villages, Bauls today have regular interactions with the larger world of Bengali and foreign elites, including scholars, journalists, musical industries, sponsors, students, and anthropologists. Also, they are not a spatially localized group, especially when one considers that there are Bauls living in Paris and touring such disparate locales as London, New York, Tokyo, Dubai, and Stockholm.

In researching Bauls, however, I was encouraged to go deep into the villages in order to find more pure, that is untarnished, Bauls. Many Bengalis as well as foreigners believe it is only in such remote places where one ever encounters "real" Bauls (though a few believe that such purity is nowhere to be found anymore).[14] I tend to believe that such a "real" Baul never really existed for much the same reason that the concept of a spatially bounded culture is problematic. Bauls do not live only in remote places; they move around, and in so doing they inevitably interact with other non-Bauls and nonrural people. This interaction has become much more common in recent years as their popularity has risen among foreigners and Bengali elite. But being a Baul often means being itinerant, and I would be skeptical that any Bauls would be isolated enough to be "pure," whatever that means.

Thus in this book, the term *bāul* remains fluid and unbounded, reflecting a diversity of meanings among the people I met. In my research, I sought to understand what being a Baul means for women, and this led to questions about gender and Baul identities. Baul women live and travel in many different contexts, brushing up against multiple and often contradictory expectations of them and their identities, and to research Baul women means to consider and to move among multiple sites. Rather than explore questions of Baul life (or "real" Bauls) in a particular place, I used concepts of "Baul women" as well as "Bengali women" and "Bauls" independently as the crucial analytical sites in my research.

Even if we accept that places, like concepts, are not bounded and discrete, the research for this book had to be done somewhere. Guided by questions of what it means to be a Baul woman, I traveled extensively but gathered my findings in specific places where I met individuals for whom those concepts held significance.

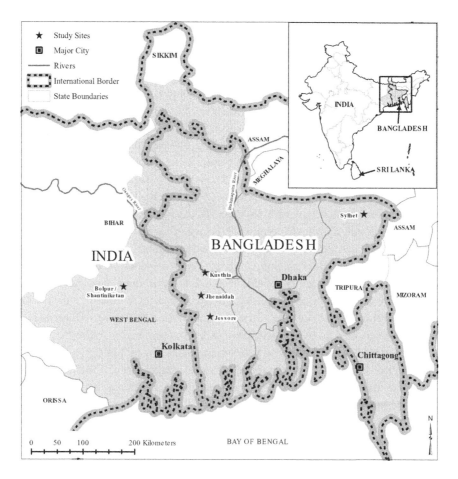

Physical research sites included locales in the districts of Birbhum (West Bengal, India), Sylhet, Jhenaidah, and Dhaka (Bangladesh), as indicated on the map, each of these areas revealing another layer to my understanding of Baul women's experiences, not the least of which is a contrast between predominantly Hindu West Bengal and Muslim Bangladesh. In the following pages I describe my primary research locales.

SANTINIKETAN–BOLPUR AREA

Most of my research in India was done from a base in Santiniketan. From there I traveled to many other areas, including to the Bankura district, Kolkata, and many villages and towns in the Birbhum district, often staying overnight. Having a base in Santiniketan was convenient because so many Bauls lived in nearby villages or would come to Santiniketan to perform at the annual festival called Paus Mela. Bauls in the area also served as links to Bauls in other regions, and at times they would lead me on journeys to villages to meet other Bauls or to attend festivals. Furthermore, I could learn much from local Bengalis and patrons on their views of Bauls. Bauls in this particular region also display certain characteristics, as will become clear, largely because they live among the community of patrons they seek to entertain.

Interacting with the urban Bengali elite, foreigners, and local villagers, Bauls regularly confront differing ideologies and expectations, and interact with people from various economic backgrounds. This is particularly evident in Santiniketan, which in many ways is an unusual small town. Situated in rural Birbhum about 90 miles (145 km) northwest of Kolkata, Santiniketan developed primarily around the reputation of eminent Bengali poet Rabindranath Tagore (1861–1941), who founded Visva-Bharati University, now attended by students from all over Bengal as well as foreign countries, such as Japan, Korea, Germany, and France. Many area residents are drawn there because of the university and the ideals of diversity and tolerance it has fostered; others are attracted to the local arts; yet others find in the peaceful surroundings an ideal retreat. There are many urban elites from Kolkata who live permanently in Santiniketan, but a great many more have second homes there or visit as tourists. Local Bauls live in villages surrounding the towns of Santiniketan and Bolpur, the nearby city and train stop. Living in these areas, Bauls have very easy access to the *bhadralok* in Santiniketan, for whom they often perform, as well as to the trains on which many Bauls sing for alms.

From Kolkata, Santiniketan is about a three-hour train ride on the Santiniketan Express or the Visva-Bharati. These trains are full of Kolkatans, many of whom commute to work at Visva-Bharati University. Other Kolkatans make their pilgrimage to see the sites of the Nobel Laureate Tagore, whose works and international recognition are a tremendous source of Bengali pride. Since 1998, banners and billboards at the entrance to Santiniketan have informed visitors that Bengal has produced three Nobel laureates: Tagore, Mother Teresa, and Amartya Sen. Even before arriving in Santiniketan, travelers are reminded that they are also entering Baul territory. As hawkers selling pens, handicrafts, and tea rush onto the train at stops near Bolpur, one or two Baul performers also slip on board. As the train leaves the station, the hawkers chant their wares, and new passengers settle into their seats. The Bauls wait quietly in the entranceway of a train car, and once passengers have settled down and the train has resumed its constant rhythmic clatter, one of them enters the car. Surveying the passengers, the Baul gets into position about a third of the way in and then begins to hum to tune the instrument. Bengalis who frequent the Santiniketan Express or the Visva-Bharati are familiar with these presentations and explain that the ocher-colored (*geruyā*) clothes, the long and often unruly hair, and the particular folk instruments used point to a Baul identity. Regular passengers may even know some of the Bauls by name or request a particular Baul song. After a few songs, the Baul walks slowly up and down the aisle, silently asking for donations, before moving to another car.

Compared to the heavily trafficked Bolpur, especially when its arteries are clogged with rickshaws and taxis vying for customers from the arriving trains,

Santiniketan is serene. Nonetheless, many visitors travel to Santiniketan throughout the year. Even during the monsoon, some brave the flooded paths in order to breathe in the clean green air and see the burgeoning, flourishing vegetation. In 1998, a retired faculty member of Visva-Bharati told me that residents of Santiniketan live long and healthy lives because there is no pollution. Most residents today, however, bemoan the rapid changes affecting this pristine environment. Every year more and more residential and guest houses are built in and around Santiniketan, and when I returned in 2007, some streets were barely recognizable to me. What had been an area of open fields and wide spaces between houses was now crowded with large and often empty new homes that mostly belong to Kolkatans who want a place to spend holidays and weekends. The streets have become more crowded with cars and motorcycles, also changing the atmosphere and pace of life. As a result of this huge influx of people seeking to escape city life, Santiniketan has become a haven for Kolkatans who bring their urban amenities with them.

The busiest time of year in Santiniketan, when the town is bursting with activity and all the guest houses and residential homes are full, is during Paus Mela, an annual festival that takes place in late December on the *melā* (festival) grounds behind the Visva-Bharati University administrative buildings and the Bank of India and across the street from the library and the boys' hostel. The festival is organized by the university and highlights regional, rural music and handicrafts. One of the main attractions is the university-sponsored tent in which musical performances, such as Baul and *kīrtan* (devotional Vaishnava music), continue from 7:30 a.m. to 8 p.m. A large area nearby is filled with tents and booths that are rented and set up by such diverse organizations as the literacy campaign, the leprosy clinic, and the bank. Bauls are also invited to sing at some of these tents before speeches and presentations.

Baul performers at this festival come from all over Bengal: Nadia, Murshidabad, Bankura, Birbhum, and occasionally even from Bangladesh. They are given a small honorarium (20–100 rupees); places to sleep, bathe, and change; and meals (tiffin). Given that the honorarium may not cover even the cost of transportation to and from Santiniketan, Bauls do not come to the festival for direct financial gain. In fact, many who are not chosen to sing on the main stage sing for even less in the smaller tents. It is, however, a chance for Bauls to network both among themselves and potential sponsors living in or visiting Santiniketan.

That potential sponsors can be found in Santiniketan is one of the primary reasons there are so many Bauls in the area. In addition to Bauls from the surrounding region who are drawn to Santiniketan for the duration of Paus Mela, many others have moved to the area permanently. Performing alone on trains or as groups for hire, they vie for opportunities to perform in lucrative settings. By the end of my stay in 1999, I knew many of the Bauls in the area and recognized most of those who lived in Santiniketan, Bolpur, or nearby villages. When I arrived in Santiniketan again in 2000, after having spent about six months away, I took a rickshaw through town to the home where I was going to stay. As we traveled along the road, I was surprised at how many Bauls I saw sitting at tea stalls or walking whom I did not recognize. It was May, not a typically busy season for Bauls in the area, yet the number of Bauls on the road had noticeably increased in just six months.

Santiniketan is strikingly different from other towns where Bauls live because Bauls are a local commodity. People come to Santiniketan knowing that Bauls perform there, often hoping to hear them sing. In addition to the common sight of Bauls sitting at tea stalls or walking alongside the road, images of Bauls can be seen all over town, in the handicrafts sold in local stalls and the paintings and sculptures on display in restaurants.

BANGLADESH

Although Bauls in Bangladesh also conjure up romantic images of rural and spiritual life, there is no center comparable to Santiniketan. Perhaps the closest is Kusthia, a small town not far from Bangladesh's western border with India. Kusthia is site of the *māzār*, or tomb, of Lalan Shah (Fakir),[15] considered the most famous Baul composer and practitioner, although Lalan never actually called himself a Baul, and two annual festivals to which his followers and many others come to sing and hear Baul songs. Kusthia was also home to the Tagore family, and their house in Selaidah is a popular tourist destination. Tagore had heard Lalan's songs and collected a number of them in his notebooks, and many claim that it was largely because of Tagore's praise of the wandering minstrels that the Bauls became so well known.

I made a brief visit to Kusthia, but I did not conduct any research among Bauls there. During a visit to the famous *māzār* of Lalan, I was approached by Bauls who indicated that they were ready to divulge information about "secret" rituals in exchange for money. Although a study of Kusthia may have made an interesting comparison with Santiniketan, in the end I researched other areas that provided an ever-expanding understanding of the term Baul. Most of my research was conducted in Sylhet, Dhaka, and Jhenaidah—three very diverse areas of Bangladesh— but I took trips to other places as well, such as Netrakona and Tongi (near Dhaka), to meet with people identified as Bauls. I became increasingly interested in the diversity of meanings of Baul in these different regions of Bangladesh. In particular, those in Sylhet seemed to have the broadest understanding of Baul, and it differed considerably from those nearer to Kusthia or in West Bengal.

Sylhet

Sylhet, a city and district in the northeastern part of Bangladesh, borders on the Indian states of Assam, Tripura, and Meghalaya. Like neighboring Assam, Sylhet is an area known for its tea gardens, which attract seasonal workers as well as tourists. Sylhet is also home to many migrant workers who travel to places in the Middle East or to Britain. In fact, there are so many Sylhetis who have a family member in London that, according to Katy Gardner, one of the villages is called *Londoni-grām*.

As Gardner states, "A House of Commons survey in 1986, for example, indicated that of the estimated 200,000 Bangladeshis living in Britain, more than 95 percent of them were Sylheti" (1998:204). As a result, Sylhet has seen many changes. First of all, overseas workers returning with extra income have built up their homes and communities. Many have also returned with the belief, gained through interactions with Muslims in the West and the Middle East, that the Arabic version of Islam is more "pure."[16] Sylhet therefore has a strong religiously conservative bent that often clashes with that of Sufi, Baul, and secular residents.

Traditionally Sylhet has been a center of Sufism, and this remains evident today through the prominence and enduring popularity of the many shrines dedicated to Sufi saints. Most notably, at the center of Sylhet is the Dargah-e-Shah Jalal commemorating Shah Jalal, a Sufi saint associated with the spread of Islam in the area in the 14th century. Within the dargah compound are a *masjid* (mosque), a madrasa (Islamic school), a *māzār* dedicated to Shah Jalal, a large kitchen to serve the many poor who come to the shrine, a graveyard, and a pond. There are a few different entrances to the site, but the main one is the dargah gate. Leading up to the shrine is a street filled with people and rickshaws jostling for a way in and lined with hotels and shops that sell Qur'ans of all sizes, writings of the Prophet Muhammad, and all sorts of religious memorabilia, from prayer beads to charms. Late at night, and especially on Thursdays, many Sufis and Bauls come to the area behind the dargah to play music, talk, and often smoke ganja (marijuana). Even though singing and Sufi devotional practices are disdained by orthodox Muslims, what goes on at these Thursday night events is generally tolerated or at least ignored. Sufis and Bauls gather near the Zamzam well. Legend has it that the well contains the same water as in the Zamzam well of Mecca, and pilgrims come to drink it whenever they visit the dargah. Also nearby is a pond full of catfish said to be the soldiers of defeated Hindu king Gaurgovinda, cursed by Shah Jalal to be reborn over and over again as catfish. Visitors to the shrine often go to the pond to feed the catfish. In these and other ways, the dargah of Shah Jalal is connected to the Muslim spiritual center of Mecca as well as to the soil of Bengal.

The first time Ed and I stayed in Sylhet, we frequented a local homeopathic doctor, Feroz Ahmad, who became our friend and contact in the area. Because of his own work, he knew a large network of people, and he often accompanied us on our initial visits to Bauls he knew. He brought us to meet Mujibor Rahman Sarkar ("Mujib"), a well-known Baul in the area and son of Mosammat Saiyedunanessa Khanum whose anecdote began this chapter. On our second visit to Sylhet, Mujib brought us to meet his brother, Munibor, who was living in the home of Rafiq Miah, a successful local businessman. Munibor was a Baul performer himself and had traveled to Britain to perform with others, including Kangalini Sufia, a famous Baul woman I had been interviewing in Dhaka. His friend and host, Rafiq Miah, had encouraged him to sing and perform. After learning about my research on Baul women in the area, they invited us to stay at their home. Although they revealed considerable ambivalence about my work with Baul women, they were immensely

FIGURE 1.1. *Waiting to cross the river Surma by ferry to go to Sylhet, 1999*

helpful and hospitable, making our stay in the area both comfortable and productive.

Their home was located in a village across the river Surma from Sylhet town. To go into Sylhet town, we had to cross over by ferry, a small flat boat that held about twelve people and was pushed along with a pole by the ferryman who stood on one end (see Figure 1.1). From there we would hop on a rickshaw and go into one of the neighborhoods where we met Baul women or one of the local cassette producers. A few of the homes we passed along the way were stately and large, but those were rarely the ones we entered. As with most bustling towns, there was a large number of transients living in rented rooms or flats, some made primarily of corrugated tin and others joined to larger, divided houses. The Baul women we visited were usually living in one of these rented homes. A few others lived on the outskirts of Sylhet, in homes in which they and their families had lived for years if not a few generations.

The Baul scene in Sylhet revolves around two general and often overlapping arenas: music and Muslim shrines. In many respects this is parallel to Sufi practices in which a number of different settings integrate with both devotion and music, including weddings, births, or celebrations at shrines. Speaking of Sufi singers of devotional music (*qawwali*), Shemeem Abbas explains that women and men performers may create diverse opportunities for devotional expression and "acquire the skill to earn a living that matches the devotion of their patrons and their audiences" (2002:2). Similarly, Baul settings are often simultaneously devotional and profitable. Many Bauls in the area are associated with singing what are locally called

bāul-gān or Jarigan. Bauls are invited to perform at festivals and programs organized by various sponsors. Some of these large programs are arranged as friendly
competitions between two or more performers in which songs are performed in a
question-answer style (Maljura) around a variety of topics involving Allah and the
Prophet Muhammad, the creation of Adam, the relationship between man and
woman, or the philosophy of the body (*deha-tattva*). For many Bauls who want to
perform at these larger settings, cassettes serve as a way of promoting their style
and talent. A few of the Baul women we met recorded their songs at home on a
boombox and later sold them to local cassette producers and distributors in
exchange for a flat fee. There is thus an industry around Baul songs in Sylhet in
which some women are highly motivated to participate.

Bauls in Sylhet are also commonly found at the *māzār* grounds of shrines, such
as the dargah of Shah Jalal, or at *urs* gatherings commemorating the death of a
Muslim saint. Lolan, a Sylheti cassette producer, took us to one festival where he
claimed we could find "real" Baul women and led us to small tents where Bauls and
Sufis were singing, talking, and smoking ganja. In these settings, singing might continue all night long, with passersby stopping in to listen for a while before moving
on to other events or to return home.

Dhaka

The *māzār*s of Shah Ali Baghdadi (see Figure 1.2) and the High Court in Dhaka are
important sites for Bauls. In fact, many Bauls have been "discovered" on the grounds
of these *māzār*s. For instance, Nur Jahan, a Baul I met in Sylhet, used to reside at a

FIGURE 1.2. *Māzār (tomb) of Shah Ali Baghdadi in Mirpur, 2000*

number of different *māzār*s in and around Dhaka, and it was at the Shah Ali Baghdadi *māzār* that a woman began to support her and encourage her singing. Kangalini Sufia also sang and stayed in *māzār*s for years before she became famous and even now goes to them to sing and visit with other Bauls. During my research in Dhaka, I visited these *māzār*s in order to get an idea of these places that were both havens and refuges for Baul women. At the *māzār*s I went to, an area was set apart for women, who gathered there sometimes for long periods. The women I saw appeared to find a sense of security by staying away from others, and they mingled, sat quietly, and helped each other. For women on their own, these female domains at *māzār*s were a refuge.

The *māzār*s felt like a refuge for me as well, as they allowed me to escape, briefly, the chaos of the city. Dhaka is a busy city crammed with people, buses, auto-rickshaws, and cars. It is a city that grew quickly, overreaching its comfortable capacity years ago, and it is busting at the seams with people living everywhere humanly—and not so humanly—possible. It has some of the wealthiest areas in Bangladesh, with gated communities and spacious homes decorated with fine original art and run by many servants. Dhaka also has many slums where people live with varying degrees of permanence. That is, people flock to Dhaka to work as rickshaw drivers, servants, and laborers in the textile factories, and from their temporary places in Dhaka they send money home to their families living in rural areas.

My work in Dhaka was scattered among a few different places. I often went to the area called Mirpur to visit Kangalini Sufia, who lived with her husband, daughter, and grandchildren in a small rented room in a crowded side street. Since they moved frequently because they could not keep up with the rent, I sometimes had to locate her through an owner of a local phone booth. I also went to one of the *māzār*s where, in addition to meeting other women and listening to Baul women and men sing, I also spoke to the caretakers. At the British Council we attended a concert in which Kangalini and her group performed, and I interviewed one of the organizers of cultural programs there. In Dhaka it seemed like I was always traveling, whether by bus, rickshaw, or foot. The people I wanted to meet were in disparate locations and were not always there when I showed up (even when my arrival was planned). Partly for this reason, work in Dhaka was particularly difficult. Unlike other places, especially Santiniketan, I too did not have a solid home base. Further complicating matters were the many calls for a work strike (*hartāl*) stemming from political conflicts between the two main political parties, the Awami League and the BNP (Bangladesh National Party), which literally shut down the city. This political uncertainty had a great impact on all of us, even Bauls who had plans to be in programs on those days.

Jhenaidah

Jhenaidah was close to Kusthia, a district particularly well-known for Bauls. Like Kusthia, Jhenaidah lies on Bangladesh's western side, bordering with India. Ed and I went to rural areas of Jhenaidah after I learned—the result of much investigation—that a Baul woman I wanted to meet was living there. Her whereabouts had been particularly difficult to determine, as she and her partner moved around regularly. Once we found her, we relocated to a circuit house (hostel for government ministers and bureaucrats) in Jhenaidah.

In many ways Jhenaidah itself seemed wild and uncertain. Not only did the monsoon pose challenges to travel while we were there, but the place seemed to be colored by lawlessness. Sometimes on buses people smoked ganja mixed with *Datura*, a highly hallucinogenic flower found on the sides of the road. It was not uncommon to see police in full bullet-proof gear riding around in armored trucks. Because Jhenaidah is close to the border with India, illegal border crossing and smuggling are constant problems. In addition, the area is still home to a number of outlaw leftist organizations known for perpetrating violence. Also, the area was a major battle site in the Bangladesh Liberation War (1971), and several people we met, including some Bauls, had recollections of it.

In other ways Jhenaidah seemed like many of the other places I visited: lush and green, with many fields ready to be plowed and farmers visiting at the tea stalls on the sides of the road. Villages we visited were small and isolated, surrounded by not much more than fields. As Ed and I walked through long, lonely dirt roads, shielding ourselves from the pouring rain with our umbrellas, the occasional villager would stop us to engage in warm conversation, often walking with us to our destination. We kept hearing about criminal activities in the area but personally felt very welcome and safe. Rarely were we met with "Salam Alaikum," the clearly religious greeting we were used to hearing in other parts of Bangladesh. Locals seemed aware of and okay with religious differences, often saying positive things about people they knew from other religions.

Bauls in Jhenaidah are similar to *lālan panthī*s, or followers of Lalan Shah, and are themselves practitioners (*sādhak*s) of esoteric rituals. Conversations with these Bauls often led to topics of philosophy, especially of the body (*deha-tattva*), and about ritual practice (*sādhanā*). The Bauls we met wore white, not the ocher-colored clothes typical of Bauls performing onstage or around Santiniketan. Positioned as they were so close to the border to India, Bauls, like other locals in Jhenaidah, reflected the diversity of religions in the area. Bauls we met talked passionately about discrimination and intolerance, and discussions of Baul philosophy were peppered with Muslim and Hindu terms, occasionally even with Christian terms and ideas.

Being a Baul means different things in these regions—Birbhum, Sylhet, Dhaka, and Jhenaidah. Not everyone who identifies as Baul, or is called such by others, performs music or practices a sexual *sādhanā* with a partner or is an initiate of esoteric practices and philosophy. But many who are called Bauls do participate in at least one of these practices. Despite these internal variances, I found some significant similarities among those considered Bauls. Being a Baul means one is outside and even critical of normative society. In most cases, this means that a Baul has a view of religion that is different from that of orthodox Hindus or Muslims in the surrounding communities. Even Vaishnava Bauls who displayed images of deities in their homes stated unequivocally that one should worship humans, not images, and that temple worship as reflected in the Brahmanical traditions is empty and futile. Muslim Bauls, meanwhile, though they did talk of Allah and the Prophet, nonetheless stated that one could do daily prayers (*nāmāj*) internally and that there was no need for external displays at the mosque. Often being a Baul also means that one's views of women's roles and abilities are different from those held by non-Bauls. Baul women and men mingled more freely than did many others in the non-Baul communities, and the status of women was often higher among Bauls. Furthermore, in all regions, whether or not one identified oneself as a Baul was integrally tied with one's own willingness to take a public stand of living outside normative rules. Thus two singers who might perform the same Baul songs may differ in whether or not they call themselves Baul. For instance, Farida Parveen, a woman who grew up in Kusthia and sings the songs of Lalan Shah allegedly with the original melodies, adamantly claims she is not a Baul, and no one would suggest that she is. Although she obviously has an appreciation for Baul songs, she is from a higher class than most Bauls and does not consider herself outside normative society. Similarly, because being a Baul implies a certain critique of society, other educated elite in West Bengal and Bangladesh claim to be Bauls in certain settings in order to suggest their own critique.

Researching what it means to be Baul in these diverse settings in West Bengal and Bangladesh has forced me to open up the definition of Baul. Although various Bauls make claims about what a "real" Baul is, I argue that being a Baul is ever fluctuating and context sensitive. While there are many things that unite the different Bauls in this book, they do not all fit into one definition, and a consideration of the various settings, regions, and discourses in which Bauls can be found make this obvious.

The Chapters Ahead

In this book, I look at issues of being a Baul from the vantage point of women, taking a cue from Bauls themselves that women are important. I argue that Baul women make choices in light of their gendered and Baul identities in order to create meaningful lives for themselves and others. Paying particular attention to the social structures that impinge upon their lives and the expectations that Bauls and non-Bauls have of Baul women, I suggest that these women sometimes draw on the tools of their encumbering in ways that suggest that adhering to some expectations may also be agency.

This book is divided into two parts. Part 1 ("Multiple Sites") situates Baul women in the contexts of locales, communities, and discourse. In chapter 2, I discuss scholarly and *bhadralok* discourses on Bauls, particularly for what they say (and do not say) about women. While these discourses reveal a pervasive view about what is considered to be a good or a "real" Baul, I demonstrate that those discourses also marginalize Baul women and contribute to the stigmatization of them as "bad" women. Notably, discourses about Bauls construct authenticity as an unencumbered life: without home or care, childless, and utterly consumed by spiritual goals. Presumably unencumbered by responsibilities to spouses (particularly to wives), male Bauls are sometimes also described as lotharios.

In chapter 3, I look specifically at those patriarchal discourses of feminine respectability that cast Baul women as "bad" women, but I do so through the eyes of Baul women, paying attention to the ways in which Baul women compare their own lives and behavior with those of their neighbors. Even though Baul views of women differ significantly, Baul women are very aware of the expectations Bengalis have of women to be mothers and wives and to act modestly in front of men. In these two chapters, I argue that Baul women are caught between having to meet the expectations of both potential sponsors seeking Bauls who act unencumbered and neighboring non-Baul community members who view such Baul behavior as antithetical to being a good Bengali wife and mother. Different in origin and ideology, the discourses described in chapters 2 and 3 contribute to the belief that Baul women are of questionable character, a view largely rooted in the perceived instability of their conjugal lives and the public dimension of performances in which some women engage.

Part 2 ("Negotiations") focuses on how Baul women negotiate the often conflicting expectations of them detailed in part 1 in order to create a meaningful life and a more just and enlightened society. Most Baul women move between contexts in which they have considerable freedom and contexts in which they act on such gendered codes of conduct as shame, modesty, and chastity. In contrast to women who are obliged to maintain propriety in order to live full lives within the homes of their in-laws and their community, Baul women, as I show in chapter 4, often draw on such codes of conduct only when they deem it beneficial to their particular situation. Although they are not generally expected to be modest, these women evoke and sometimes even subvert social constructions of appropriate gendered behavior in order to save their sense of dignity.

Bauls are best known for their songs, and Baul performers use songs to spread their messages to others and to cultivate deeper knowledge among the initiated. In chapter 5, I look closely at the songs performed and sung by Baul women. I argue that these songs are by nature transformative and are used to further personal as well as social changes. Baul women, like Baul men, utilize the performance setting to cultivate their identity and to communicate the kinds of messages they believe are important. I particularly examine the ways these songs relate to the lives of women who sing them.

Renunciation (*sannyās* or *bhek*) is potentially the most radical form of unencumbering. Found throughout India, renunciation is typically seen as a formal rite of severing ties with family, community, and worldly concerns for the pursuit of spiritual goals. Although not an expected stage among Bauls, renunciation is sometimes used as a strategy by Bauls for gaining a more respectable status and the concurrent entitlement to alms. I demonstrate in chapter 6 that, for women negotiating their place and status in society, renunciation becomes a means of stepping out of normative roles and expectations. These women renounce above all society's claim on them, creatively interpreting their lives and their options. As they renounce their position as a traditional married woman with all the associated benefits and restrictions, Baul women create a life of increased mobility.

Issues of reputation, respectability, and gendered codes for behavior go to the heart of questions of power and agency. In negotiating their social identity, Baul women engage in and manipulate the very structures and discourses that encumber them and jeopardize their social standing. Rather than seeing them as victims of contradictory standards of "good" Bauls and "good" women, I demonstrate in this book the ways in which these women actively engage in the production and maintenance of their identity by utilizing a variety of strategies in order to improve their livelihood, social standing, and sense of dignity. But before I do that, I turn to discuss constructions of Baul identity and the marginalization of Baul women in discourses about Bauls.

2

"Real Bauls Live under Trees"
IMAGININGS AND THE MARGINALIZATION
OF BAUL WOMEN

When I first went to West Bengal to test the feasibility of my dissertation project in the summer of 1997, I spoke with a well-known scholar in Kolkata who tried to discourage me from researching Baul women by insisting there was no such thing. "Only men are Bauls," he claimed. "If there are women around, they are only to serve the men; they know nothing." I understood immediately that his reaction stemmed from the view that Baul philosophy and rituals are, as among many Tantrics, primarily for the benefit of men, and women's involvement is usually considered to be that of a *sevādāsī*. As the name implies, *sevādāsī*s are women who are dedicated to serving others: a deity, a temple, or other devotees. The term *sevādāsī* also suggests a woman who serves others sexually, sometimes in a ritual context. Although *sevādāsī*s are arguably also very worthy of study, I also understood that this scholar was essentially dismissing the women who were involved with Bauls.

Over a year later when I arrived in Santiniketan to begin my research, I went to register at the police department in Siuri, a nearby city. After I finished filling out pages and pages of paperwork in triplicate (without the benefit of a copy machine), the police inspector grilled me about my project on Baul women. Already wary of his suspicious tone, I added that I had received a Fulbright grant for this project, hoping that would give me and my work the necessary credentials. The inspector was not easily thwarted from his role as investigator and patroller of foreigners. "But," he said, "there are maybe only a couple of Baul women." I explained some more, trying to remain upbeat as I rubbed my hand after completing the many forms, wondering if I would soon be turned away. I clarified that I was interested also in women who were associated with Bauls though perhaps did not actually identify themselves as Bauls, and yet he insisted: "You're going to spend a whole year talking to just a couple of women?" Despite my insistence that I knew there were several Baul women, he remained convinced that there was no such thing, and even if there was, why would I spend so much time talking to a couple of women? I began imagining further hurdles I might have to overcome in order to get the appropriate approvals from the regional police inspector, but he finally shrugged his shoulders, signed the paperwork registering me as a foreign researcher, and handed me my copies.

These initial responses were echoed by many other Bengalis throughout the course of my time in both West Bengal and Bangladesh, and I came to realize that the absence of women in many people's accounts could not be attributed merely to skewed research tactics or misrepresentations of life on the ground because of a tendency among (predominantly male) researchers to ignore, or have little access to, women's perspectives. The image of Bauls as wandering solitary male minstrels, depicted romantically in literature, is shared by a significant number of Bengalis who live in places where one might expect such a view to be challenged by regular personal contact with the many very visible (and audible) Baul women. Two locally available bits of information challenge (or presumably *should* challenge) the view that only Bauls are men. First, performing women Bauls are visible on trains that leave Kolkata for many destinations in Birbhum, Bankura, Murshidabad, and Nadia and are seen singing at functions in Kolkata as well as the very popular Paus Mela in Santiniketan. Second, for those whose knowledge about Bauls is limited to literature, many books, especially those published since *Bānglār bāul o bāul gān* (*Bengali Bauls and Baul Songs*; Bhaṭṭācārya 1971[1968]), at least allude to Baul sexo-yogic rituals and implicate both men and women as practitioners. Even the person skeptical about women's agency in such relationships would need to concede that women are involved. So why this pervasive denial about the existence of women Bauls? I believe that much of the imaginings of Bauls among *bhadralok*, the elite who figure among the main patrons of Baul music in current-day West Bengal and Bangladesh, has grown out of a body of literature that made Bauls a popular and exciting Bengali phenomenon and, at the same time, marginalized women participants.

Scholarly Constructions of Bauls

SETTING THE STAGE

Scholars date the origin of the Baul tradition to sometime between the 14th and the early 20th century. However, Openshaw 2002:19–32 shows that mention of them in official texts (census reports, early Bengal District Gazetteers) and in Bengali scholarly or other literature is scant until the end of the 19th century, when discussions of Bauls begin to move from "near total obscurity relieved only by the odd reference to Bāuls as godless and debased entertainers of the common folk, to their apotheosis as bearers of a glorious indigenous heritage" (19; see also Urban 1999). Part of the problem in tracing the origins of Baul, as Edward Dimock (1966) points out, is that though the term *bāul* occurs frequently in medieval literature, it is unclear when, or if, it referred to such a group of people. Since *bāul* also means "mad" or "crazy," it could have been interpreted as such in the texts.

Mentions of Bauls in scholarly texts from the middle and end of the 19th century mostly condemned them as degenerate, filthy, and immoral (Dimock 1966:253; Openshaw 2002:22–23). For example, writing in the 1890s, J. N. Bhattacharya considered Bauls one of the "disreputable Chaitanyite sects of Bengal" and described them as "low class men ... [who] make it a point to appear as dirty as possible.... Not only their dress, but their musical instruments, their dancing, and their songs are all characterized by a kind of queerness which makes them very amusing" (1968[1896]:381). According to the description in Bhattacharya's index, "Baul" means "Batul [from Sanskrit], a madman. [They are] a class of beggars who pretend to be mad on account of religious fervour, and try to uphold their pretension by their fantastic dress, dirty habits, and the queer philosophy of their songs" (446). He adds that the appeal of such music and merriment is to the lower classes (381). Indeed, given the tone of his portrayal, it is clear that "respectable" Hindus would not associate with the likes of such people.

Hindus were not alone in their dislike of Baul practices and dress. Bauls and other fakirs (Muslim mendicants, a term often used for Muslim Bauls) came under attack during the Islamic reformist period in the late 19th and early 20th centuries. Bengali Muslim reformers denounced Bauls for their heterodoxy as well as their esoteric beliefs and practices, and they condemned Baul music as being un-Islamic. In fact, both orthodox Muslims and orthodox Hindus criticized Bauls for practices they deemed tainted by the other religion.

Although the more orthodox of West Bengal and Bangladesh remain critical of Bauls to the present day, some of the negative attitudes toward them began to change in the late 19th century as other upper-class Bengalis took an interest in Baul songs and philosophy. Rabindranath Tagore, a Nobel Laureate Bengali poet, is frequently credited with raising the status of Bauls in the eyes of the Bengali *bhadralok*. Although he and his friend and scholar Ksitimohan Sen certainly praised Bauls and contributed considerably to making their public image respectable, they were not solely responsible for the increasingly positive view of Bauls. Already some *bhadralok* were turning to idyllic village life as a source of nationalistic and regional images, and from the 1880s on, others were writing and publishing songs, which they called *bāul-gān* (Baul songs), suggesting that at least the songs were becoming appealing to more people, particularly the educated elite. Bengalis (like Indians in other regions) turned to village icons as sources of national and regional pride during a time when they were trying to assert a distinct and positive identity separate from British rule. A similar trend happened later as Bengalis from East Pakistan struggled for independence from Pakistan, eventually becoming the nation of Bangladesh. Due to the often violent attempts of Pakistan to suppress the Bengali heritage of Muslim Bengalis, Bengalis in turn responded by trying to find "an identity rooted in the soil of Bengal, rather than based on Islam as practiced in Arabia, [and thus] Muslim Bengalis exalted literary figures, whether Hindu or Muslim, who expressed nonsectarian humanistic beliefs" (Salomon 1991:269), including Rabindranath Tagore, Lalan Shah (Fakir), and Kazi Nazrul l Islam. The status of

Bauls in what is now Bangladesh thus improved in a way similar to what occurred in West Bengal; in creating a unique identity, whether in West Bengal or Bangladesh, Bengalis looked toward cultural symbols on their own soil, and in the Bauls they found much that was worthy of praise and pride.

Although Tagore was not alone in increasing the popularity of Bauls and Baul songs, his particular portrayal of them has had a significant, continuing impact on popular and scholarly constructions of Bauls. In 1915–16, Tagore published several songs by Lalan Shah, considered a great Baul poet, and around the same time played the role of a blind Baul in his play *Phalgun*. Tagore also openly acknowledged his debt to Bauls for inspiring and influencing many of his melodies and his poetic imagery.

For Tagore, Bauls were not only a source of indigenous wisdom; they also embodied a spirit of freedom and creativity. He praised them for their spiritual pursuits and their blanket disapproval of orthodox traditions, sectarian divisions, and religious institutions, such as temples and mosques. Tagore viewed these ideals and their expressions as both an inspiration and a goal. Believing in the unity of religions, he found in Baul songs a "clue to the inner meaning of all religions," which has to do with the "divinity of Man" and "the God of human personality" (Tagore 1963[1931]:12).

The Baul of Tagore closely resembles a *sādhu* or *sannyāsī*. He had no worldly attachments, family or even kin, and he wandered around the countryside of Bengal, singing and spreading his message of love. He was also exclusively male; not only did he not have a spouse and family, but there is scant evidence of his participation in any sexo-yogic practices involving the sexual union of a male and a female Baul. Furthermore, Tagore translated the phrase *maner mānush*, the realization of which is a goal of Bauls, as "Man of the Heart." Translated literally, however, *maner mānush* means the "person of the heart or mind." Openshaw found in her fieldwork that the term also referred to " 'a/the person (suitable) for me' or 'a person one finds particularly attractive.' In all these senses, it refers as often to a woman as a man, as indeed does the word *mānus* itself" (1993:21). In Tagore's portrayal, Bauls became spiritualized, male, and without female partners. He and Sen ignored the sexo-yogic union of male and female Bauls, the very practice of which would bring one to the realization of *maner mānush*, focusing instead on the love between the Baul and *maner mānush*. Considering that Bengalis had condemned (and would continue to condemn) Bauls for their "deviant" sexual practices, Tagore's portrayal of a more idealized and "clean" Baul is not a surprise. In addition, by situating Bauls within a larger *sādhu* or *sannyāsī* community, Baul behavior and appearance became much more acceptable.

Tagore's Bauls, however, had only limited connection with actual Bauls of Bengal. As the popularity of Bauls increased, however, more scholars began to research the subject, eventually leading to more complex and context-sensitive views. Upendranāth Bhaṭṭācārya, in his extensive book *Bānglār bāul o bāul gān*, provided one of the first real challenges to the Tagorean view of Bauls. Bhaṭṭācārya emphasized that one of the most important aspects of Bauls was actually the eso-teric doctrines and practices that had previously been ignored or denied by such scholars as Tagore and Sen. He also argued that the ritual *sādhanā* practiced by Muslim and Hindu Bauls was essentially the same and the basis of their doctrine. Furthermore, he argued that only an understanding of the sexo-yogic rituals and their purpose would lead to an actual appreciation of Baul songs. Thus previous renderings of the songs and their meanings, having ignored *sādhanā* and *deha-tattva*, completely missed the point. Based on over twenty years of fieldwork, Bhaṭṭācārya's book was the first extensive field study of Bauls. It also provides interpretations of Baul songs, more than 500 of which are included.

Bhaṭṭācārya's argument of the centrality of sexo-yogic rituals to Baul identity was met with a good deal of resistance, particularly initially. However, many early Baul scholars did make veiled references to the rituals without going into specifics. For example, in his important work on religious sects in Bengal, Shashibhusan Dasgupta (1962[1946]) appears to strike a balance between the views represented by Tagore and those later espoused by Bhaṭṭācārya. In asserting his approval of the Tagorean Baul in search of *maner mānush*, he in effect dismisses Bhaṭṭācārya's claim that sexo-yogic practices are at the heart of Baul philosophy and songs (161–162). Dasgupta concedes that the esoteric rituals of the Vaishnava Sahajiyas (another loose category embracing practices and beliefs similar to those of Bauls) "were also known" to Bauls and describes those rituals in chapters focused on Sahajiyas. But he asserts that the search for the "unknown bird" (*acin pākhi*; another name for the Divine located in the body) is the defining characteristic of Bauls, and in his chapter on Bauls he includes songs about this search, whether composed by Bauls or other poets, including Tagore. Dasgupta's preference for the Tagorean Baul is underscored in his conclusion to his chapter on Bauls: "Tagore has been the greatest of the Bauls of Bengal" (187).

Despite very adamant contestations of this portrayal by later scholars, many *bhadralok* have continued to hold on to Tagore's version. For a while Tagore's ide-alized Baul persisted because Bauls became emblematic of national pride among Bengali and Bangladeshi nationalists. The image has been difficult to contest also because for many urban Bengalis Bauls conjure up a romanticized view of rural Bengali life. Even with the introduction of information about sexo-yogic *sādhanā* into the corpus of literature on Bauls, many writers have preferred less controversial portrayals of Bauls. For example, in his ethnography of Bauls, R. M. Sarkar (1990) glosses over Baul ritual practices, focusing more on the state of mind of Bauls and the goal of rituals than the details of the rituals themselves. Thus concerning the ritual of *cāri-candra bhed*, or the "piercing of the four moons," Sarkar explains that the "four essential elements of the body—semen, the menstrual flow, stool and urine...[are exchanged by ritual partners] *of course, psychically*, so that each of them would acquire a perfect mind to win over all the bodily and worldly affairs" (33; emphasis added). Baul ritual practices are controversial not only because they go against conventional norms but also because they problematize idealistic

imaginings of Bauls. Furthermore, although acknowledgement of these various rituals may imply the presence of women, authors have generally been more concerned
with exploring the less controversial subjects of philosophy, songs, and historical
origins of Bauls than with delving into the circumstances and views of women
themselves.

ON BAUL WOMEN

Until quite recently, mentions of women among Bauls—be they women identified
as Bauls or women partners of Baul men—are limited in the literature. Usually
when writers mention women, it is in the context of sexo-yogic rituals. In such situations, women appear to be present for the benefit of the male ritual practitioners,
are called *sevādāsī*s, and are viewed, to use Sarkar's works, as "helpers of the [male]
Baul concerned in proceeding in the long path of devotional practice" (73). One
gets a sense also that these women are easily replaceable. We see this in Sarkar's
account, for instance, when he claims that male Bauls may easily leave women partners who become pregnant and that Bauls tend to look for new *sevādāsī*s at *melā*s,
or fairs, where they attract women with their song and dance. The other context in
which women may be mentioned is while discussing so-called domestic Bauls. Since
in this case men and women are married and usually have children, discussing the
presence of women is unavoidable. Manas Ray (1994), in his ethnography of Bauls
in Birbhum, states that in ideal circumstances a Baul does not have a traditional
family but lives in an ashram with his guru and *guru-mā* and his *sādhanā saṅginī*
(female ritual partner). Although the Bauls he researched were settled into domestic
life, his information about women Bauls in particular is limited. Charles Capwell
(1986), an ethnomusicologist, also mentions women in the context of ritual and
domestic life—when he discusses the wives, sisters, mothers, and mothers-in-law of
his main informants. Capwell and Sarkar each mention one woman who is an
exception in the community. Capwell describes the woman he saw as dressed like a
Baul and as being "more expressive and mobile than was usual among women
singers" (1986:18). Sarkar refers to one Baul woman as a *sādhikā* (female practitioner of *sādhanā*). Neither author attempts to contextualize these women or to
reconcile the disparate images of the *sevādāsī*s who are "helpers of Bauls" and the
sādhikā who is actively pursuing her own path.

   In much of this literature, very few Baul women stand out enough from traditional gender roles to bear mention. Even when the situation of these Baul women
is considered, writers continue to see their influence among Bauls as minor. A few
recent scholars, however, do take the role of women more seriously and show Baul
women in quite a different light from that in most other texts. This section will
address some of the scholars who discuss, in varying but greater degrees, the role
and position of women among the Bauls.

   Sudhīr Cakrabartī (2001), though he devotes some discussion to women in his
book *Bāul phākir kathā*, appears to view women among Bauls as being particularly

vulnerable and their role as minor. Reflecting on his impression of two Baul women, Cakrabartī wonders why they remain with partners he believes are likely to leave them. He discusses one woman who is the *saṅginī* (companion) of a Baul he admired until that Baul man went overseas to sing and was corrupted by white women (161). Now looking at the Baul's *saṅginī*, all Cakrabartī sees is the tenuousness of her situation. Another women is Maki,[1] a Japanese woman he says feels fortunate to have found a guru in Sadhan Das (172). Cakrabartī speculates that as *sādhikā* and *saṅginī*, these women do not know where their path will take them; they follow their guru (here, partner), not worrying about being abandoned. Nowhere in this work does he directly ask women to reflect on their own position and future.

Līnā Cākī (2001, 1997, 1995) has a similar view of Baul women as reflected in her book *Bāuler caraṇdāsī* (*Servants of the Baul's Feet*) and in articles devoted to the subject. A journalist in Kolkata, Cākī traveled to spend time with Baul women and to learn about their circumstances. Unlike previous writers on Bauls, she states that there are indeed numerous Baul women, though she does hold that among these there are very few who are genuine. Like the *bhadralok* discussed below who have become disenchanted and cynical about Bauls, Cākī (1995:88) thinks the Baul sect is almost extinct. She also believes that most women associated with Bauls come from the pool of widows, women abandoned by husbands, or poor families. Discounting any significant agency to these women, she depicts them as victims of circumstances, subject to likely abandonment by men who will not hesitate to leave them on a whim or when they become older. She argues that women are merely the steps on men's path to perfection (*siddhi*) and that they know very little if anything about *sādhanā* (85). One of the objectives in Cākī's work, it appears, is to counter idealistic and overly romanticized views *bhadralok* have of Bauls by revealing that life for women called Bauls or partners with Baul men is not at all idyllic. Her work is successful in showing that although Bauls may say they value women, in practice this may not be the case.

While it is notable that field experience with Bauls has led Cākī and Cakrabartī to discuss women, a lack pervasive in the earlier material, their work continues the marginalization of women. Cakrabartī does not foreground women's voices but uses his own voice to articulate his opinions based on his observations. Although women are described, their own views and actions do not come through in his writing. And even as Cākī offers valuable glimpses of life stories and interviews, her general argument is the victimization of women.

Whereas Cakrabartī and Cākī focus on the tenuousness of Baul women's circumstances, June McDaniel, in her article "The Embodiment of God among the Bauls of Bengal" (1992), seeks to demonstrate that women and men are equally valued in the ideology and ritual of Bauls. She shows that unlike women in most other religious traditions, Baul women are considered ritual equals and that the female body "is sacred and the dwelling place of a deity which is neither male nor female, but includes aspects of both" (27). Also unlike most other traditions, Bauls view menstrual blood as not just a highly charged substance, but also a positive one indicative of the overflowing nature of female power. Although McDaniel finds evidence for an ideological valuation of women among Bauls, she does not tackle the question of whether or not this translates into higher status for Baul women, particularly in comparison with non-Baul women living in otherwise similar circumstances. McDaniel seems to rely primarily on the ideological information available in other texts written about Bauls, which are written from a male perspective, and the words of informants, which also describe the ritual and ideology from only a male perspective.

For example, McDaniel describes part of *sādhanā* as the union of male and female during menstruation when the deity inside the woman is believed to be present in her menstrual flow. The man then "goes fishing" through ritual in order to capture this aspect of the divine and unite it with his own (28). In a footnote, McDaniel adds that "this aspect of the practice is written primarily from the male perspective. The woman is understood to unite with the divine aspect within the man, but her technique of doing so is unspecified in the literature. It is unclear if the woman can 'go fishing for her own fish'" (28–29).

Clearly one source of McDaniel's literature is *bāul-gān*, or Baul songs, particularly those written by Lalan Shah, and this would explain why the rituals are discussed from the male perspective. As she writes, "it is unfortunate that virtually all Baul songs have been written by men, for it is thus difficult to gain access to women's religious experience" (37). She then continues to say that in her fieldwork she observed Baul men and women of both the ascetic and householder types. She notes that householder "couples acted fondly toward each other" and that "the women participated in conversation and seemed equally involved in religious practice" (37). Did she conclude from her observations that Baul women's status was high? In talking of ascetics, she notes that men and women have a more casual approach to marriage, as they are supposed to be detached from the world and such relationships. In these cases, women were not considered wives "but rather *sevadasis* or *bhairavis*, handmaidens or ritual assistants" (37) and thus either "professional assistants or ascetics themselves" (38). She also notes that "partners seemed interchangeable among renunciants who were seeking to overcome both lust and human love" (38). What then does it mean for women's position among ascetics that their role may be temporary and interchangeable professional ritual *assistants*?[2]

Two recent publications deserve mention. *Song of the Great Soul* by Parvathy Baul 2005 and *The Honey Gatherers* (first published as *Baulsphere* 2009) by Mimlu Sen 2010 are both written by Bengali women in English and describe their personal journey among Bauls. Both women came from high caste and well-educated backgrounds, took initiation with a Baul guru, learned Baul songs and philosophy, and have been active in the community of Bauls. Their books are not concerned with an analysis of gender, but they provide insight into the appeal of this path to educated women.

The final two scholars I discuss not only offer more information about women among Bauls, but they also demonstrate their importance. Jeanne Openshaw's

Seeking Bāuls of Bengal (2002), based largely on her dissertation (1993), discusses in detail, among many other things, Baul views on women in ritual practices and philosophy. Kristin Hanssen's dissertation (2001) and chapter in Khandelwal et al. 2006, based on fieldwork with two small Baul families in Rampurhat, Birbhum, incorporates the life experiences and views of women members of the families. Both of these anthropologists take the view of women seriously, though gender is not their central analytic concern.

Openshaw's excellent work is distinguished by being specific and context-sensitive. Aside from a thorough analysis of literature on Bauls and an overview of Bauls in West Bengal, Openshaw focuses largely on one guru, Rāj Khyāpā, and his followers.[3] This gives her a concrete context for an in-depth discussion of some Bauls, whom she calls *bartamān-panthīs*,[4] even as she highlights different perspectives about philosophy and practice among other Bauls. Her work on women surfaces in three main areas: in the idea of woman as a guru, some *bartamān-panthī* views on women, and the woman in ritual practices.

While Bauls tend to recognize three different types of gurus (*dīkshā, śikshā, bhek*) whose roles are often performed by three or more people, Openshaw demonstrates that many *bartamān-panthīs* emphasize the importance of their female partner, often viewed also as a *śikshā* guru, over their other gurus. Part of the reason for this is that women are viewed as "naturally perfected without having to undergo esoteric practice, and therefore need no guru [themselves]. What a woman is and does naturally, a man must achieve through cultivation and practice" (Openshaw 2002:147). *Bartamān-panthīs* believe women are to be worshipped and that "a man's success in esoteric practice depends largely (some would say wholly) on his female partner" (146). Although *bartamān-panthīs* value different gurus, they clearly emphasize their female partner as a significant guru in her own right.

Openshaw also explains that *bartamān-panthīs* tend to extol women as a generalized form called variously *nārī* (woman), *meye* (girl), *śakti* (female power, the goddess, or power conceptualized as female), *mā* (mother), or *prakṛti* (nature, seen as female), and most do not pay credence to a named individual (177). Rāj Khyāpā, however, does do so by ending his songs with the name of his beloved partner, Rājeśvar, alongside his own instead of the guru, as done by most others. He also dedicates his written text on theory to Rājeśvar (147; see also Openshaw 2010). Although naming one's female partner is rare among Bauls, even among those who clearly value women, Rāj's example underscores the importance placed on women.

Openshaw suggests that the "vilification of woman is yet another manifestation of the *hiṁsā* [ill will] of householder society combated by Rāj, his disciples and other *bartamān-panthīs*" (177). One of the followers of Rāj, Satīś, wrote extensively on his views of the nature and role of women, criticizing conventional views on women that often depict women as the gateway to hell. I quote a portion of Openshaw's summary of Satīś's views at some length:

Woman is the creator of all, without her, and intercourse with her, nothing would exist. If anything, man is the woman's gateway to hell, he argues. Because of his lust, she suffers the pain and dangers of child-birth. Sometimes he even abandons her when she gets pregnant.... [Satīs] contradicts many renouncers in maintaining that if a man loses his semen, it is his own fault, not the fault of the woman. Women are not tigresses (as some renouncers affirm) but givers of joy. (176)

Openshaw claims that Satīs's views on women and women's sexuality are shared by many *bartamān-panthī*s (177). *Bartamān-panthī*s believe in the worship of the human being, and for many this translates to the man worshipping the woman and the woman the man. Their view is held in direct opposition to worship directed toward images, or *mūrti pūjā*, as is the common form of worship among Hindus. Thus in one song, Maṇi Gosāi, a disciple of Rāj, states:

Deluded people worship images of clay, metal and stone....
Maṇi relates the words of Rāj—do not worship an unknown treasure.
First comes the worship of the one who eats, sleeps, shits, and speaks with me. (184)

They also share the idea with orthodox *sādhu*s of the value of retaining semen, yet they approach this altogether differently. Instead of celibacy, which they mock, they embrace sexual union as their *sādhanā* and use it to transform lust (*kām*) into love (*prem*). They also conflate the notion of woman as mother and lover, often referring to their wives as *mā*[5] (177–79). Openshaw's work on Rāj continues in *Writing the Self* 2010, which focuses on his biography. That book further demonstrates Rāj's devotion and respect for his partner, even sacrificing his own social standing for his relationship with her.

Hanssen (2006:106–107) discusses, among other things, the ways in which the Bauls she lived and worked with explain ritual; for example, they believe that seed is present in both male and female sexual fluids and is viewed as both the same substance and of different qualities. The "seed" in these fluids, as well as in food, is seen by the Bauls Hanssen worked with as life-sustaining, allowing them to live in good health, be strong, and sing. The seed women possess is highly charged, particularly in a young woman's first menstruation, and is considered nourishing for those who ritually ingest it (107). Not only are women's fluids valued, but Hanssen's interlocutor Tara also believes "women are afforded a central place" in rituals (2001:63). Furthermore, Hanssen explains that Tara consciously avoided following traditional roles for women, being "weary of ending up like her mother, having to cook and clean for a husband who might abandon her, as her father did" (2001:55). Unlike traditionally married women, Tara stated that she goes out of the home regularly, does not wear the vermillion line in her hair parting, and mingles with non-kin. Hanssen suggests that Tara's choice to become a Baul singer was in part motivated by her gender (56).

Although I have touched on some of the major threads, my main concern here is the depiction of women—or significant lack thereof—in this literature. Most of this literature relegates women to a lesser status—as *sevādāsīs*, replaceable partners in men's rituals, or through their relative absence in the literature in favor of a more pure and idealized Tagorean Baul. Other scholars suggest that Bauls regard women highly. These more positive views on women are consistent with the understanding that Bauls (or *bartamān-panthī*) are *ulta-pathik* (one who travels the reverse path, i.e. goes against conventional society), as evident also in their disregard of the caste system and orthodox rituals. Despite Bauls commitment to their oppositional views, there are likely disjunctures between ideology and practice. Openshaw (2002) does not analyze such disjunctures, but she notes that discrepancies between Baul views of women and women's actual roles and experiences are to be found. Other writers, such as Līnā Cākī (2001), June McDaniel (1992), and Carol Salomon (1995:195), speculate that the sexo-yogic rituals are for the benefit of men, though they do not pursue the question with women practitioners.

This literature is important because, as we will see, it has an impact on the perception that Bengalis (and foreigners) have of Baul women and, consequently, influences women's lives. Tagore's portrayal of Bauls pulls at the heartstrings of many Bengalis (and others as well) and remains influential even though more nuanced and context-sensitive writings have begun to emerge. Even when people realize that there are women among Bauls, they tend to either dismiss those women or hold those women to the same expectations as they hold Baul men. In other words, they expect women to behave with the same freedom as evidenced in men. This, as I will show, poses problems for Baul women.

Popular Imaginings of Bauls

Tagore's version of Bauls endures in the minds of many *bhadralok* and is reflected in the material culture of Santiniketan and the dress of performing Bauls. Although Baul women are indeed very visible in Santiniketan, performing regularly at functions, they remain at the margins of this discourse on Bauls. In Bangladesh, where one of the most popular Bauls today is a woman, Kangalini Sufia, it is perhaps even more surprising to find, as I did in Sylhet, people who claim there are no Baul women. My experience in Bangladesh leads me to believe that the marginalization of women has a slightly different motivation there, the local enhanced valuation of purdah perhaps being an influence. (The term *purdah* comprises a complex of practices by women, such as veiling, seclusion, or silence, with the aim of displaying modesty and protecting their honor as well as the honor of their families; see chapter 3.) However, ideals of the Tagorean Baul as well as expectations for appropriate behavior of women (such as purdah) influence the situation of Baul women in both regions, though to different degrees in different locations. In this section, I examine some of the popular Bengali conceptions of Bauls that influence Baul women.

FIGURE 2.1. *Hindu Bauls performing at Paus Mela, 1998*

FIGURE 2.2. *Muslim Bauls (Fakirs) performing at Paus Mela, 1998*

For the larger public, it is predominantly the performance context that provides information about Bauls. Baul performances are hugely popular in both West Bengal and Bangladesh. During the annual Paus Mela (see Figures 2.1 and 2.2), Kolkatans flock to Santiniketan, filling the area's numerous hotels that have been constructed largely for this event. The festival celebrating the famous Vaishnava poet Joydeb also features Baul songs (see Figure 2.3). Located in rural Kenduli, about 40 km from Santiniketan, Joydeb Mela attracts people from the region as well as from the city.

In Kusthia, a district in western Bangladesh, two annual festivals celebrate Lalan Shah and draw Bauls from both sides of the border as well as large numbers of people from the local area and from cities like Dhaka and Rajshahi. In 1999, I saw Kangalini perform onstage with a group of Bauls at the British Council in Dhaka before an audience of predominantly well-dressed *bhadralok*. The Narigrantha Prabartana, a feminist bookstore in Dhaka, also housed a Baul performance during my stay in Bangladesh. In addition to these larger performances, Bauls regularly perform at *melā*s, or festivals, held throughout the countryside and are invited to

FIGURE 2.3. *Ananda Gopal Das, performance at Joydeb Mela, 1999*

FIGURE 2.4. *A man from the audience pins money on a Baul woman's sari at Joydeb Mela, 1999*

sing at the death anniversaries of *pīr*s (*urs*), at village festivals, and at *pūjā*s (worship) for a deity, saint, or guru. *Bhadralok* also invite Bauls to perform for a group of friends at their home. In whatever setting, audience members typically express their appreciation for Baul performers by giving them money, sometimes pinning it onto their clothes (see Figure 2.4).

Because Bauls are often idealized for their rhetoric of antidiscrimination and a life unencumbered by (excessive) propagation, they are frequently hired by the government or by NGOs to sing at events oriented toward promoting awareness of such issues as family planning, AIDS, or the problems of caste privileges and religious prejudices. One day when I was visiting Kangalini, she and her husband were writing songs about family planning for a television program (see Figure 2.5). Jaya and Niranjan, a young Baul couple living outside Santiniketan, performed in many villages around the region for UNESCO to promote fair treatment of daughters. Rina and Dibakar, also in Birbhum, performed at functions organized to educate rural people about AIDS and leprosy. Farhad Mazhar, one of the organizers of Narigrantha Prabartana, uses Baul songs and ideas to communicate the NGO's messages to an audience consisting of rural as well as urban people.

Whatever the type of event, performing Bauls are usually recognized by their appearance. Men typically wear an ocher-colored *pānjābī*[6] (a long shirt usually worn with plain drawstring pants), and often they have a long piece of cloth wrapped around their waist or as a turban on their head.[7] Many also wear a patchwork jacket made up of pieces of leftover cloth. Women usually wear saris of the same ocher color, and sometimes their long hair, which traditional South Asian women

FIGURE 2.5. *Shekham and Kangalini Sufia, composing songs on family planning, Dhaka, 2000*

typically pull back into a neat bun, hangs loose as they sing.[8] It is usually expected that Bauls will dance, the expression of their devotion and marginality pouring out through their joyful jumps and twirls. These images are prominent in the minds of urban *bhadralok*, and public performances, television, and newspaper articles usually confirm these images.

When I saw Kangalini and six other Bauls perform at the British Council in Bangladesh, I was struck at how it seemed they intentionally sought to fulfill people's expectations of Bauls. They performed after several other singers of folk songs, including Farida Parveen, a distinguished professional singer of Lalan Shah songs. My field notes from September 2, 1999, based on initial impressions, record that the Baul performance highlights the ways in which the Baul performers had the "Baul look":

> I was first struck by what was an echo effect on the voice. None of the previous singers had it, but now suddenly the "spiritual" singers used it to create an affect of the mystical. Most likely it was the producers who suggested it. The two performing in front also appeared to have the "Baul look": long hair, flowing robes. The first singer wasn't all that good, but he seemed to know what was expected of him and swayed in dance.... Next to the front came Kangalini Sufia. Everyone seemed very excited to have her sing, and the audience applauded as she came forward. She was wearing a wrinkly orange sari with an orange scarf that she had over her shoulders sometimes and waved around in both hands other times. At first she carried a little *ektārā* in her

hand, and this she waved around as she danced. She didn't play it, but used it as a prop. Her voice didn't seem particularly strong, but it was hard to hear her as she was far from the microphone. She seemed somehow very self-conscious as she sang and danced, and I got the impression that her image was cultivated. She wore her hair loose and often swung it around as she danced. She used the *ektārā* or the scarf to accentuate her swaying and movements, holding them above her head as she twirled around and swayed from side to side.

It was later that I began to get to know Kangalini, and to say she merely acts a role does not do her justice. She is a complicated woman who is very aware of her own position in society. At the same time, there is something completely honest and carefree in her dealings with the world in which she lives. Her story I take up later. For now, I will say that she does have an awareness of people's expectations of her as a performer and tries to fulfill their wishes. When I asked her and other Baul performers why they dress in ocher-colored clothes when they perform but ordinary clothes the rest of the time, they always responded that they wore onstage what was expected of them. As a TV producer in Dhaka told me, he hires Kangalini because she gives people the kind of performance they want. Another man, when I asked what he thought Bauls were, came up with the English word "supernatural," suggesting that there was some mystical power to Bauls. So, add to Kangalini's performance a bit of echo effect, and the impression of the mystical Baul is complete.

Several Bengalis I asked to explain how they know when someone is a Baul cited the ocher-colored clothes and instruments as the identifying markers. Once when I was interviewed by a journalist in Dhaka, I had been asked to bring photos of Baul women. When the photos I brought showed women who looked like ordinary women with their hair tied back and wearing printed green or blue saris, my interviewer looked disappointed and asked if I might have some other photos; from these photos—even one of Kangalini Sufia, the most famous Baul singer in Bangladesh—the journalist could not recognize them as Bauls. But these women, as well as men, usually dress in ocher-colored cloth and carry an instrument only when they are going to perform or be interviewed. The rest of the time they look mostly like any other women from their class (see Figures 2.6 and 2.7 for comparative examples). A major exception to this is that Bauls from the western parts of Bangladesh, such as Jessore, Jhenaidah, and Kusthia, wear only white.

For many urban Bengalis, Bauls embody a certain "realness": the simplicity of village life, the purity of spiritual pursuits, the passion of singing from the heart, and a longing for an experience of the Divine. As the organizer of the British Council cultural events in Dhaka told me, Baul songs remind urban people in Dhaka and Kolkata of their connection to the villages where many of them still have ancestral homes. The material culture in Santiniketan shows Bauls as still being idealized for their connection to pristine village life and mystical knowledge. Representations of Bauls in the shops of Santiniketan target and perpetuate these ideas. One of the most common images of Bauls is of a man with a beard who wears a turban and a

FIGURE 2.6. *Kangalini Sufia wearing a pink and green sari in her home in Mirpur, 2000*

FIGURE 2.7. *Cover illustration of cassette produced by Electro Voice featuring Kangalini dressed in the bright orange sari she wears during performances and holding an ektārā*

long *pānjābī* or *ālkhāllā*. In his hand he holds an *ektārā*, and he gazes up into the sky as he sings. He is often also posed to look like he is dancing and twirling. This ubiquitous image is painted on buildings or molded in terra-cotta on the outside walls of many hotels and guest houses as well as residences (see Figures 2.8 and 2.9). Local tourist shops sell batiks and carvings of this Baul man (see Figure 2.10). Only

FIGURE 2.8. *Terra-cotta Baul decoration on wall of a Santiniketan home, 2000*

FIGURE 2.9. *Statue of a Baul standing in front of a home in Santiniketan, 2000*

occasionally are women depicted: on shelves next to wooden images of men fishing and Santal women dancing (both equally exotified) stand small wooden Baul couples decorated with ocher-colored paint, a cloth turban on the man's head, and an *ektārā* in his hand (see Figure 2.11).

FIGURE 2.10. *Batik of a Baul man performing in a village setting (center) flanked by batiks of the Goddess Durga (left) and a Santal couple (right) in a shop in Santiniketan, 2000*

FIGURE 2.11. *Small wooden Baul couples on display alongside other wooden items depicting typical village scenes, including (bottom shelf) fishermen wearing wide-brimmed hats and (top shelf) drummers performing, Santiniketan, 2000*

FIGURE 2.12. *Mural in Jessore, Bangladesh, depicting (far left) a Baul man wearing ocher-colored clothing and carrying an ektārā and (to the right) a triumphant Sheikh Mujib, first prime minister and the traditional father of Bangladesh, 2000*

On my return in 2007, I noticed that one shop had acquired wooden images of a single Baul woman. Like her male counterpart, she held her *ektārā* above her; she stood four inches tall, and her painted eyes, rimmed with long lashes, were fixed toward the sky. Although Baul women have received more recognition in the past decade, I saw in 2007 that most of the new representations of Bauls in Santiniketan are still male and much the same as those conceptualized and publicized by Tagore.

Figure 2.12 shows a similar portrayal of a Baul man in Bangladesh. Painted on a wall along a public street in Jessore, the Baul man, dressed in ocher-colored cloth and carrying an *ektārā* in one hand, is positioned directly to the left of the first prime minister of Bangladesh, Sheikh Mujib. Given the sometimes very tense relationship in Bangladesh between conservative Islam and Bauls (as well as other "non-Muslim" groups and/or the question of the permissibility of music in Islam), this juxtaposition on a mural is not only a political statement of a more moderate Bangladesh; it is also a testament to the positive view of Bauls shared by many Bangladeshis.

Bengali *bhadralok*: Searching for Real Bauls

Although educated elites, including many who consider themselves Marxists, have admired Bauls for their ideals of egalitarianism and social reform, many are now cynical about Bauls because they believe Bauls have succumbed to materialism and the concordant states of responsibility, anxiety, and dependence. They see that instead of being carefree and unconcerned about material wealth, many Bauls are actively and aggressively looking for sponsors who will provide them with fame, money, and international exposure. Very ironically, Bauls are no longer meeting the expectations of many of the *bhadralok* who used to treasure their ways and their music. Speaking of Muslim Bauls, one *bhadralok* in Santiniketan said: "They had been my last hope, but now they just sing the same fucking songs of Lalan! And they no longer dress in rags. They dress better than many of us do! They used to hit themselves on the head right onstage and bleed as they got involved with the music. Now they're looking more and more professional and *still* sing the same songs."

What many *bhadralok* valued in Bauls was something considered to be "genuine"—reminiscent of the indigenous knowledge of Tagore's spiritualized Bauls. Many *bhadralok* claim that you can see someone's genuineness in their eyes: "There's something—a spark—in their eyes. You can tell they're doing their *sādhanā*." And when I would tell someone I had met an interesting Baul, often they would ask if I had seen "it" in their eyes. What they usually had in mind was an inner feeling or emotion (*bhāb*) viewed as highly developed in only some Bauls and other holy people. Although they were not able to be much more specific about what they were hoping to see in a Baul's eyes, they were often very clear that they knew the difference between "real" Bauls and "fake" ones. This kind of dichotomy, constructed in several different ways, was prevalent in conversations I had with *bhadralok* as well as with Bauls and villagers. Distinguishing between different kinds of Bauls is one way of dealing with the disappointment that many Bengali elite have of Bauls. In that way they can continue to hold onto the ideals of Bauls and yet criticize what they see to be shortcomings.

Distinguishing between "real" and "fake" holy women and men is common in South Asia, where various people regularly evaluate the power and authority of religious people. As Ann Grodzins Gold states, "wandering holy men—whether genuine selfless saints, pompous and self-important platitude-spouting preachers, or fraudulent self-serving rascals—are stock figures in classical Sanskrit theatre, simple vernacular tales, and oral epics" (1992:54). The *sādhu* (holy man or saint) who is really a dacoit (robber) or the yogi who uses his or her powers for selfish or destructive ends is a common image in narratives.[9] In her work on women renouncers (*sannyāsinīs*), Meena Khandelwal (2004) argues that potential disciples and laypeople base their evaluations of the genuineness of various saints on personal sets of criteria, there being no established objective standards or institutional enforcement regulating sainthood. Like the *bhadralok* I met, she encountered various and often contradictory views on what constitutes a real saint. Khandelwal further suggests that "ultimately, however, saintly authenticity is a question of inner attitude" (142), a reflection of which some of the *bhadralok* I met sought in the eyes or practices of Bauls.

There are two criteria for real Bauls that *bhadralok* I met frequently stressed: freedom from societal bonds and responsibilities and *sādhanā*. At a party in the house of a Bengali intellectual in Santiniketan, a Bengali woman, elegantly dressed in a pressed white sari with a green, sleeveless blouse, asked me what I was doing in Santiniketan. When I told her I was researching Baul women, she replied, laughing, that I should interview her too: "I'm a Baul too! Why not? I want freedom.... sure I'm a Baul." Another upper-middle-class woman from Kolkata whom I met at the Joydeb festival, held not far from Santiniketan, expressed similar sentiments. She had taken a Baul woman as a teacher both because she loved the songs, which she was learning, and because she valued the life of freedom she saw in Bauls. As a result, she had taken this trip to spend a couple days at a festival, being able to leave her husband and worries at home in Kolkata. These two women, both very well educated and wealthy, saw Bauls as representing freedom and independence. Although neither one of them, I believe, would really consider themselves Bauls, they want to share in that freedom.[10] In fact, as elite women, they are able to enjoy what they see as the positive aspects of being *bāul* and then return to their urban homes without having to contend with the more difficult and daily consequences of what being *bāul* actually means for women.[11]

While this sense of freedom is reflected in Tagore's discourse on Bauls, the emphasis on *sādhanā* as central to Baul identity came about during the middle of the 20th century with the publication of numerous books describing the secret sexual elements of the ritual, discussed earlier in this chapter. Baul *sādhanā* includes sexo-yogic rituals involving seminal retention, and knowledge about its practice is passed down from guru to disciple. As a result of these publications, however, many *bhadralok* have an idea about the existence of these rituals as well as the assertion that childlessness is proof of successful *sādhanā*. Therefore, according to some people, Bauls with no children are often considered more "real," since having children is considered proof that they are not doing their *sādhanā* (correctly).

Also as a result of awareness about Baul *sādhanā*, Bauls have gained a reputation, especially around the Santiniketan area, for being promiscuous. Usually men are described this way, and people gossip about the number of "wives" a Baul has. Some *bhadralok* warned me about the reputation of certain Baul men, explaining that one was a ladies' man and that another had a seductive or mysterious look about him. Most of the people I spoke with in Santiniketan who mentioned the promiscuity of Bauls merely accepted it as a characteristic of men and women Bauls. I did notice, however, that some enjoyed talking about this, winking their eye conspiratorially as if to suggest that I, as a Westerner, would surely also understand. A few times people talked of Baul women in terms of their sexual independence, but I found actual examples of this rare. One older *bhadralok* who helped me meet Baul women early on in my research urged me to ask my interviewees whether or not they believed Baul women could leave their husbands easily. He felt that the answer to this question would clarify whether or not that woman was really a Baul. As an example, he told me of a "real" Baul woman he knew years ago who would just get up on a whim and leave her husband to travel alone without so much as providing an explanation.

To exotify or make an Other of others is not unique to *bhadralok* and Bauls, or to Bengal. Urban elites in other parts of India are nostalgic about aspects of rural life and exotify rural traditions and arts, for instance, by drawing on them in Bollywood films and in fashion. William S. Sax (2002) has demonstrated that creating an Other is universal, as all people tend to focus on the differences evident in other groups. (In other words, Bauls also see *bhadralok* as Others.) Furthermore, the Other is not necessarily or completely inferior. As Sax argues, "The Other is also a reflection of the self, at times resented, at other times emulated" (191). This is certainly true of *bhadralok* views of Bauls.

Bhadralok imaginings of Bauls as materially, socially, and sexually unencumbered say much more about *bhadralok* and their particular relationships with Bauls than about Bauls themselves. *Bhadralok* seem to have a particular vested interest in Bauls, as they conjure up many images *bhadralok* long to identify with. This is not hard to see in the Tagorean Baul, for it is this Baul who embodies the mystical knowledge rooted in Bengal's soil. Even Tagore identified with Bauls by acting the part of a Baul in his play and by acknowledging his debt to Bauls like Lalan Shah. *Bhadralok* share Baul feelings about music, and many *bhadralok* are casual singers of Baul songs or Rabindra Sangeet (songs by Tagore, at least some of which are inspired by *bāul-gān*). It seems that even the view that Bauls are sexually free elicits *bhadralok* fascination with—and often disdain for—"free love." Although probably only a few *bhadralok* have positive views of promiscuity among Bauls, the idea that Baul men and women are unencumbered by traditional family mores may be appealing to many others, including those who embrace the common Indian construction of the Western liberated individual. As many visitors to India have noted, Indians tend to characterize themselves as more concerned for the greater good than the individual. This concern is cited as the reason why it is crucial that individuals suppress their personal desires, including love marriage, by following tradition and family instead. Indians contrast this concern for society with what they view as an obsession by Westerners to satisfy individual desires, even at the expense of parents and spouses (hence the high divorce rate in countries such as America). Urban and rural Bengalis asked me countless questions about "free love" in America, and many also assumed that the interest Westerners have in Bauls stems from shared practices of promiscuity. Although *bhadralok* do not condone promiscuity, at least not openly, the idea that Bauls follow their desires despite "tradition" may be appealing to some urban elite in a society that has become more driven by individual desires than was perhaps the case in the past.

Bauls symbolize many important ideas for *bhadralok*, and for that reason many *bhadralok* have developed a particular relationship with Bauls. While Tagore's version of Bauls shares some similarities with the characteristics of *sannyāsī*s or *sādhu*s, *bhadralok* have a distinct relationship with Bauls that is different from what laypeople have with *sannyāsī*s. Although many *sannyāsī*s follow their own path while maintaining a distance from householder life, some *sannyāsī*s become gurus of householders, offering advice on spiritual or material matters. Especially when seeking a potential guru, householders evaluate the characteristics of *sannyāsī*s and *sādhu*s; once they accept a guru they tend to justify discrepancies or apparent deviances from ideals. Generally speaking, this is not the kind of relationship *bhadralok* have with Bauls. Even though some *bhadralok* may learn Baul songs from Bauls, most of those who view Bauls positively position themselves as patrons of Bauls. Because this relationship is hierarchical, *bhadralok* continue to evaluate Bauls, and they tend to reward those who meet their expectations. Similarly, Bauls who subsist on contributions from *bhadralok* seek to meet those expectations. Although some Bauls are valued for their particular contributions (musical talent, songs, etc.), it is the ideal that tends to be elevated, not actual individuals.

Why There Are No Real Baul Women

In the beginning of this chapter I wrote about individuals I met who dismissed the idea of Baul women. I would like to suggest that there are two reasons why some claim there are no women who are "real" Bauls. The first reason, shared by those who uphold some version of an ideal Baul, is that only a few men manage to become real Bauls. This view is reflected in the statement made by the Kolkata scholar who argued that women are only ritual servants to Baul men. It is also reflected in the idea that all Bauls should meet the same standard and that women frequently fail in exhibiting that ideal. A second reason is that Baul women contradict notions of good Bengali women, and therefore their very existence is suppressed or denied. These two reasons for denying the existence of Baul women are rooted in ideologies that are clearly in tension with each other, yet together they challenge women's ability to be accepted as real Bauls.

To be fair, both Baul women and men usually fail in exhibiting the ideals *bhadralok* have of them. Whether Bauls are viewed as spiritualized village icons, purveyors of humanistic ideals, promiscuous opportunists, sexual deviants, or transgressors of boundaries, they often fail to meet most everyone's expectations. This is particularly true because Bauls do not form a unified group, and most Bauls do not conform to ideals held by *bhadralok*, even if some try. If being carefree means having no house and family, very few Bauls would actually fit that category. Although many Bauls travel regularly, most have a home to which they return. Furthermore, Muslim Bauls, following the Islamic emphasis on family and work, generally have occupations in addition to singing or begging for alms. This Islamic ideal contrasts with the Hindu ideal of *āśrama* (stages of life) that culminates in *sannyās*, characterized as a renunciation of all previous stages, social ties, and possessions. But whether living in a Hindu or a Muslim context, actual Bauls do not readily conform to expectations that they be utterly carefree.

Furthermore, the expectation that Bauls not have children—whether that idea comes from the view that they are akin to *sannyāsī*s and therefore celibate or from knowledge about a sexual *sādhanā* that results in no pregnancies if performed correctly or from the conviction that family life inhibits spiritual progress—contradicts the reality that most Bauls do have children, many of them quite happily so. When I confronted Niranjan, the husband of Jaya (and parent of one daughter), with the idea that Bauls are "not supposed to reproduce," he chided me for reading too many books on Bauls and cited the large number of well-known Bauls who had children. But having children also has a benefit that pertains directly to the Baul community. Proving that a couple is able to reproduce may also strengthen their claims of doing *sādhanā* correctly. One Baul woman, Bimala, now in her forties, has had no children. Her husband claimed they had no children because of their *sādhanā*, but neighbors—including other Bauls—cited barrenness as the cause. In this case, having no children weakened her husband's claim that they were successful at *sādhanā*. Thus *bhadralok* expectations that Bauls have no children or home contradict the reality of the majority of Bauls who may in fact be responding to other ideals, including ideals they hold as Bauls.

But the expectations *bhadralok* have of Bauls to be unencumbered by home, family, and responsibilities marginalize women in ways not experienced by their male counterparts. First of all, for Baul women who go out of the home to wander and sing, the larger socioreligious context influences their ability to act and feel independent and carefree. When I first began my research, I asked Baul women how their lives differed from that of other women, and "going out" (*baire jaoya*) was the central difference they cited. Although at the time I had been hoping for a more elaborate and profound answer, I quickly realized that the implications of "going out" were plenty significant. Given the expectation that women not "go out" into public streets to meet the gaze of unrelated men, stemming from the wide range of local purdah customs,[12] neighboring married women generally did not go out beyond their village, at least not without an accompanying male kin or spouse, and then only rarely.

Second, in areas where outsiders know about Baul sexo-yogic rituals and/or think of them as promiscuous, Baul women have the added concern of being perceived as deviant from traditional marital norms. Although many Bauls assert that Baul couples should never split up and severely criticize the practice, Bauls in Birbhum and particularly those living in or near Santiniketan have the reputation of having impermanent marriages. This reputation is actually well founded, as it is not unusual for Baul men to leave their wives to be with another woman. In rural Bengal where arranged marriages are the norm, any such blatant displays of marital instability are looked down upon. However, it is the rare Baul man who suffers from the fruits of his actions, even if he may also be laughed at. As Niranjan revealed when he told me that nearby villagers ribbed him about his success at having secured for himself a foreign woman, Baul men are often praised for their sexual exploits. Although Niranjan attempted to defend the honor of his wife and me by insisting to his neighbors that I was her friend, their assumption was that I was having some sort of dubious relationship with Niranjan because it happens so often in that area.

Third, although having children, particularly after renunciation, is an indication of failure in *sādhanā*, women without any children are likely to be stigmatized by the communities in which they live. In Bengal, as in other places in South Asia, women's status is considerably improved when they have offspring, particularly male children, and a woman who does not reproduce is considered unfortunate and is often shunned as inauspicious. Unlike her husband, who incurred no blame or stigma, Bimala was treated as a barren woman by her neighbors and was systematically avoided lest her unfortunate condition transfer to others. Jaya admitted that it would have been very hard for her in the village had she not had children.

Niranjan's criticism of my own privileging of discourse over practice concerning Bauls and children points out that Bauls, like everyone else, live in a social world comprising people, attitudes, and ideals that may not match their own. The multifarious ways in which practice differs from discourse reveal that these broader social contexts do matter. And it is with that larger context in mind that I give the next two examples, to help set the stage for the next chapter, in which I discuss local expectations of feminine respectability in greater detail.

Kangalini Sufia, a woman whose life trajectory has touched upon many of the diverse definitions of Baul, exemplifies this tension between a "real" Baul who resides in *māzār*s, wanders freely, and remains obscure[13] and a good woman who adheres to the socioreligious norms in Bangladesh. After leaving a failed marriage, she was for a time a woman far from public view, singing Baul songs and practicing rituals. She visited temples, shrines, and *māzār*s, sleeping under whatever shelters she could find and subsisting on alms. It was at a *māzār* in Dhaka where she became recognized for her talent. She converted to Islam and remarried. Kangalini explained to me that it was impossible to remain unmarried, that women cannot get around by themselves in the society in which she lives. She started getting invitations to perform at programs, and today there are several recordings of her songs, and she has performed in places like Korea, Hong Kong, Bangkok, New York, and London. She currently lives in a small rented room with her daughter, grandchildren, and husband, but it is her identity as a Baul that has made her famous, and she fulfills most peoples' expectations of someone who represents the simplicity of village life, sings Baul songs (many of which she spontaneously composes), and performs with emotional abandon. But for precisely the changes she makes to the definition of Baul in order to be accepted as a proper woman living in her society (e.g., marriage and living under a roof), some people criticize her for failing in their expectations of being a Baul.

Late one morning I went to see Kangalini in her rented room in Mirpur. Finding her home was always a challenge because she and her companions had to move frequently due to their inability to pay the monthly rent, particularly during the summer and rainy seasons, when there were fewer programs in which to perform. When I arrived that morning, the director of a local Dhaka TV station was sitting on her cot amid piles of clothes and blankets and heaps of cassettes, awards, and plastic flowers. Kangalini was rushing around, looking slightly flustered, and disappeared into the back room. The director and I talked about our different work with Bauls, and he, as many others have done, urged me to find "real Bauls." As Kangalini served us tea and biscuits, he told me in English that she is not a real Baul. If she were a real Baul, he claimed, she would be living under a tree. Instead, Kangalini has a roof over her head, has a family and fame. For the director, these possessions and being a Baul were mutually exclusive, and because Kangalini feels responsible for assuring the subsistence of her family, she is not a Baul.

To the extent that Kangalini accepts being encumbered, she disappoints those evaluating her as a Baul. That women may respond to local expectations (or their own desires) as opposed to ideals of Bauls as unencumbered is one of the reasons why many claim there are no women who are real Bauls (after all, it is the woman who gets pregnant, incurring both the praise and blame for motherhood). Yet, it is often still those very behaviors questionable for women that Bengalis expect of "real" Bauls.

But whereas *bhadralok* and other potential sponsors apply their ideas of the ideal Baul (whatever that might be) to Baul women, others, including non-Baul neighbors and orthodox Muslims and Hindus, evaluate them against standards of feminine respectability and conclude that Baul women are problematic.

This tension between the "real" Baul and the "good" woman initially became clear to me when I was researching in Sylhet, a city and district in the northeast of Bangladesh, where I was repeatedly dissuaded from meeting Baul women. But it is a challenge faced by Baul women elsewhere as well. Although a few Baul men in Sylhet were criticized for their indulgence in intoxicants, most men were praised for their musical talent and their knowledge of a variety of subjects, including theories on the body (*deha-tattva*) and Ma'rifat, their form of religious practice. In contrast, however, Baul women were repeatedly and almost comprehensively condemned. Under pressure to follow the Shari'at by refraining from singing and by following purdah, for instance, any woman who does not behave "appropriately" threatens the socioreligious standards, and as a result her very existence is often denied or criticized. This was illustrated by a comment made by one of the committee members of the *māzār* of Shah Ali Baghdadi in Dhaka: "Women here [at the *māzār*] do not sing." So this administrator of the *māzār*, being interviewed by a foreign woman, stated what is ideally the case: in Muslim society women do not sing in public. He knew quite well that they do indeed sing, despite the decrees of Islam. In fact, as we were discussing whether singing in public was a woman's prerogative in Bangladesh, we could hear a woman singing in the grounds of the *māzār*. But to admit that fact would be to challenge the integrity of this Muslim society and his role in overseeing the *māzār*. Similarly, the several men in Sylhet I questioned about Baul women told me what is ideally the case: there are no Baul women. When I insisted I knew that such women existed in Sylhet, they would say: "Oh, those, yes, well … they are not good women." So if such women had to exist, then of course they would not be "good."

Conclusion

These various discourses on Bauls are important not merely as a scholarly study but also because they have a direct impact on the lives of many Bauls. It is precisely the *bhadralok* in areas like Santiniketan, Kolkata, or Dhaka who are some of the main sponsors of Baul performances. If they expect Bauls to behave in certain ways, they are likely to reward those who do, for example by inviting them to performances, and bypass those who do not. As mentioned above, Kangalini gets hired because she gives people what they want.

Even the *bhadralok*'s knowledge and expectation that Bauls perform *sādhanā* is well known to Bauls. Niranjan, who criticized me for listening to what books say and not what Bauls do with regard to having children, also knew that such books discussed *sādhanā*. During a conversation that had led to the subject of *sādhanā*, his wife Jaya had tried to hush him up to prevent him from talking about confidential matters. Niranjan responded, however, by telling her that such matters were already written in books and that I had access to them. Furthermore, many researchers, laypeople, and foreigners armed with some ideas of these rituals approach Bauls for further details. Bauls in Santiniketan and Kusthia are used to being asked about secret rituals and on their own initiative may offer to reveal such information in exchange for money. Bauls are possibly even more willing to divulge such information to foreigners since as transient outsiders they seem less likely to spread the information to neighboring Bengali non-Bauls, who would highly disapprove of Baul *sādhanā*—if they actually knew the details. But this publicized knowledge also means that many performing Bauls (*śilpī bāul*) who have no commitment to learning anything about *sādhanā* will nonetheless tell researchers what they think they want to know.[14] This discourse about Baul authenticity is therefore not at all merely academic; it is integrally intertwined with Baul motivations for meeting expectations.

As this chapter suggests, all these multiple layers of discourses marginalize women by excluding them in most of the representations and by emphasizing—and often exoticizing—Baul characteristics and beliefs that undermine Baul women's status in their local communities. In the following chapter, I examine more closely the local expectations of women that have an impact on Baul women, and in chapter 4 I discuss how Baul women negotiate between these conflicting paradigms of the Good Baul and the Good Woman.

3

"I've Done Nothing Wrong"

FEMININE RESPECTABILITY AND BAUL EXPECTATIONS

Reflections on Feminine Ideals and Betrayal

SNAPSHOT ONE: KANGALINI SUFIA

In an interview with Kangalini Sufia in her crowded room in Dhaka, I asked her about her past and the circumstances leading up to her entry into the Baul path. She described a poor childhood and marriage as a young girl to a man who regularly abused her.

> I really took a beating from him. A girl like me: I was a simple village girl! I grew up in my parents' mud hut. [When I was married] I used to get up at 3:00 a.m. I cleaned the house, swept, and washed the courtyard. I was a Hindu, you know. We were very clean. Everybody loved me then. I used to wash all the clothes. Then I'd cook all the rice, I ate, and then I'd sleep. I used to get up at three in the morning, and I would bathe. I was a Hindu, you know? If you're a Hindu you have to wash your body and clothes before you go in the kitchen. Imagine, my husband never gave me anything. I worked so hard, and I never got any remuneration for any work.

The marriage failing, Kangalini's mother finally came to retrieve her, and she stayed with her parents through the birth of her only child, a daughter. But Kangalini described being ambivalent about ending her marriage, and it is not clear if she left or if her husband told her to leave.

> I wanted to go back. I got along really well with my in-laws. I just had to leave. My father used to go and say, "My daughter is a little crazy, but she can do all these things in the house. She's talented. She knows how to sing. There's no work she doesn't know how to do." I can still do all that. I am a really good cook. If you want me to cook five different kinds of vegetables, I can.

Because her parents did not have enough money to feed her regularly, Kangalini described having to drink the water in which rice had been boiled or wait for leftovers from nearby weddings. Not knowing what else to do with the young woman, who no longer fully belonged in her natal home,[1] Kangalini's mother finally gave her and her infant into the care of a *sannyāsī*, and it is from that beginning that she eventually became a Baul. Not surprisingly, Kangalini's views on her position as a woman are complex, but she claims that she had done everything right as a woman.

> I used to look at men and be disgusted.......Do you understand? What
> could I do? I couldn't go anywhere by myself. I had to be escorted by men.
> I was disgusted. When I was married, I used to keep my head covered. I was
> very shy and modest [*lajjā*]. I acted in a way that people couldn't say anything
> bad about me.

In a later interview Kangalini argued that a woman is expected to worship her husband,[2] regardless of his treatment of her. Women, she and others in Bangladesh and West Bengal told me, are supposed to be shy and modest (*lajjā*). Despite this awareness of appropriate feminine behavior, Kangalini is quick to say that behaving well as a young woman did not lead her to a happy marriage life. Kangalini's disgust, as described above, likely stems from the betrayal she experienced as a young married woman who tried to please her husband and in-laws.

When one looks at Kangalini Sufia today, however, adjectives like shy and modest are not likely to come to mind. She is an outgoing woman with a strong and often brusque presence. She seems to speak without thinking, seldom hesitating to speak her mind. Her worn-out saris appear carelessly draped over her body, defying her occasional gestures to cover her head with the loose end of the sari. Not only does she run the household from the inside but she also goes daily to the nearby market with a bag in hand to purchase food for meals, a task usually undertaken by men in Bangladeshi households. But even more unusual is that Kangalini herself negotiates performances with potential sponsors for popular radio and television shows or other functions, which often take place long distances from her residence in Dhaka. Once onstage, she captivates her audiences with her passionate singing and expressive dancing. Her lyrics may encourage love and a quest for the Divine, but sometimes they directly instruct people to respect underprivileged groups, such as rickshaw drivers. Adjectives like determined, passionate, and probably even defiant are more likely to come to mind when describing Kangalini today.

SNAPSHOT TWO: MADHABI

Everyone loves me [here in my natal village] ever since I was little. I've done nothing wrong. I haven't caused any harm. I've harmed no one. So everyone loves me. I've caused no harm. Otherwise people will call me bad. One must follow the rules.

My grandfather named me Radharani. I was born on Radhashtami [Radharani's birthday] in the month of Bhadra [August–September]. He named me Radharani.[3] I was treated with affection when I was young. But now that I am grown, I haven't found peace. I don't like it anywhere. See how my life has turned out! For this reason I said that there is something called happiness in this life, and I attained this bit of happiness [when I was younger]. [But] it hasn't gone anywhere. [Now] I don't travel anywhere. Living in this house, I listen to tapes, turn on the fan, study, and sing. I don't go anywhere outside. [When] I go out on programs, I go with *dādā*. And I don't associate with [men] ever. I don't.

Like Kangalini, Madhabi claims she did everything right when she was younger. Although Madhabi's parents and her husband were already on the Vaishnava and Baul path when she was married, she believes that she followed the rules of society and that, like Kangalini, no one had any reason to say anything bad about her. Yet despite their "good" behavior, both women were abandoned by their husbands, Kangalini's marriage failing before the birth of her daughter and Madhabi's marriage failing soon after the birth of her daughter. As Madhabi states, "I [should be able to] hold my husband's hand and go [though life]. That isn't happening though. And whose hand will I hold now? It's the age of betrayal now. Which era? It's the Kali Yuga.[4] I'll grab its hand, and it will take me in that direction."

Kangalini and Madhabi's lives are parallel in other ways as well. They both assumed sole responsibility for raising their daughters and arranging for their marriages, they did not have any more children, and both claim that being abandoned by their husbands is what led them to take renunciation. In Kangalini's case it also led her to the Baul path, something she would not have done otherwise. The two have also turned to singing as a way of supporting themselves.

When I met Madhabi, it had been about a year since she had taken the step toward formal renunciation. She wore a white sari unless she was going out to perform Baul songs, in which case she wore ocher-colored clothes, and she was living with her fictive brother (*dādā*) in Bolpur, some ten miles from her natal village and ashram, where her parents currently were living. When we talked, she repeatedly returned to the subject of her husband's abandonment of her and her daughter, even though it had happened more than six years previously. I had wondered if the birth of her daughter had somehow initiated the demise of their marriage, as she claimed it began soon after the daughter was born. But in this and most contexts she claimed that gender was insignificant. So when I asked her if she thought things would have been different if she had had a son, she was adamant in claiming that the gender of her child would have made no difference to her circumstances. "No. No, she's a boy. She's a boy. I gave a girl and got a boy. I gave a girl and got a boy, so it's a boy. One, two: I gave away my girl in marriage [and gained a son]. They'll look after us. Now they have to take care of me and my parents." In identifying her own daughter (*meye*) as a boy (*chele*), Madhabi emphasizes that having a daughter is as valuable as having a son. This view contrasts significantly with more predominant views that having a son is more desirable because daughters typically are seen as requiring expensive dowries and will move to their in-laws' home at marriage. Moreover, she stresses that she gained a son when her own daughter married and that the two of them will take care of her—a role usually expected of a son. In other conversations she also frequently referred to herself as the son (*chele*) of her parents. Madhabi's views on having had a daughter were in some ways quite pragmatic. When I presented the argument that parents would have to provide a dowry for a daughter—a formidable feat indeed for people who lived off of alms—she countered that if her child had been a son she would have had to provide him with a house and land for his family. Thus, she claimed, there was no difference between having a daughter and a son, and she never suggested that her husband might have stayed if she had given birth to a son.

When it came to being abandoned and living her life without a husband, however, it was clear she saw gender as a significant factor in her troubles. It is in this context that she argued that things would have been different had she been a male: "If I'd been a boy... *sampatti* (wealth, riches, fortune, excellence). Then I'd have fortune. But girl... girl [pointing to herself]. I've given the girl in marriage. And [now] I'll get no more. I'll get the ashram no more." Kangalini's view on gender is very similar in that she too believes that being a woman has been a deciding factor leading to her current situation. For Kangalini it is precisely being a woman that led her to the Baul path. "If I was a man, I would have stayed in their world. Whatever my caste occupation [*jāti byabasā*], I would just have done that. In the present time, the way I am now, radio and television: they're my mother and father. So now I'm known as a radio and television artist. That's where I am right now." Both recognize that if they had been men they would have had direct access to whatever wealth, land, and occupation had been a part of their birth lineage. They would not have had to depend on men and marriage for those, nor would they have felt the precariousness of being both dependent on others and abandoned by them. As Bauls they have room to maneuver, yet they still advocate behaving "right" and demonstrate that even Baul women's lives are circumscribed by their gender.

Many Baul women, like Kangalini and Madhabi, live in households and travel to other settings in which they do not need to behave in the same ways as expected of their non-Baul neighbors. Indeed the mere act of traveling outside their residential communities defies normative expectations of women in rural and some urban Bengali communities. However, because expectations for Bauls and for women often clash, Baul women feel marginalized by local and regional perceptions that they are not respectable women. As the examples in this chapter suggest, Baul women are very aware of these feminine codes of behavior and often consider themselves encumbered by them. While we saw in chapter 2 that the expectations patrons have of Bauls marginalize Baul women, in this chapter I focus on the problem from the angle of local societal expectations for women.

Baul women care about normative expectations of women for at least two important reasons. First, they are judged by those expectations by their neighbors and others who see them on the street or stage. For that reason, even though Baul women may not need to conform to gendered expectations in certain situations, they often will in others. Second, as Bauls, some of those expectations are the very societal assumptions they wish to challenge, either through their own actions or their songs.

Both Kangalini and Madhabi, despite their gutsy behavior, are well versed in feminine ideals in Bengali society. Their situations as single mothers and public performers are not unusual for Baul women, and they have support from other Bauls to earn a living and remarry. But when they talk about their failed marriages, they orient themselves toward normative society in order to free themselves from blame.

In both the examples above, *lajjā*, often translated as shame, modesty, or shyness, emerges as a term used to describe appropriate feminine behavior: many Bengalis explain that a "good" woman in their society exhibits *lajjā*; Kangalini describes herself as having had *lajjā* as a young woman, suggesting that her behavior had been according to normative expectations; Madhabi also argues that "one must follow the rules" in society. As will become even more evident below, *lajjā* is an important concept that is used in multiple contexts, and I will spend some time discussing it. In chapter 4, I suggest further that shame reflects dynamic power relations and applies in significant ways to men as well as women.

Women's Position in Bengal

Many scholars have written about the status of women in South Asia, and I will not summarize those views here. In much of this literature, there is a tendency to overgeneralize and to simplify what is of course a vastly diverse and complex subject mediated at the very least by differences in caste, class, and geography, though some excellent critiques and more nuanced descriptions have emerged in recent years.[5] Instead I will defer primarily to the views of Bengalis I interviewed, especially the observations of Bauls, for it is those perspectives and concerns that are most pertinent to the lives and choices of Baul women. When talking about expectations for women, Baul women cite familiar themes: the expectation of being a wife and mother (discussed in chapter 2), a lack of formal education, and pressure to be modest and restrained. Although Baul women often emphasized that it was their neighbors who had to conform to those expectations, several of the Baul women I met often also feel encumbered by them. I begin with Jaya's observations on gendered norms.

WOMEN ARE UNEDUCATED

I met Jaya within a few weeks of beginning my fieldwork in West Bengal in 1998, but I quickly dismissed her as being merely a performer of Baul songs, not a practitioner with a deep commitment to Baul ideology. She was young and appeared in many ways to be a regular Bengali woman living in a rural community, her daily life intertwined with her neighbors, family, and domestic concerns. When at home, she looked and dressed no differently from her neighbors, with old, inexpensive cotton saris of various colors and ready-made blouses. She wore the *tulsī mālā* (necklace made of *tulsī* beads) that only a few of her neighbors wore, though a good number of rural Bengalis wear the *mālā* after taking initiation with a Vaishnava guru. But it was when she went out to perform that her appearance suggested a difference from her neighbors: she dressed in a bright ocher-colored sari and a matching blouse, and wore long strands of beads around her neck and a *tilak* (sectarian mark) on her forehead. As a result of my initial impressions that being a Baul for Jaya was no more than the means of earning an income and playing music, I let several months slip by before I visited her again.

I began to visit her more often during a time when I was particularly frustrated with my work and found reassurance in her warmth and openness. It was a relief to find that my questions seemed to make sense to Jaya, and it was not long before I realized that Jaya kept her feet in two worlds. I had not been wrong in viewing her as an ordinary Bengali married woman living in a village: that was an identity she actively cultivated. I also was not totally off the mark when I evaluated her lifestyle and concluded that being a Baul was an occupation: that too was the image she wanted her neighbors to have of her. Jaya, as it turned out, was keenly aware of her position in the community of non-Bauls in which she spent most of her days, and she was very concerned with fitting into that community. What I came to realize over time was that she also deeply believed in Baul ideals and philosophy but that she recognized the ways in which those ideals put her at odds with the society in which she lives daily. It is likely that this self-awareness of her own positionality is what made her take such an interest in my research, particularly in showing me how difficult life is for Baul women. We sat together for hours at a time, talking about the situation for her and other Baul women, about the obstacles they face in society, the questionable reputation of Bauls in Bengali villages, and the challenges of negotiating between the conflicting ideals and expectations of Bauls and of Bengali women.

In the summer of 2000, I returned to Birbhum after a few months at home in Chicago. I spent the long, hot days of that summer with Jaya, moving from in front of her newly purchased fan in her mud hut to the shade of trees behind her house when the electricity was off. We both approached the stove reluctantly, and Jaya kept all chores at a minimum during the day. Jaya was as uncomfortable in the heat as I was, and we relished any breeze and shade we could find. Her village was a 20-minute bicycle ride via a shortcut across the train tracks near my home and through several fields. I arrived most days in the morning and stayed often until nightfall. On a few nights I shared the verandah with her and her family, but I generally avoided spending the night, uncertain what message that would give her neighbors about my relationship with them.

My conversations with Jaya that summer covered more territory than my previous visit with her. We talked about personal matters—both hers and mine. We compared experiences in America and India, gossiped about other foreign women and other Bauls, and discussed a variety of other subjects as diverse as astronomy and Indian cinema. Taking the initiative to help me with my reseach, she described to me women's position in general in order to emphasize the challenges that she and other Baul women face. She explained that the women in her society, like the girls living in her village, are not allowed to speak for themselves. They have no voice, she said; they are raised to be quiet, to do what they're told, and to stay indoors. She described women as having no freedom or independence (*svādhīnatā*, a word I heard frequently from that point on). Furthermore, she complained that girls are not encouraged to study, as parents claim there is no need for them to get an education,[6] and that girls do not get fed as well, or as much, as boys.

While we were having one of these conversations, a 15-year-old non-Baul girl who was getting married in a few days was sitting with us looking at photos of Jaya and her husband, Niranjan, several of which had been taken at music programs. She was a dark girl with a sweet, bright smile. Like other young unmarried girls in her village, she was wearing a dress with worn-out frills on the front and no pants or *salwar* (loose-fitting, pajama-type pant). Her hair was pulled back loosely in an unkempt braid. By Friday, she would be transformed from a young girl to a young bride in a bright sari, henceforth wearing only saris and binding her hair back carefully. She appeared to be only half listening to Jaya's criticisms of the limitations placed on girls' education, and still concentrating on the photos in her lap she asked Jaya "why?"

> Jaya answered her question harshly: "Are you in school now?"
> "No."
> "Well then. That's what I mean."
> I asked the girl, "Do you have brothers? Are they in school?"
> "No," she answered.
> But Jaya explained, "That's because they don't want to study anymore. It's a different matter."
> "Do you want to study?" I asked the girl.
> "Yes, but *mā* took me out of school."

During another conversation, we were talking about programs when Jaya brought out a book called *Mina, Learning to Count Chickens* (*mīnā murgi gunte śikshā*), published by UNICEF, that explains in story form that little girls should be fed the same as boys and should be allowed to go to school. Jaya, Niranajan, and a few other Bauls had done about ten programs in villages in the district of Nadia, singing songs given to them by the organizers on improving women's position in society. Jaya had taken several copies of the book home with her and had offered them to her non-Baul neighbors, but she complained that they were not interested. The books on Mina were still out on the ground when later two young mothers were standing around holding their babies and listening to our conversation. Jaya held one of the books out and asked, "Would you read this book if I give it to you?" The girl with a class five education offered a noncommittal yes. The other one, with a class two education, said nothing. The first one said she'd come for it later. Jaya looked at me and shrugged: "There's no point; they don't want to understand. They'd take the books, never look at them, and then not return them. It's useless."

Jaya's statement that most women are unable to get an education reflects her perspective on the plight of women around her. Unlike many of her female neighbors, Jaya is literate, reads frequently, and is pretty well informed about Indian and world news. Although she knows she could have studied more, she is proud of her education. She uses descriptions about gendered expectations in order to highlight the obstacles and prejudices she encounters regularly as well her own ability to overcome them.

Although Jaya may be better educated than some of her neighbors, I found that women's lack of education is one of the reasons given for dismissing Baul women in Bangladesh. Mujib, a Baul in Sylhet, told me that women's position (*meyer sthān*) in society is very low because they are not educated (*śikshita nai*). As a result, he went on to say, women are not able to be Bauls because they do not understand the meanings of songs and philosophy. When pressed further about whether this was an innate defect in women or a limitation brought about by society, Mujib stated that women and men's abilities (*adhikārī*) are the same, but women's low status is a result of their low economic status. "Women get involved with Baul songs, and maybe they are serious at first. But they are poor, and soon making money becomes the reason to continue on that path. They change directions; they're no longer serious about real Baul stuff. They may have a pretty face, and they ride on that. Women of higher class status tend to be more serious because they are not in such economic need."

Mujib's older brother, Munibor, a hafiz[7] as well as a Baul, also was very critical of women's lack of education. Although he has several disciples who learn songs from him, he is very reluctant to take on women students. According to his view, a student has to have a working knowledge of the language, and women often do not. He also was concerned about pronunciation, mentioning one woman who had a good singing voice but always mispronounced words. Not only did he find this embarrassing, but he knew that there would be educated people in the audience who would hear that something is wrong or would misunderstand the song.

He also mentioned a trip to India with several performers, including two women who did not know how to write. At the border crossing into India, everyone leaving had to sign their name with the Bangladesh Rifles (BDR, the border police). The two women gave their finger prints, and a little later the police said to Munibor, "What's this? They can't even sign their name? And they're going to India to represent our country? How embarrassing! Couldn't you have taught them to write their name?" Munibor answered, "No, they live in one place; I live somewhere else." But he too was embarrassed.

While the underlying reasons for women's lack of education are certainly complex,[8] they are partly connected to a system that values women's success in the domestic realm over more public work, such as receiving an education and interacting with a wider world through activities like work, shopping, or travel. In Sylhet, observance of purdah was often enforced and frequently limited young girls' education and minimized women's contact with the world of men. During the months I was in Sylhet, I visited a number of households, often with my hosts. In most of the households we visited, women were secluded in the inner rooms. When I was urged to go talk with them, I found their Sylheti version of Bengali extremely difficult to understand, and they also had difficulty understanding my more urban and western Bengali. Unlike the men of these houses, who circulated throughout Sylhet and often to other regions of Bangladesh as well, many women I met remained in the home and could only speak the local dialect. Since men spoke to these secluded women in the local dialect, the women often had little exposure to the forms of Bengali used more in urban settings and toward the western parts of Bangladesh (where Bengali is more similar to what I had learned).

Whereas many men were quick to criticize women for their illiteracy and pronunciation, I found that several women also were clearly self-conscious about their lack of education. Kangalini speculated that it was in part her lack of education (as well as her dark skin) that caused problems with her first husband. Given that few other girls of her age and socioeconomic status at the time of marriage would have been educated, it is unlikely that illiteracy had anything to do with the failure of her marriage. Nonetheless, Kangalini regrets her lack of education, something she had as little control over as the color of her skin. Nur Jahan, respected by many in Sylhet for her singing, bemoaned her inability to read and write and claimed that she would feel much more accomplished if she were able to write a book than if she were to record a cassette of her songs. Phulmala, despite having composed numerous songs, also remarked that she was limited in her abilities to succeed because she is illiterate.

Jaya's observations about women in the society in which she lives are confirmed by the views of a number of other Bauls I met. In addition to comments about women's lack of education, women's conversations about women's status in Bengali society are peppered with statements that women cannot go outside of the home, that they are dependent on men at virtually every stage of their lives, and that they have no independence or freedom. To a large degree, Baul women are familiar with the images of women as oppressed, dependent, and silent—ubiquitous in literature about South Asia—though they usually use such images to describe their neighbors and local expectations rather than themselves.

WOMEN CANNOT BE *PĪR*S

Expectations and ideals about feminine behavior and demeanor are echoed also in statements about what Baul women cannot do. As discussed at length in chapter 2, many Bengalis claim that women cannot even be Bauls, just as the administrator of the Shah Ali Baghdadi *māzār* said that women do not sing at the *māzārs* even though we could all hear a woman's voice raised in song in the background. For rather similar reasons, most Baul women and men I met in Bangladesh also stated that women cannot become gurus or *murśids/pīrs*.

Knowing that Kangalini had several disciples, I was curious how all this made sense to her. When I asked Kangalini if women could be *pīrs* (or *pīrānī*), she repeatedly answered that they could not. In what seemed like another contradiction, she also stated that in *sādhanā*, a woman is the guru of the man as well as vice versa. As she got increasingly frustrated with my probing about women's abilities to become *pīrs*, she stated that women can be *sādhaks* (ritual practitioners), "but [for women] to be on the level of Olis [Auliyas⁹], that's not written. It's only written that men can become Olis." And later she explained, "Women can have *murīds* (disciples), but they can't be *pīrs*. They can't be gurus; they can be *mā*." Finally in the third conversation we had on the subject, I began to see what kind of distinction she was making in her mind.

> KANGALINI SUFIA: No, listen to me. A woman can't be a *pīr*. Women can't be Auliya. She has the right to be a mother. Men are *pīrs*. Sometimes the guru will say, go to your mother, she will teach you something. The mother can give instruction, show the way. The guru is a man.... Women can only pray. I do my prayers. I do my *nāmāj*. They can't become religious leaders. They can pray to Allah. Mother Rabbeya did her *nāmāj* in mid air and on top of the water. Air, on air. Can you see the wind? You can feel on your body the wind when it comes, [but] that's it. Did you ever see what wind looks like? No, you can't. But you can see the form of water. In your home, you can keep water in a glass. But you can't keep wind in your home. So she was able to say her prayers on the wind. From her prayers, Allah was very pleased. But even though she was so powerful, Allah never gave her the title of Auliya.
>
> LISA KNIGHT: Meaning, women can do the same thing as a man, but they won't get the title?
>
> KS: Yes! Yes! [But] women have the *right* to do anything. Even more than men.

Kangalini believed that women are capable of doing pretty much everything that men can do, but in society's eyes it is not seen in the same way. Even though a woman, like Kangalini, may have disciples, she is not called a guru, *murśid*, *pīr*, or Auliya—the many titles given to such teachers. The rules of society confer these titles only on men. Kelly Pemberton found a similar disjuncture among Sufis in two important Indian shrines (associated with Mu'in ud-din Chishti in Ajmer, Rajasthan, and Sharaf ud-din Maneri in Bihar) where women are usually not called *pīrs*, though their actions situate "them squarely in the realm of *piri-muridi* [pir-disciple]" (2004:1). Pemberton argues that one of the reasons women are not called *pīr* is that they are not given official sanction by Sufi orders that closely regulate initiation and the succession of *pīrs*. Furthermore, this "classical" form of Sufism has an ambivalent view of the authority of women mystics, particularly as a result of Sufi reform efforts that seek to emphasize purdah observance, among other things. In some cases, however, women who fulfill the roles of *pīr* may also informally be called *pīrs*. Joyce Flueckiger (1997, 2006) gives examples of women married to *pīrs* who are themselves healers and spiritual guides and are informally called *pīr* (or *pirānimā*). In these cases, the question is not so much whether women have the ability to perform some of the functions of a *pīr* but, rather, whether the term will be used to identify them. Kangalini's assertion that women cannot be *pīrs* reflects, I believe, the expectation, particularly evident among orthodox Muslims (who tend to have problems with many aspects of mystical Islam, including the institution of the *pīr* and women mystics) and many "classical" Sufis, that they not fulfill this role and/or are not given the title of *pīr*. Among Hindus, as Kangalini also admitted, women are more likely to be given the title of *guru-mā*, and this is particularly evident among some Vaishnavas in West Bengal. Vaishnava Bauls and Muslim Bauls in western parts of Bangladesh and in India regularly identify women as gurus (*guru-mā*) in their various forms (wives of gurus who may also be viewed as gurus in their own right; one's own wife as guru). Among Hindu and Muslim Bauls, *guru-mā* is a common title for the partner of one's male guru, though both partners are often viewed as one's guru. As Phulmala, a Vaishnava Baul, said, "Women are the supreme gurus. We—those who are women—are in fact the immortal *śiksha* guru, the goswami." Kangalini also stressed the importance of women as gurus among Bauls, and her assertion that women cannot be gurus/*murśids*—a view shared by most every Baul I met in Sylhet and Dhaka—is a reflection on women's status in the predominantly Muslim society in which she lives.

HAVE YOU NO SHAME?

Couched in these denials of what women are capable of doing is an understanding of local expectations of women. The complex of restrictions on women's behavior, seen in these various denials of what women can do, is reflected in the term *lajjā*, usually understood as modesty or shame.

Shame, often conceptualized in scholarly work as the feminine counterpart to a code of honor, can be expressed physically through practices of purdah, such as veiling and keeping silent. Although the literature on this subject is more diverse and nuanced than I can present here, the general notion is that the honor of a man, and by extension the whole family and often lineage, is in part dependent on the appropriate behavior of women considered to be under his care. In South Asia, this includes daughters, daughters-in-law, wives, sisters, and mothers. Particularly crucial to maintaining the honor of one's family is the vigilant control of women's chastity, and therefore in communities that stress such control, women are kept secluded or protected as much as possible.

This was the case to varying degrees in the areas of Bangladesh where I conducted my research, but purdah was especially evident in Sylhet, where there is a strong presence of orthodox Islam and foreign influences, mainly Middle Eastern (though often indirectly through London).[10] In the areas of West Bengal where I worked, the outward signs of purdah—such as veiling—were less obvious, but Baul women I interviewed were very clear that neighboring women were generally expected to stay in their village and close to their homes and courtyards. In both places, *lajjā*, a word meaning shame, modesty, shyness, and embarrassment which translates quite well in the expression "Have you no shame?" was frequently used to describe a good woman, and a bad woman was described as having no *lajjā*. In making a comparison with Western women, undoubtedly like the anthropologist in their presence who was persistently trying to go out into town for research, men would tell me that Bengali women were *lājuk*, ashamed or shy, and would not go freely around outside. Also in contrast, Baul women were often dismissed as bad women who did not display *lajjā*.

Lajjā is thus in part a code for gendered behavior and is used in evaluations of women's conduct and reputation. To the extent that it is related to a specific complex of behavior, which includes physical expressions of purdah, actual demonstrations and expectations of *lajjā* varies with context. As has been described of purdah, it is also an internal state that can be strategically employed in different settings so that normative rules are not necessarily broken when leaving seclusion. This has been demonstrated of purdah through work on women activists (Forbes 1982, Minault 1982), women who perform in street theater for a living (Seizer 2005), and women who are beyond a certain age (Wadley 1992) or have already established themselves as respectful (Gardner 1998, Kotalova 1993). There are, for all women, contexts and situations in which they do not need to overtly display shame or purdah. This is especially true of Baul women who, by virtue of being Bauls, are already precariously outside of normative roles for women.

AN EVENING IN SYLHET, SEPTEMBER 20, 1999

Sitting in the inner room of a house made of corrugated tin that kept the heat in as much as it kept the rain out, I had been listening as, one by one, several Baul women of Sylhet town sang to the accompaniment of a harmonium and tabla. We were in a room full of men and women; many were singers and others were spectators. This event had been reluctantly organized for my benefit by Munibor, one of my hosts, so that I could finally meet some local Baul women that he had tried to convince me I should not meet. Early in the evening there was a sudden hush between songs as people shifted in their spots and quieted others still talking. Latifa, wearing a black *salwar khamiz* and black shawl, put one end of her narrow shawl over her head, a symbolic gesture, as the shawl covered very little of her head and hair. Someone leaned over to Ed and me and whispered "*Nāmāj*": the call to prayer had started. Even though we could hardly hear the call, some of those in the room must have been expecting it. After a few minutes of silence, the shuffling began again and singing resumed.

By this time I had seen such behavior among Bangladeshis countless times as they paused in their activity to observe *nāmāj*. Of course many people would mark *nāmāj* by going to a *masjid* (mosque) or pulling out a prayer rug, but others would merely quiet down their activity for the duration of the prayer. Often women would pull the edge of their sari or shawl over their heads, if they were not covered already. People would keep their eyes downcast. It visibly marked the passing of the day and reminded me of my status as outsider, and I had seen it so many times that I should not have been surprised when it played out in a room of Baul performers. But up until the call to prayer, I had been taking note that I was sitting among people who in so many ways appeared to be going against normative Bangladeshi society, some women even seeming to recklessly abandon codes of modesty.

In my field notes from that evening I describe the following episode:

After the two, Latifa and Aisha, sang, they moved towards the back, still sitting on the floor. I then noticed that they were actively making sure that each of the other women got a chance to sing next. They would usher a woman forward if she hesitated too much. Their behavior also changed somewhat— became more casual. Again, they had their heads uncovered, and sometimes stretched their arms outward and leaned back on the bed, behavior that looked more appropriate for a man. [Despite their young age and gender, they seemed completely at ease in this group of mixed company and were not hesitating to assert themselves and their wishes.] They leaned over to one another and talked, and often they would say something loudly to someone across the room. When *pān* was being offered at that end of the room, the two became very animated, gesturing for someone to give them some *pān*. When they got it, they shoved it into their mouths. Latifa then leaned back over to the direction of the person with the *pān* ingredients, and waved her arm for attention. Nobody noticed, so she gestured more emphatically. Meanwhile the song was going on, and Aisha was playing cymbals. Someone finally handed Latifa more lime, which was most likely what she was wanting, and Latifa put some in Aisha's mouth. That wasn't enough for Latifa too, so she waved again for more. A short while later Aisha indicated that she wanted more. I'm not sure exactly how this happened, but she was still playing so her hands weren't free, and the owner of the house, who was sitting between the women and the door to the kitchen, reached over with some lime on his finger which Aisha sucked off. I was taken aback at what seemed to me like a disrespectful and rather bold act toward an older man. But in general, I was also seeing in Aisha and Latifa some of the behavior which most likely was what Munibor found so problematic. These women seemed loose. They had none of the refinement that [many Bangladeshi] women have; they were not demure and reserved. They certainly didn't embody modesty. They were surprisingly outgoing, forward, and unconcerned about what others, including us, thought about them. Either that or they were very unaware of themselves and their behavior.

As I was observing Latifa and Aisha, I thought immediately of Munibor, who had warned me repeatedly about Baul women and tried his best to dissuade me from seeing them. In conversations about women in general, Munibor was adamant that they should be modest and shy (*lājuk*). Women in this country, he explained, cannot walk around freely like they can elsewhere. I personally felt this during my stay with Munibor and Chacha, as Munibor told both me and my husband (who always accompanied me in Sylhet) that I should not go certain places. He would warn us that there are bad people outside and instruct us to return before the sun sets at 6:30 (a very inconvenient restriction considering Bauls usually gather late). Although Munibor and Chacha always showed me a great deal of respect, they both were very critical of women and had little good to say about most of them. Baul women, it seemed, exemplified the worst. They were illiterate, untidy, immodest, and crass; "uneducated," as I discussed previously, was the word that usually summed it up most succinctly for our hosts and other Sylheti men I met. By the time I was sitting in the room with these women, I had spent enough time in South Asia, Bangladesh, and particularly Sylhet to understand what he meant, even as problematic as those characterizations felt.

My initial problems interpreting Latifa and Aisha's seemingly contradictory behavior help highlight both the expectations placed on women and their local significance. Although the situation in Sylhet bears some important differences in the nature of the pressure on women to follow normative roles (discussed below), it nonetheless is suggestive of similar tendencies elsewhere in the Bengal region. I was jolted by what I saw as a disjuncture between immodest behavior one moment and modesty the next. As I pondered my feeling of surprise at the momentary displays of modesty during *nāmāj*, I realized that I had internalized some of our hosts' prejudices against immodest behavior, brought to the surface by a shift in these women's behavior.

Probably too I had merged Islamic religiosity with modesty, and so I had expected these women, who clearly did not care much about being *lājuk*, not to show respect to *nāmāj*. On the one hand, I was mistaken in my assumptions that modesty in front of men and modesty in prayer were one and the same. Surely the contexts require significantly different kinds of attention, even if some visible markers (e.g., veiling, downcast eyes, silence) might be same. And I had seen enough religious women in Bangladesh who appeared not at all modest and shy. On the other hand, this conflation of the religious with the social is characteristic of Islam, evident in Shari'at law that specifies appropriate behavior in particular circumstances and Islamist ideals that often equate women's proper behavior and attire with being good Muslims. Studies such as those done by Saba Mahmood (2005) and Sadaf Ahmad (2009) demonstrate continuity between modesty and Islamic piety among women in some Islamic movements, suggesting that the deliberate enactment of these feminine ideals may be reflective of or eventually lead to actual piety.

Furthermore, the Islamization campaign of Bangladesh from the late 1970s onward[11] put particular pressure on families and communities to enforce modesty among women, and these concerns were cast largely in religious terms. Writing of

Pakistan where a similar politicization of religion occurred, Farida Shaheed explains that "gender definitions were central to this new politico-religious discourse, and women became easy targets of Zia's [prime minister of Pakistan, 1977–88] version of Islamization. For the first time, the state led an offensive against women's rights through legislation and administrative directives, and attempted to restrict women's mobility, visibility, and access to economic resources (Rouse [1998])" (1998:146). Bangladesh experienced a very similar trend as the nation struggled to find its identity in opposition to a Muslim Pakistan and a Hindu Bengal, and in 1988 President Hussain Muhammad Ershad (1982–1990) declared Islam the state religion. This Islamization gained strength when, in the 1990s, Khaleda Zia of the Bangladesh Nationalist Party began negotiating with the Jama'at-i-Islami (a fundamentalist Islamic party) in order to secure more votes during election, precipitating an increase in the legitimization of openly enforced restrictions against women. It is not only national politics that fosters the Islamization of social roles and a separation of men's and women's realms, however. Many Bangladeshis migrate abroad in order to work, especially to the Middle East, and in addition to this trend, a significant number of Sylhetis migrate to Britain. Families of foreign migrants often become both wealthier and stricter in their religious observances. When abroad, migrant men come in contact with what they perceive as being more "pure" forms of Islam[12] among Muslims in Britain and the Middle East, and when they return to Sylhet they bring this religious ideology with them, enforcing purdah among their women. And because these households are also now wealthier, they can afford to keep their women secluded (and out of the workforce). Additionally, since many of these men return to Bangladesh for only short periods of time, often to marry, their absence breeds suspicion that their young wives may not remain faithful during long months alone. Bangladeshis from Sylhet critical of this tendency have told me that sometimes young, newly wedded women are locked in the house for fear that they may create a scandal while their husbands are abroad.

Certainly the stronghold of orthodox Muslims in Sylhet is one reason observance of purdah is so high among certain classes there. Alpana, the daughter of our host, Chacha, was about 13 years old and was being taught proper behavior for a young woman when we were there. While in the house, she kept a shawl ready to cover her head and remained mostly out of sight. The one time I saw her outside was when we all went to the house of the in-laws of her older sister in order to bring the young married woman back for a visit with her natal family. Alpana spent a great deal of care applying makeup and dressing up in fancy synthetic *salwar khamiz* and gold jewelry. She insisted that I borrow one of their saris, made out of a heavy, shimmery green synthetic cloth, as she did not consider my dull cotton saris nice enough for the occasion. By the time we left, Alpana's finery was completely covered by a black *burqā* (an overgarment and veil), and, thus shielded, she traveled with us in an auto rickshaw to see her sister who had become pregnant during one of her husband's visits from the Middle East where he worked most of the year.

Although modesty in front of men and modesty in prayer are not the same thing, as demonstrated by Latifa and Aisha's behavior above, the social and religious realms are not necessarily distinct. I had conflated the social with the religious by expecting a certain degree of consistency in the behavior of these Baul women, but I was not alone in doing so. Katy Gardner explains that in the Sylheti village where she conducted her fieldwork, village men told her, after a missionary event organized to spread "correct" Islam, that the "*mullās* instructed them on how to lead more pure lives: keeping women in stricter *pardā*, and rejecting charismatic *pīr* (Muslim saints) and 'un-Islamic' behavior, such as dancing, drumming, gambling, or smoking ganja" (1998:209). As among Muslim women's revivalist movements in Egypt and Pakistan, showing modesty, observing purdah, going out in public only with a *burqā* and accompanied with appropriate male relations are all considered by many Sylhetis as signs of a good Muslim woman. Nonetheless, almost all the activity considered impure or un-Islamic by the mullahs Gardner mentions was going on in that room with Latifa, Aisha, and other Baul singers that night.

It is likely that the main reason for the display of modesty in that room during *nāmāj* was the conservative nature of Sylhet such that not respectfully observing *nāmāj* was out of the question. After all, we were sitting in mixed company with at least a few Muslims who did go to the *masjid* regularly. Pressure in Sylhet to worship at the *masjid* was evidently intense, as I heard a number of men complain in whispers that they felt forced to go and were repeatedly criticized when they did not.[13] Even some Muslims who followed a mystical path sometimes found it hard to avoid going to the *masjid* for prayer. Tanjul, a Sufi Baul I interviewed at length, argued that going to the *masjid* was not necessary because one could do *nāmāj* internally and privately. He claimed that mullahs had no power over Bauls, but sitting in that room with those women I felt that probably it was thought best to avoid confrontation when possible. In fact, when I had begun my first interview with Tanjul in the waiting room of a homeopathic doctor friend of ours, there was another man present who was unknown to me. Tanjul had seemed tense and reluctant to talk, but as soon as the man left, he relaxed. It was then that I realized that I had put him in an awkward situation by talking about being a Baul in front of a conservative Muslim. When I apologized for my ignorance, Tanjul dismissed the man as a mullah and *ṭupi-wallah*.[14] Nonetheless, Bauls are clearly aware of more orthodox expectations and views.

"His Life Is in Woman's Hands": Discourses in Tension

Baul women may be particularly aware of gendered expectations because they are simultaneously aware of—and usually subscribe to—a contrasting perspective. Although the actual status of Baul women in the home varies considerably, and oftentimes appears not to coincide with ideological pronouncements, Baul ideals nonetheless place Baul women's roles at odds with their status as good, respectable,

Bengali women—especially as wives and mothers. Just as the expectations sponsors have of Bauls fly in the face of expectations of good feminine conduct and behavior, Baul views about women also pose challenges to women's everyday lives. Although the tensions between these often opposing discourses may create challenges for women, we will see later that they also open up possibilities for diverse ways of acting.

Baul ideas about women do not come out of a vacuum: they are directly related to normative views about women and often address very similar concepts. Whether solicited or not, I frequently heard both men and women Bauls stress the value of women, claiming that women are more powerful than men. The view that women have more power (*śakti*) than men is common in South Asia and is the reason cited for many of the restrictions placed on women. Looking at normative society, South Asian views on *śakti* appear paradoxical. On the one hand, *śakti*, understood as feminine, is the active and creative power of the universe as well as the name for the Goddess.[15] All women are said to have *śakti*, and it is likely an awareness of this power in women (and the images of such strong goddesses as Durga, Kali, and Parvati) that contribute to the possibility that women can also be political leaders (for instance, Indira Gandhi, India's long-serving prime minister beginning in 1966). Thus in South Asia there is clear evidence of female power. On the other hand, while women are seen as more powerful, Brahminical society also asserts that women are unable to control themselves because they lack education and knowledge (even though, as suggested earlier in this chapter, it is societal restrictions on women that limit their access to education).[16] According to this high caste perspective, women are likely to get themselves and their families into trouble if they are not contained, and thus it is the responsibility of men, particularly fathers, husbands, or sons, to protect women from their own lack of self-control. Dominant Hindu society therefore claims that women's power reflects a potential that usually needs to be restrained, lest it become destructive. In other words, power in this sense is typically not the same as agency because of societal expectations that most women should not act on their own. In some senses women's *śakti* is celebrated but more in the sense of its potentiality.

Bauls also celebrate the potentiality of women's *śakti*, but there is more evidence among Bauls for making this potential concrete through ritual and everyday life. The reasons different Bauls give for women's greater power are slightly varied, though usually it is rooted in the importance of women to Baul *yugal-sādhanā*. To quote Kangalini:

> KANGALINI SUFIA: There are many obstacles against women in this country. But you know, women are the most important. If a woman doesn't give permission, he [her partner] can't be a *sādhak*. A woman can save him and can kill him too. His life is in woman's hands. That's why I said for a woman the *sādhanā* is greater. Woman has nine qualities, her strength is greater. A man has six.... Every human being has six qualities: eyes, nose, etc. But a woman has three more than men.

LISA: You said that men can't practice *sādhanā* without women; can a woman practice without a man?

KS: Like, you are the guru of your husband and your husband is your guru. One is not complete without the other. You two are complementary. God loves the devotion of a wife and husband which is put together. An individual worship is not much rewarded, whoever the person is, be it a man or a woman. If a man thinks that he can be a *sādhak* without woman, he can do it with his physical strength. Yes, a man may be physically stronger than a woman. But the fact is that a woman is really stronger than a man.

According to Kangalini, men have the advantage of physical and social strength. But the strength that women have is connected to female sexuality. The idea that women have more strength (*kshamatā*; *śakti*) than men was repeated by a number of the Bauls I met. I had a funny interaction with Jaya about this topic, and her hesitation to speak freely reflects how concerned she tends to be about societal expectations, even when she discussed Baul ideas that she values. To illustrate women's greater power, she asked me: "How many husbands can a wife have?"

"I don't know," I answered. Thinking she intended a literal and social understanding of husband and wife, I suggested, "One."

"No, many. But how many wives can a husband have?"

"Ummm...many. But there will be problems." Again, I was thinking of the social implications of her scenarios. A wife would not be allowed to have more than one husband.

"No! He can only have one."

"I don't understand."

"Say, there's a husband and a wife. If many women come to him, what will happen?"

Silence.

"But a woman can have many men," Jaya concluded, hoping I had figured it out.

The following day, her husband, Niranjan, followed up on this conversation, avoiding the euphemisms that had thrown me off in my conversation with Jaya. Niranjan was several years older than Jaya, and he had taken on the role of teaching Jaya about Baul philosophy, trying to empower Jaya with knowledge and confidence. He asked me if Jaya had told me the story of the prostitute to whom many men would go. Comprehension about the previous day's conversation dawned on me: Jaya had equated women's strength with their sexual power. Niranjan explained that despite the prostitute's "dirty" behavior, she was good; her mind was good. Women's power is greater, he explained, because they can handle things like this, much more so than can men. But, in quick succession he added that men's power is also great. Pointing to the top of his head, he explained that "Brahma" lives inside men, and when it goes out (he moved his hand quickly from head to sexual organs and out, indicating the path), then he loses his power and life force.[17]

There is great variety among Baul ritual practices, and it would be misleading to generalize too much. However, a few explanations are pertinent here. Baul philosophy holds that the body is a microcosm of the universe and that the Divine, located also in the body, has separated into male and female principles in order to experience pleasure. In the body and in Baul sexual rituals, there are a number of different ways of conceptualizing the male and female principles.[18] Bauls generally believe that the male and female principles exist in both men and women, but in the man's body the Divine is more difficult to perceive. In the women's body the active form, usually conceptualized as female (*śakti*), is more predominant, and once a month it overflows in the form of menstrual blood (sometimes called seed or *bīj*). Some Bauls believe that it is during this time that, if the right techniques are applied (*yugal-sādhanā*), the divine unity may be directly experienced by practitioners (*sādhaks*). This is particularly the case for the man for whom, without a woman's help, this would be virtually impossible. A woman, on the other hand, is believed to be already more in touch with her divine essence.

Like Tantrics, Bauls view bodily emissions, such as semen and menstrual blood, as powerful substances. However, while Tantrics generally view the emission of both semen and menstrual blood as decreasing the health and power of men and women, Bauls argue that while this is true for men, women have an abundance of this powerful substance, resulting in a monthly overflow. It is because of this power in women that many orthodox Hindu *sādhus* condemn women as being dangerous, as leading men into temptation and death through loss of their life essence or semen. Orthodox renouncers therefore seek to retain their semen through celibacy. Some Tantrics seek to overcome this tendency to weakness by absorbing the power of women, but according to Jeanne Openshaw (2002:220), many Bauls view this as stealing women's essence for men's benefit.

Women's monthly impurity, given by Brahminical society as a significant reason for limiting women's activities, including preventing them from being educated in Brahminical scriptures, is thus challenged by Baul beliefs and practices. Bauls argue that partaking in rituals during a woman's menstrual cycle makes use of the gift she is capable of offering naturally and without detriment to herself during that time. Unlike the view of normative society, menstruation is not regarded by Bauls as polluting but, rather, as the highly charged and often ideal time for *yugal-sādhanā*.

Various goals are said to be behind Baul *yugal-sādhanā*, including good health and longevity (perhaps even immortality), unity, and wholeness. For some practitioners, the couple aim to reach equilibrium, balancing the different properties in their bodies through a sharing of their substances. Because a woman is usually seen as already perfected or whole (or at least more whole), the man may be made more complete through drawing in the already whole essence in the woman's body. Furthermore, while Tantrics generally use sexo-yogic rituals to destroy and transcend worldly illusion manifest in lust (*kām*), Bauls' sexo-yogic rituals aim to transform lust into love (*prem*). Finally, Bauls argue that by turning inward and doing *yugal-sādhanā*, they seek to realize the internal divinity of all human beings, regardless of societal constructions like caste, religion, and often also gender.[19] With these aims in mind, Bauls argue that women are to be valued and respected, and *yugal-sādhanā* cannot be done without a woman's help.

Baul terminology for women also suggests the high ideological status of women and illustrates how Baul views oppose normative society. Bauls have a number of terms for women, including *mā* (mother), *saṅginī* (partner), *nārī* (woman), *bāulinī* (female Baul), and *sevā dāsī* (woman who serves others). A brief consideration of a few of these terms will help us understand Baul views of women and the status of women.

The significance of these terms is evident in a discussion I had with Jamal, a Baul man living in Jhenaidah, Bangladesh, about women and marriage. He told me that he disagreed with societal marriages in which women are called wife or "*strī*." When I asked him to clarify, he answered that in regular society it is okay to beat your wife. He then asked, "Which is greater, woman [*nārī*] or man [*purush*]?" Answering his own question, he said, "Woman is greater because woman is mother. All women, no matter what their age, are mothers. They have the essence or quality of '*mā*.' Therefore, all women should be respected. The problem in this society is that people don't understand this, that all women are '*mā*.' That's why men beat their wives."[20] He and several other Baul men I met called their wives *saṅginī* instead of *strī*. A few Vaishnava Bauls do have traditional social weddings with a Hindu priest and a dowry, but others practice *mālācandan* or *mālābadal*, an exchange of garlands done with the guidance and blessings of a guru. Some Bauls considered this type of exchange more binding than a regular social wedding since it is done in the presence of one's guru, whom disciples are expected to obey, but there is considerable debate and variation on the permanence of Baul marriages done this way. Jamal, however, believes that *mālācandan* was also just to show society. The goal and the binding glue of any union, in his mind, is love (*prem*), whether that union is overseen by a priest or a guru. "So what does marriage entail? Two minds. If two hearts/minds [*man*] become attracted to each other, if two people's minds mix with each other, then that is a marriage. If two people stay together and their minds mix, then they've come together. So what is this marriage? What's marriage [besides this]?" Bauls, like Jamal above, criticize society's treatment of women, arguing that conceptualizing women as dangerous and in need of control misses the point that women's power should foster respect, not fear.

Bauls frequently claim that all women are *mā* and deserve respect, and it is not unusual for Baul men to call their wives or ritual partners *mā* as well. Among non-Bauls, calling older women renouncers or the wives of gurus *mā* or *mātā–ji* can establish a nonsexual and respectful relationship.[21] Meena Khandelwal (2004) shows that cultivating motherly attributes desexualizes women renouncers and can be a useful strategy for women to dissuade the unwanted advances of men. However, for Bauls the implication of the term *mā* is not the desexualization of women but, rather, recognition of the sexual potency inherent in all women that give them the potential to create and to become mothers. Although many scholars have posited a split image of women as *either* mothers *or* sexual beings, emphasizing that the maternal and sexual attributes are conceptualized as being in opposition, Bauls provide an additional example that such split images are not shared by all.[22] In explaining what he believes is wrong with the social construction of marriage that relegates women to an inferior position, Jamal emphasized the sexual power of motherhood in all women. Directing his explanation to Ed, he said:

> This woman here, this is your wife, but in our *sādhanā* language, you are not supposed to call her your wife. You're calling her your wife, but can you call your mother your wife? Your mother took this form, so you came through the door [vagina] of your mother. The mother whose door you came through— that mother and this mother—how different are they? That door is the same. Do you understand me? It's the same thing.

Jamal emphasized that all women are mothers and that all humans are essentially the same but have split into male and female in order to enjoy play.

> We think we're many different mothers and fathers, but we're really just one mother, one father. There's only one father and one mother, and that's all there is in this world. It's all the play of the mother and father. This one mother and father are playing, and my situation is just another one of this play.

Bauls embrace the view that their sexual partners and their daughters, whose premarital chastity is valued by most everyone in South Asia, are mothers. But it is clearly their potential to become mothers that is celebrated, not necessarily actual motherhood as stressed in normative South Asian society. While women are valued among Bauls in part because of their sexuality and procreative potential, it is non-reproductive sex that characterizes Baul *sādhanā*, and is considered the means for transforming lust into love. Given the importance of doing *sādhanā* correctly, being physically capable of having children is crucial. A couple living in Bolpur was said to be able to do *sādhanā* correctly, but they were criticized by other Bauls for falling out of practice, being instead distracted by earning money and having had an "operation"[23] to prevent further pregnancies. While having the "operation," encouraged by many local government organizations,[24] is an option that Bengalis might take in order to avoid further straining the family resources, Bauls view any kind of surgery as a violation of the body. In fact, many Bauls argue that someone who has had surgery, particularly to remove or alter a part of their body, cannot be a Baul because the body needs to remain intact and whole in order to gain the fruits of *sādhanā*.[25] Miscarriages and barrenness are also problematic, since in those cases a woman does not embody the potential to be a mother. Two couples I interviewed in Jhenaidah regularly criticized each other behind the others' backs by stating that the other really was not doing *sādhanā* correctly. Proof of their failures, not evident to me, was claimed to be multiple miscarriages and indiscriminate spilling of seed. Bauls celebrate women's potential to become mothers, rather than actual motherhood, but they do not condone preventing motherhood by any other means than correctly performed *sādhanā*.

Among the various discourses that give shape to Baul women's lives and choices, there are some interesting patterns about curbing potentialities. In normative society, it is women's *śakti* that is valued as a potential yet is frequently limited by societal restrictions. In most cases, especially in higher caste rural families, *śakti* is celebrated in women so long as women do not actually become too powerful. In contrast, Bauls seek to draw on women's *śakti*, not celebrating it in the abstract but channeling it as the source of their own possible transformation. In this case, women are viewed as gurus who are capable of helping Baul men during *sādhanā*. On the other hand, normative society celebrates women's creative potential of motherhood not in the abstract, but in the flesh: women are born to be mothers, and it is through the actualization of this role that women's status is raised. Again in contrast, Bauls value the potential of motherhood in all females, but actual motherhood is often viewed as an impediment to spiritual work. Women's potentialities are celebrated in both cases, but those ideals are curtailed very differently.

Wynne Maggi's study (2001) of indigenous conceptions of ethnic identity and women's agency among the Kalasha of Pakistan demonstrates that a group's ethical model may not necessarily match actual practice, an idea that is relevant here. In her study, women's freedom emerged as a significant ethical model and marker of that identity, made all the more concrete in comparison to neighboring Muslims. This ethical model highlights a potential to move about rather than an empirical fact, as many Kalasha women seldom travel far, though claiming women's right to do so is a source of pride for both Kalasha men and women. Similarly, the ethical model purportedly embraced by Muslims in nearby villages included women's adherence to forms of purdah. These women "represent themselves as people who stay put" (2001:82), yet again this ideal did not match Maggi's observation that Muslim women spent plenty of time traveling to visit distant relatives—perhaps even more so than did Kalasha women—even while maintaining purdah (81, also 38–39). Baul rhetoric about women's high status, value, procreative potential, and mobility emphasizes a central ethical model embraced by Baul men and women. Indeed, Baul women I met claim that what they love most about being a Baul is the freedom to move around ("Who likes to live at home?" some asked rhetorically) and the respect Bauls claim women deserve. One might conclude that where Baul ideals overlap with sponsors' expectations, Baul women would be empowered to actualize those ideals, yet it is not as simple as this. Unlike the Kalasha, who live together as a community surrounded by ethnic boundaries, Bauls live in small family units and interact daily with people who have very different ideas about appropriate behavior. Baul women are thus not only aware of regional gendered expectations, as are the Kalasha, but they also are motivated to strategically orient themselves toward normative society. It is not a surprise then that what Baul women say women *can do* and what they as women *actually do* are often very different, as demonstrated by some of the women discussed above. Unlike the Kalasha women who emphasize their ability to move while in fact often choosing not to move, Baul women emphasize what normative society expects of them (to stay put, have children, and be silent) while in fact often moving and singing (and maybe having a child or two). Therefore, while it may well be that some, such as the administrator of the Shah Ali Baghdadi *māzār* who denied the existence of women singers at the *māzār*, may underscore the expectations in order to dismiss the exceptions, Baul women seem to highlight societal norms in order to underscore their own defiance.

In the next chapter I discuss how Baul women negotiate among often conflicting ideas of feminine respectability and the ideals and expectations of behavior for and among Bauls themselves. It is here that Baul women emerge not as victims of a variety of social forces that appear to leave women with no agency, much less any chance for success, but as women who consciously and actively engage with the choices and expectations presented to them. Moreover, they often use those very ideals of gendered respectability in ways that enhance their position and options in society.

PART II

Negotiations

4

Negotiating between Paradigms of the Good Baul and the Good Woman

"All This I Have Done"

Phulmala often met me at the station nearest my home in order to bring me back to where she was living in 2000. I was never convinced that this was convenient for her, though for reasons of her own she usually insisted that she take the train to meet me. Phulmala is on the trains nearly daily, singing for alms (*madhukarī*). She has a particular train she boards each day, and she knows the schedule and trains on which several other Bauls work. The advantage to working the same train is that she gets to know people pretty well. She told me that some of her best connections— that is, those that led to big programs, often abroad—were made on trains. I suspect she remained hopeful that other similar connections would be made in the future.

When Phulmala sang on the trains, she never paid the fare. It was the right of alms seekers and hawkers to get on the trains for free and conduct their work; so long as their work was evident, they were not asked to show a ticket. When I rode with her, I bought her ticket as well as mine before we boarded. She did not sing, and we would sit or stand as space allowed. There were often several people on the trains who seemed to know Phulmala when I rode with her.

When I was with her at the station or in the train, she would typically start a conversation with someone else who was waiting. Invariably they would ask about me: where I was from, if I knew Bengali, and so on. Sometimes they would eventually ask me something, but usually they just continued speaking to Phulmala. I was not inclined to join in because I was tired of these kinds of conversations about myself, and it seemed like they were benefiting Phulmala more than anyone so I did not interfere or correct her if she misrepresented me. She would continue on by telling them how many foreigners came to see her, how she spent three months in France and a few months in America. She would describe how in France they almost went crazy at the program she and other Bauls gave. And she would tell them something about how Americans live, how busy they all are, how the houses are large, and so on. And then when she had sufficiently convinced them that she knew, from personal experience, what other countries and people are like, she would return to talking about how many foreigners came here to learn Bengali or about the Bauls. She would tell them that I was studying Bengali at Visva-Bharati in Santiniketan (not true) or that I was researching her life and music. And she would add that I was her friend.

These conversations always seemed about the same with Phulmala telling her listeners about me but mostly about how she has socialized with foreigners and performed many programs abroad. It was my impression that she was working these conversations to her benefit. People on the trains or at the station were curious about me, but after giving them only a few vague details about me, she instead revealed to them how experienced and impressive her own life had been. Most of her listeners would never have such an opportunity, even if they were much wealthier than Phulmala.

Standing next to her listeners, Phulmala was a tiny, older widow wearing a worn-out and graying white sari with purple trim. It was cold during the month or so I visited her most, and she wore daily the same purple sweater with holes in it. Her hair was pulled in a bun with split ends sticking up here and there. She kept her *ektārā* in a cloth bag when she was not using it, and she tied up her money into the end of her sari which she then would fling over her shoulder. The men and women she engaged in conversations towered over her and were sometimes dressed up for the job they were either going to or returning from. Undaunted by their relative wealth and social standing, Phulmala told them just who she was and what she had been able to accomplish. They often seemed to be put into their place and got increasingly quiet as the conversation went on. By the end I think they just might have felt slightly intimidated by her experience and clout.

Phulmala certainly impressed and usually intimidated me. She was a determined woman who had a lot going against her. She had been a widow from the time she was a young woman with three children. Although by the time I knew her she was an older widow and was entitled to a degree of freedom of movement and speech not as acceptable for younger, married women, I suspect she gained her commanding presence through years of necessity and hard work. Sarah Lamb (2000) writes on the situation of widows in West Bengal and shows that the degree of freedom a woman experiences is related in part to her age. Because of what is viewed as an abundance of bodily heat (sexual potency) of women in their reproductive years, women who become widows at a young age are contained through certain dietary restrictions that are said to keep them cool and prevent sexual transgressions. Widows and women who are older have naturally cooled down and are therefore more pure, more like men, and more free to roam. But women like Phulmala and Kangalini had been young mothers without husbands and had to learn how to survive during those years when ideally they should remain enclosed and contained.

Phulmala's natal family was from Faridpur, Bangladesh, and she said her marriage was arranged when she was about three years old, "back when I had no sense about domestic life." She and her husband came to West Bengal about 25 years ago. He used to sing *kīrtan* (Vaishnava devotional music), and then he served in the military. "What happened, I don't know. He was crippled and stayed in the home—for 9–10 years. He died over 18–19 years ago." She and her husband both took *dīkshā–śikshā* and began learning songs long after marriage, but when her husband was confined to the home, she took over learning songs and earning an income.

Phulmala's two sons and one daughter were grown and married by the time I met her, and in 2000 she lived with her sons, two daughters-in-law, and some grandchildren in a small house next to the unitrack railway. Her sons contributed financially to the family (one was a tailor with sporadic jobs; the other sold lottery tickets), but the decaying condition of their cramped house and Phulmala's own frequent requests for assistance suggest that they did not have an easy time making ends meet. She lost a fourth child, a daughter, whom she said was talented in singing and would have carried on her music tradition.

Phulmala's features are delicate, but her eyes are strong and set, and her mouth is firm. Even a photograph of her when she was younger reveals a woman one would not want to cross. When she breaks into a smile, though, she completely lights up, and she finds many things funny and endearing. When one day in her home I was recording her interview, which she took very seriously, ever conscious of the microphone, her smallest grandson came into the room giggling and unable to control himself when Phulmala told him to be quiet. Phulmala did not get stern with him, though his father tried, and she broke into a big smile and turned toward me, laughing.

I ran into Phulmala at the Joydeb Mela in January 1999, and we spent the greater part of one of the days walking around, meeting people. When she saw Gaur Khepa, a well-known Baul performer who is on several CDs and has toured abroad frequently, she led me toward him. He was sitting on the ground smoking ganja with a few people clustered around him. He cleared a space next to him as Phulmala made her way through the crowd. I sat nearby. Gaur Khepa leaned over to show me a certificate stating he performed at Brown University in about 1989. It was not unusual for Bauls who performed abroad to show evidence of their performances years afterward. As we sat there, more people gathered around, hoping to hear an intimate performance of Baul songs under the tent and away from the various stages on which Bauls and *kīrtaniya*s (performers of Vaishnava *kīrtan* songs) were playing. Gaur and Phulmala seemed playfully close, bantering back and forth. After a while Phulmala began singing a song, and then Gaur jumped in and sang the next line. While he was singing, she laughingly nudged him and then stood up in the middle of the circle of listeners that had grown quickly since they began singing. Standing there she sang the rest of the song alone. Her voice was not as strong as Gaur's, who performs with the abandon suggested in his name Khepa, or, mad. But as was stated by a poet from Hooghly who had come to Joydeb to hear Bauls sing, Phulmala sings with real feeling (*bhāb*). Because she had suffered so much and yet sang so well, he believed that Phulmala ranked up there with the "real" Bauls and had gone far on the path. Still, as a performer, Gaur Khepa, with his booming voice, could have easily dominated the impromptu performance. Yet Phulmala, laughing playfully, silenced him by standing up and, without further interruption, singing the rest of the song she had begun.

Such behavior was not unusual for Phulmala. She has experienced multiple dismissals herself and has learned to exert herself and be heard. Līnā Cākī (2001:94–99) describes seeing Phulmala in the 1980s perform on a stage at Joydeb. Before she began, a well-traveled Baul man with a strong and dynamic presence and a host of foreign admirers performed. Cākī describes his command of the audience, and when he was done the musicians and foreigners, satisfied, left. As Phulmala entered the stage, there was no one left to play with her, and she turned to the Baul musicians who were departing to ask if some would accompany her. A fakir offered to play the *cimṭā* (iron tongs used for cooking and as a rhythmic musical instrument), but she was not able to get anyone to play *khol* (two-sided barrel drum). Cākī described Phulmala as not having a strong voice, yet making all the more effort. Interviewing her later, she found Phulmala to believe strongly that despite discrimination that privileged men's voices, dance, and needs, she had as much right as a man to sing publicly, to get programs abroad, and to earn a living. From what I have seen, Phulmala is still actively trying to gain those things for herself. Standing up among a group of seated listeners and a well-known Baul performer at the Joydeb Mela I attended in 1999, she made sure that she was heard.

One Bengali friend in Santiniketan who knew Phulmala agreed that she was a strong and complicated woman but believed it was because she was up against men all the time. He said he once saw a Baul be condescending toward her in a train station, and she responded by telling him forcefully not to talk to her like that. My friend was surprised by Phulmala's response because, in his experience, most women would not defend themselves so strongly in public. The cultural behavior he had in mind is that Bengali women tend to hide being harassed (whether through insults or what is regionally called "Eve teasing") rather than to draw attention to themselves, as they have too much *lajjā* to confront someone or ask for help from others. Phulmala clearly disagreed.

When I saw Phulmala again in 2007, I mentioned Cākī's 2001 book on Baul women since it had a section on Phulmala's life. Phulmala exploded in anger. She said that a friend had read portions of the book to her, and she became furious about the descriptions of Baul women as destitute and desperate. Based on her friend's summaries, Phulmala concluded that Cākī did not speak poorly about her but that the author had negative things to say about Bauls she loved and respected. She was so angry that she refused to take a copy of the book home because she did not want to spread the bad name given to Bauls.

Phulmala has a strong sense of self-worth and expects people, whether journalists, sponsors, Bauls, or ordinary people, to treat her appropriately. When she interacts with people on the train or in the festivals, she lets them know with confidence just who she is and why she is worthy of respect. For her, it seems, her worth lies in her Baul path and in all that she has built up on her own. There was some appreciation for Vaishnava music in her home growing up, but she established herself as a Baul singer with a reputation all on her own. Nonetheless, she describes being saddened because there is no one else in her family who is continuing the tradition: her sons, daughter, and daughters-in-law are all busy with family life and have not learned Baul songs. But even if she was not able to teach them songs, she believes her Baul path and her own actions have left a legacy for her family.

> How will it remain after my death? Do you know Lisa? Suppose, saints, gurus, or Vaishnavas come from somewhere. [My children] will serve them [*sevā karā*], love them, and see that they get food. They will keep these original customs of Bauls [*sevā*]. Music practice—it may happen, or it may not. I can't tell for sure. Someone may still wake up—as my parents who did not sing at home or abroad…[but I began singing and] I went all over the world. Many people know me, and because of this they [my children] are glorified. People come also to know them. These works of research are going on. Nobody knew about them [before]. But if you publish this research in a book, they—my sons, my daughters, my father-in-law, mother-in-law, or my parents—they will remain immortal for centuries. This immortality came from me. They will become elevated and remain immortal. More Vaishnavas, more devotees will look after them. They will look at their names and see that they are really original Vaishnavas, they are original Bauls. This history will remain for centuries. All this I have done. If anyone enters my place, that person will awaken our memory.

Phulmala is undoubtedly overestimating the longevity of ethnographies, never mind my own personal contribution to the field, but it is clear she believes that she has had a positive impact on her family—despite the fact that as a Baul and widow she has struggled to make ends meet. Her situation has become even more complicated since I recorded this interview. In 2007 Phulmala left the house she had bought for her family in order to live on her own. Although her departure was motivated in part by a tense relationship with her daughter-in-law, she interprets her new situation as one that is appropriate for this late stage of her life. Her belief that her reputation among Vaishnavas and her own teaching of Baul ideals and customs as well as her interviews with researchers will immortalize her and her family suggests that she sees herself as a powerful actor in the world around her. Even her current situation she chooses to view as a step in her spiritual journey. Rather than bemoan her struggles, which she does acknowledge, she actively attempts to create for herself and others a meaningful life. Questions of textual longevity notwithstanding, it is because of her clearly stated desire to be immortalized through research that, after some contemplation, I have included her real name in this text.

Although Phulmala feels the tension between being a good Baul and being a mother (as she says, "How can I be a Baul? I have been consumed by family."), it is her identity as a Baul that helped her support her family. Being a widow with children necessitated her pushing the boundaries of what is generally considered behavior suitable to women in Bengal. Phulmala's background is Vaishnava (*jāt baishṇab*), and some Vaishnavas, like widows whose lives may be characterized by asceticism, abstain from eating rich foods, often also wearing white. Although Phulmala wears white, her life is not so much characterized by enforced self-denial as by a determination to succeed as a Baul performer who can support herself and her family. Phulmala not only travels widely she also asserts her self-worth regularly, interrupting another's singing, relating her accomplishments to strangers, and, as I discuss more below, demanding financial support from Bengali elites and American anthropologists.

As an older widow Phulmala no longer faces the same pressures to be a respectable housewife, and she can act in ways that belie *lajjā*. In this way she differs from several of the women I discuss below, many of whom are young and married. But Phulmala's fate of having to raise a family without a husband is feared by most of the women I discuss here, and their worries reveal from another angle the hardships Phulmala has faced. Although I have only a little information about Phulmala's early life, it is my impression based in part on Cākī's observation of her in the 1980s and mine in 1999 that Phulmala has had to learn through challenges how to get what she wants and needs. Some of the younger women I discuss below, like Jaya and Madhabi, are clearly in the process of learning how to negotiate between being a Baul and the expectations people have of them as women. Today Phulmala is indeed a determined woman who feels she should get what she believes she deserves as a Baul. Her gender, though an obstacle in society, should not, she believes, prevent her from being respected and remunerated as a Baul singer.

Defying Obstacles

Being a Baul can in itself be read as an act of defiance against societal expectations, and all Bauls, whether male or female, decide to what extent they will be open about their choice of rejecting certain societal norms. Some Baul women, like Phulmala in Birbhum, Kangalini in Dhaka, and Siuli in Sylhet (discussed below), scoff at the obstacles they have faced, highlighting their successes despite a society that aims to restrict them. For them, being a Baul is at least in part a means of achieving freedom, independence, and self-sufficiency. These three women see their Baul identities as a way to create a meaningful life for themselves.

Like Phulmala, Kangalini is an older woman who has struggled alone to make her place as a Baul artist. Both eventually gained the presence and "protection" of men, though only after a long period without them. Phulmala's sons finally grew up; Kangalini, the mother of only one daughter, eventually became a Muslim and remarried. But in both cases it is still clearly the women, not the men, who are the main sources of income and prestige in the households. In fact, it appears that these men are not actual wielders of domestic power or even figureheads in the household. Phulmala's sons, though they work, bring little income into their household, and Phulmala, as seen in the beginning of this chapter, clearly sees herself and her Baul ways as the source of prestige in her family. Even now that she is no longer living with her family, she argues that all of the wealth they now enjoy (e.g., house, television, mobile phone) came from her. Kangalini has been married a few times, and her current and previous husbands, both about half her age, accompany her in musical performances in which she is definitely the star. Although Phulmala has had some success, performing abroad and at many programs, Kangalini has become very widely recognized for her musical talent.[1]

Perhaps because of her success as a Baul singer in Bangladesh, Kangalini, who is often in the public eye, appears more conscious of or cautious about her image as a woman than does Phulmala. However, Kangalini may claim that she has done everything right as a woman, but she by no means merely acquiesces to those gendered expectations. Rather, she states them, sometimes appearing to support them, but in action tends to ignore them. Thus, as discussed previously, although she says women cannot be *pīr*s or gurus, she herself has many students, playing the role of *pīr* or guru. Also, she argues that women should remain with their husbands no matter what, yet she herself left her first abusive husband and has remarried a few times since then.

Although Kangalini's words often appear to support normative expectations for women, when I asked her about the obstacles she has faced as a Baul woman, her voice was defiant and unwavering:

> Yes, if a woman becomes a Baul *śilpī*, she faces lots of obstacles. Let the obstacles come [I say]! When the mind enters the Baul path, then it won't be bothered with such obstacles anymore. I will try to keep the Baul tradition alive. Isn't it?
>
> When I took a guru or *ustād*, when I took the cloth off of my head, when I didn't have any disgust for anything, then I thought, well, let me see how I can keep the Baul *dharma*. I am keeping it in that way. I don't give a damn about anybody. I don't care what people say. I'm living like that. I'm not controlled by the obstacles that people give me. I only—I'll die, I don't care—but I'm going to keep the Baul tradition.
>
> For example... so many of my relatives have been disgusted with me, thought badly of me. Kangalini Sufia, she's gone bad. How can she go for this stuff? None of this is in the Shari'at. You've become a Baul; you've gone down the road of a Baul.
>
> Whatever insults I get, I think that this type of music, my voice—I've done it! I don't care about anybody; I just care about the music.

Like Phulmala, Kangalini recognizes that her achievements have been earned despite significant obstacles. As rural Hindu women who face discrimination because of widowhood or a failed marriage, both have indeed gained an independent source of income and prestige against substantial odds. Hindu widows in South Asia, generally expected not to remarry (though some do), have few options available to them. A widow's future depends largely on whether or not there are family members willing to take care of her: in-laws who might still value her contributions within the household; grown children (especially sons) who can support her; parents who still feel an attachment and are financially able to take her back in or arrange a new marriage. When family members are not able, or willing, to support a poor widow, she may need to resort to begging, sometimes also retreating to monastic settings or religious sites where householders are more motivated to support those in need.[2] A few also become renouncers, joining one of the many monastic orders or religious paths.

Phulmala and Kangalini both had young children to support when they lost their husbands. When I asked Phulmala what troubles she has faced as a Baul woman, she answered that it was hard to earn enough to support her family: "With children our Baul life is very difficult. Our Baul lives depend on doing *madhukarī*. Meaning, our family life is not comfortable; we have to manage our family with music. Most of the people's lives are happy with children. [But] we [Bauls] feel pain at this." Although Phulmala has done some programs abroad, her main day-to-day income has been from *madhukarī*. That Phulmala's main concern has been raising and supporting her children is not unusual for widows with children. As Lamb (2000) describes, widows who have children tend to construct their identities more as mothers than as widows. Being a widow with young children compounds the challenges of being a Baul who earns a living through *madhukarī*. "By doing *madhukarī* life can more or less go on. But it's not really for supporting a family," Phulmala explains. But although she says she does not want her children to face the challenges of the Baul path, supporting a family through *madhukarī*, she believes there was no other way for her: "I like this path, so I am crazy!" The defiance in Kangalini's voice when I asked her about the obstacles she has had to face is thus not surprising. She too has had to support herself and her daughter alone by doing *madhukarī*. Yet despite the hardships, she has not only managed to support her family, but she has also gained nationwide recognition.

In the passage above, Kangalini notes several times that she has gone against normative expectations: she took the cloth off of her head, no longer following purdah. She also took a guru when a woman's only lord and teacher should be her husband. This transition was marked when she left conventional society and marriage life to follow a *sannyāsī*. As a result of becoming a Baul, she claims that relatives have been disgusted with her, viewing her actions as going against religious norms and doctrine, and that people have insulted her. It is interesting that Kangalini says her family criticized her actions for not being in line with the Shari'at since her natal family was Hindu. First of all, she claims that she no longer has a natal family: "I have no relatives. No one from my mother's family or from father's. I am an orphan. I am the only kin of my daughter, and she is mine." It was her mother who had given her to a *sannyāsī* after the birth of Kangalini's daughter, so it is unlikely that her family, even if they were still alive, would be in a position to criticize Kangalini when they lacked the resources to provide her with another option after the failure of her marriage. Furthermore, except for her first husband, who was also Hindu, the rest of her marriages have been with Muslims, but those men were also Bauls. I suspect that the family she is referring to is a broader community of Muslims, not natal or conjugal. Or, it is possible that she did receive criticism from her first husband and his family (she mentions that she did in another conversation) but that here she confers on them a Muslim identity. Such re-creations of her past are not unusual; they reflect her own ambivalence about her place and her past in the predominantly Muslim society that is Bangladesh.

But despite using such re-creations of her past to put herself in a better light (as a Muslim), she argues that she does not care what others think about her. In fact, it is precisely the Baul path that has led her to "not be bothered with such obstacles anymore." Thus while the Baul path is the source of people's criticism of her, it is also the source of her own personal and public transcendence of societal norms. As other Bauls have explained, being a Baul means that one should love human beings and not discriminate against them. Kangalini states that in "becoming Baul *śilpīs*, we came to know that every human being is equal to others: either she or he is a Muslim or a Hindu, either a Buddhist or a Christian. Everybody's identity is that of human being. There must be no discrimination [*hiṃsā*] of others."

Despite Baul views that being a Muslim or a Hindu make no difference, Kangalini all too painfully knows that in Bangladeshi society it does matter. Religion has affected both her own personal options and her public status. Her father and brother were killed in the Bangladesh Liberation War (1971) because they were Hindus. Instead of becoming remarried, an unlikely possibility given family circumstances, she took renunciation and eventually became a Baul singer. But it was not until she became a Muslim that she says she received respect within the larger Bangladeshi society. "When I converted to Islam, I got respect from all. I also got love and care. But when I was a Hindu, I did not get any care. You know that ours is a Muslim country. Muslims could not tolerate Hindus, and Hindus could also not [tolerate Muslims]." In a later interview she added, "[When I became a Muslim] I could stand on my own two feet. I could go out and make some money. Then I was able to be a little happier." Not only did becoming a Muslim give her respect; it also gave her the public sanction to remarry, and having a husband further improved her social standing.

While, on the one hand, Kangalini seems full of contradictions, what she says and does makes sense when considered in the larger context in which she lives. Presenting her past and current identity as a Muslim does not contradict her Baul convictions about religion. While Bauls argue that all religions are the same, they claim that differences are merely apparent in the names used. Kangalini has basically substituted Hindu terminology with Muslim ones. For example, she uses Shari'at when referring to the religious doctrine of her "relatives," and she uses guru and *ustād* or *pīr* as well as *bhek* and *khilāphat* interchangeably. This is actually common among Bauls who discuss the same basic philosophy using either Muslim or Hindu terminology, usually depending on familiarity with a particular background but sometimes also with the intention of erasing differences among them. Thus the underlying ideas and her convictions have probably remained essentially the same.[3] But what she has gained in the process of "conversion" is respect in the predominantly Muslim Bangladesh.

Words thus do matter, and encoded in one's choice of words are careful considerations about one's place in society. Kangalini largely presents herself as a Muslim Baul, though she does not deny her Hindu background. Claiming that she gained success and happiness when she became a Muslim is probably quite accurate, though that statement can be interpreted in different ways. For example, the reason for her happiness could be her newfound faith and belief system implied in her conversion, or it could be that as a Muslim she is more accepted socially. Therefore although Bauls argue against distinctions among religions, Bauls with different backgrounds not only tend to use different terminology; they choose their terminology carefully in order to respond to perceived expectations and requirements in their immediate contexts. This is also the case with whether or not a person may call her- or himself a Baul, as being a Baul can have very different connotations regionally. I take up one aspect of this issue in the following section, in which I examine more closely one woman's assertion of her Baul identity in Sylhet.

The Power of a Name: Baul Identity as a Proclamation of Social Defiance

In Birbhum when I asked women if they were Bauls, their answers often suggested that being a Baul was a process or a goal and not simply a label one gains through initiation. Women, as well as men, often rhetorically asked me questions like "How can I be a Baul? I have a home, a family, and responsibilities. I am not a Baul yet." Women's reluctance to claim Baul as their identity reflects at least in part a sentiment of humility in which one tends to deny any achievements or favorable qualities. Although the reasons behind this reluctance are undoubtedly more complex than can be explained here, the point I wish to make is that being perceived as a Baul is generally viewed more positively in Birbhum than in other areas. This is true even alongside concerns that Bauls have the reputation of being promiscuous. Being a Baul woman in Sylhet, on the other hand, has very different connotations.

Like in Birbhum, the Sylhetis with whom I spoke (mostly Bauls themselves or supporters of Bauls) stated that being a Baul means being carefree, unencumbered by social constraints, and knowledgeable about the body. Munibor summed up that a Baul is one who does not care about worldly possessions, does not care if there is a bed, a car, or a roof over one's head. Such a person can still have a family and live at home, as his father (a famous Baul *sādhak* and *śilpī*) did, but emphasis is not placed on possessions and material comfort. His brother, Mujib, emphasized the knowledge of the body that Bauls have. Paraphrased from an unrecorded interview at his home in Sylhet city, he gave the following explanation of Baul:

> There are Hindus, Muslims, and Christians, but being a Baul is something different. People recognize that a person with long hair is a Baul. But that's not what being a Baul is about. The sky, the earth, the stars, the sun, and the moon—just because you don't see them in the body doesn't mean they're not there. You can't see the top of your head, or your backbone, but they are there. There are 7 worlds, 24 moons, 24 suns: they all reside in the body. One who knows this and has knowledge of the body is a Baul. Bauls also sing. If a person says he can't sing, a Baul can fix it. Like a car: if it doesn't start then a mechanic looks around, finds the problem, and fixes it. A Baul also can fix the body because he knows it.

Other Sylhetis emphasized these two aspects of being Baul—being carefree and having esoteric knowledge of the body—to varying degrees. To my knowledge, being a Baul in Sylhet does not indicate participation in the sexual rituals associated with the term in the areas of western Bangladesh and West Bengal where I conducted my research, yet broad understandings of the term are somewhat similar. In both contexts, being a Baul suggests that one is outside social norms, particularly as laid out in Hindu or Muslim orthodoxy. In Sylhet, Bauls are *māraphati*s (those who follow the Ma'rifat) or Sufis; they follow *pīr*s and visit *māzār*s for all-night musical gatherings. In areas where being a Baul is viewed as a challenge to normative society, the willingness of women to identify themselves as Bauls may be seen as a marker of a willingness or desire to challenge those norms. Since in Sylhet being a Baul woman is fraught with negative connotations, including being thought of as uneducated and morally loose, not all who sing Baul songs or engage in Baul practices associate themselves with the term itself. When they do, however, I suggest it is used to communicate a certain challenge to or deviance from normative Sylheti society. This became clear through discussions with various individuals who either shunned the term or embraced it, as with Siuli below.

It was weeks after Ed and I had arrived in Sylhet, and after much protesting with our hosts Munibor and Chacha (who discouraged us from meeting what they described as "shameful" women), that we finally were able to meet some Baul women. After the gathering described in chapter 3 where several women performed for us, we arranged to meet some of them again.

Kasem took us to meet one of these women, Nur Jahan, late one afternoon. Living with her in a rented house was her husband and another woman performer, Siuli, with her husband and children. To get to their house we walked through several narrowing streets and some twists and turns around and behind closely packed houses in Sylhet town. By a dirt courtyard surrounded by houses and a big tree, we took a final left through a rickety gate and made our way into an outwardly small house. There were several people around, and it looked like a few families were living together in one place. On the inside, the house did not seem especially small;

there were several rooms, most of which we did not see. We were led to an inner bedroom, and we sat on the bed; to the right of us was a fairly large shelf full of makeup, hair oil, plastic flowers, and cassettes. Across the room was a table on which a harmonium and a violin in its case were placed. Among those in the room was an older man dressed in a white sarong-like garment or *lungi*, a white *pānjābī*, and a light-colored scarf. His grey hair hung about two inches below his ears, and he had a light beard. He was introduced as Siuli's *ustād*; soon after we arrived, he arose to leave, his departure accompanied by lots of hustle and bustle.

Everyone was very friendly and welcoming, and after a short while I had an opportunity to explain to Siuli why I had come to visit. When I told her that there were many books written about Bauls but nothing about women, adding that no one seems to be asking women what it is like being Bauls, Siuli gave a knowing laugh and nodded her head. Nur Jahan returned from another room, sat down on a stool near the wall a short distance from us, and I explained my project to her as well. When I was finished, Ed added that we had been looking everywhere for women to talk to but that people kept telling us there were no women Bauls, and with no further prompting Nur Jahan launched into a story about her own life. (Some of this story is relayed and discussed in chapter 6.) There was a relaxed manner in the way these women related to each other and to the men around them. They were not at all shy or quiet; they talked, interrupted, and laughed loudly. In their presence I found myself finally feeling very comfortable. But I was struck by the disparity between the behavior and perspectives of women in this room and the expectations other local Sylhetis have of women. I wondered how these women navigated the restrictions I had observed and come to experience in Sylhet. Furthermore, after the preceding difficult weeks trying to find women to talk to, I was intrigued to find that those I finally met had a clear idea of a story they wanted to share as well as an understanding of the social structures that denigrated and excluded them. This latter perspective was particularly evident in Siuli's speech.

Siuli was born in Jhenaidah, a region in western Bangladesh near Kusthia, also considered to be full of Bauls. Her father sang songs by Lalan (*lālan-giti*), and she learned singing from him. Although she has since learned all kinds of songs, on her business card she identifies herself as "Baul *śilpī*." After some difficulties she moved to Sylhet, and it was here, she said, where her music life really began. She got married and had children, but that marriage failed because her husband tried to put a stop to her singing. Siuli defiantly declared, "Though I am willing to leave my family for music, I cannot leave music. I love music so much that I just can't live without it. If someone gives me the crown for leaving music, I won't take it. It is simply impossible for me to live without music because this is mixed with my blood." After being separated from that family, she got married again. She told her current husband that she had one requirement, to be allowed to continue singing. Her husband, sitting nearby and listening throughout our interview, nodded his approval. They have children, and when I met them she had begun teaching the oldest girl to sing.

But although Siuli has the support of her current husband to pursue a career singing Baul songs, she does not always get that support from others. I did not need to ask her what kinds of obstacles she faces as a woman or as a Baul because she immediately began to describe them to me.

> Many times I perform onstage. Mullahs sometimes oppose us doing a program. I feel very distressed at this [and wonder], why have I learned all these things? I am well off with my present husband. He can afford every-thing. Meaning, it's not that we can't live—can't make ends meet—without my singing. Even though we can live with comfort like others in this society, I can't live without music, because music is my life. I go to many places [to perform]. Sometimes we are chased away by mullahs. Then I'm stricken with sorrow. Then I think that I will not sing anymore. But at the same time, I realize that it's impossible for me to live without music. That's it.

Siuli described the peace of mind she gets from singing and said she realizes that pain often inspires music. Struggles to perform as a woman in a conservative envi-ronment appear to be intertwined with the joy she receives from her accomplish-ments. "Without getting pain, *śilpī*s cannot sing," she says. Baul men in Sylhet also have complained about mullahs disrupting their performances, but they usually declare that Bauls ultimately have more strength than the conservative Muslims. Siuli, on the other hand, seems to stress her discouragement about these struggles and reflects that women are doubly disadvantaged. Indeed, it appears that through performing she intends also to challenge gender roles.

> I think women are defenseless [*asahāẏ*], especially in Bangladesh. Women are treated as worthless. People don't value women. I think, why do they not pay any attention to us? I am a human being too. I have the right to live my life just as a man does. I must establish my rights by myself; that will be the greatest achievement. Why don't I get my rights [*adhikār*]? I have my hands and legs. I can live by working just like anybody else. Why should I depend on others? I want to establish my rights myself. In this way it will be established for all women.

We saw evidence of this desire to achieve rights for women on a following visit to their house. We arrived at about 5 p.m. a few days later to find Siuli and Nur Jahan sitting in one of the bedrooms drinking tea with several neighboring women. We sat and joined them while several of the household men and women walked around us, tending to their daily lives. Siuli had recently taken a shower; her hair was shiny and black, and it was pulled back neatly in a bun at the nape of her neck. Her gray sari with a reddish border looked unwrinkled from the day. Nur Jahan was wearing a house dress with a shawl over her shoulders.

While we were drinking tea and eating a snack of fried flattened rice (*ciṛā*), Siuli told us and the other women in the room that she was tired of women being treated as second-rate and not given respect. "Why should we be treated badly?" she asked.

"We're just as good as men." She told us that she was tired of the insults that men throw at women who sing. Siuli was clear that the way women were treated in Sylhet was unfair, and she communicated this view to her listeners. Furthermore, she believed that women's voices and opinions were just as valuable as men's. When someone new in the room asked what I was doing there, she explained my project with such clarity that I felt elated and relieved to find my questions resonated with at least one of the women I had been trying to meet since arriving in Sylhet. For further emphasis, she added that I am not researching men, only women.

An older woman sitting with us told me that her daughter-in-law also sings, and she invited us over to her place. Siuli and the older woman led us out of the house and over to another home a few doors down. We only entered as far as the first room, which housed a large bed with bedposts and beautifully carved wooden furniture, but the place looked more spacious and appeared to belong to a family of a higher economic class. Anuwara, a young woman in her late twenties who wore a sheer sari, came in. She had a delicate face and a pleasant smile. Her mother-in-law told us that Anuwara sings songs of Arkum Shah, a Chisti Sufi some call a Baul because of his songs emphasizing *deha-tattva*, and suggested that she sing one now.

Anuwara joined us on the bed, and someone handed a harmonium to Siuli, who placed it in front of her. Two men came in and took up cymbals and a drum, and soon all four performers were sitting on the large bed near me. The young woman launched immediately and confidently into a song written by Arkum Shah, and as the musicians joined her, the room filled with enthusiasm. She sang another song, and Nur Jahan, who had since showed up, went to the center of the room, encouraged the older mother-in-law to get up, and they began to dance. Soon two young girls joined them, and the women began to dance a line dance. The room was booming with music and dancing, and everyone was clapping along. Many women from nearby houses had meanwhile come in to watch, and they too filled up the room. It was a moment that I felt celebrated women: women danced, women sang loudly, women clapped, and everyone enjoyed themselves.

After the revelry quieted down, Siuli explained that when she had first suggested to Anuwara to sing three years ago, she had refused. Siuli told us Anuwara was so shy that she never went anywhere and always covered her head. The first time Anuwara went onstage, she had her entire head and face covered and tried to sit in the back behind all the musicians. Siuli demonstrated this by pulling her shawl over her own head, and then Anuwara imitated herself from a few years ago by also pulling her own sari over her head. Teasingly, Siuli tugged the end of the sari further so that none of Anuwara's face was visible. But today, Siuli proudly stated, this once shy (*lājuk*) woman sings confidently, with her head uncovered, for ministers and other officials onstage in front of hundreds of people. Anuwara appeared pleased with her own accomplishment and transformation, but for Siuli it seemed to fit the larger objective of trying to encourage women to assert their own rights and value in society.

Although not only women were present at this impromptu gathering (a few of the musicians sitting on the bed with us were men), for those several moments women were clearly the center of attention, and they reveled in it. For the duration of my afternoon visit there, the women in that home created a space in which they were the agents as well as the subjects of social and personal transformation. It was a moment created around the demonstration of one woman's transformation from a shy, modest housewife to someone who performs in public. I had not originally been interested in interviewing Anuwara, whom I had been told was not a Baul, but a few women present insisted I interview her about her life. At their direction, I had pulled out my tape recorder. Siuli and others present believed Anuwara's transformation was important and that if I wanted to learn about women, Bauls or otherwise, I should pay her some attention. It was a community that laughed at the memory of Anuwara hiding behind her scarf and took pride in her accomplishments. When I asked Anuwara how it felt to perform onstage for the first time and how she feels now, she answered, "Of course it was difficult. Even though I was happy and gained pleasure [from singing], I was also very afraid. Now [I feel] 'free.' "

That it was Anuwara's mother-in-law who brought us over to meet Anuwara also is significant. In the home of one's in-laws, women are generally expected to be modest and to place the welfare of one's husband, children, and in-laws before one's own interests. In this household there was a transgression of that norm, but it was one that was tolerated and even celebrated by at least the mother-in-law, who in many South Asian families is the enforcer of proper displays of respect within the household. Anuwara's entrance into the public arena, particularly as a singer, could be interpreted as a scandalous endeavor for a young, attractive wife and mother of her economic status in Sylhet. But Anuwara is also, it appears, a successful mother: she has five sons and one daughter, all studying at various levels in school. Her well-to-do in-laws are tolerant enough of this new interest to allow one of the sons to learn music.

But Anuwara appears also to be cautious about her reputation in the community. When I asked her if she had faced any difficulties as a woman performing, she was clear to state that male relatives absolutely always accompany women outside; women cannot go anywhere without men. Like a good many other women discussed so far, Anuwara knows that her actions are circumscribed by local expectations for women, and so she bends some norms (by performing in public) while following others (by being accompanied by men).

Furthermore, while Siuli declares *herself* a Baul, Anuwara states that *she* is a *śilpī* and *not* a Baul. Even though Anuwara sings songs by a man, Arkum Shah, called Baul by some people locally, she is very clear that she herself is not a Baul. This is no casual issue of identification. Recalling that in Sylhet being a Baul implies a challenge to normative society, Siuli is quite clear that she wants to challenge local Bangladeshi treatment of women. That her business card labels her as a Baul *śilpī* shows to what extent she publicly embraces this objective. Anuwara, on the other hand, has a lot to lose from being identified as Baul. Although it is clear that she and others in her community are pleased with the ways in which she has successfully broken out of some local norms about women's place in public, she nonetheless sees herself as a respectable daughter-in-law, wife, and mother. If wealth is any indication, I suspect that her in-laws have some standing in the community, and though that may give Anuwara room to maneuver, it also means that they have a reputation to maintain. Being a Baul is generally not something for the wealthier classes.[4] Thus, while Siuli has something to gain by being called a Baul, Anuwara would lose something if she did so. Anuwara is not trying to transform society, only herself, and only to the extent that she can do so without jeopardizing her and her family's standing.

Portraying an Image of the Good Wife

Kangalini, Phulmala, and Siuli appear to embrace their freedom from social constraints, demanding that others treat them well because, as Siuli says, "I have the right to live my life just as a man does." Rather than focusing primarily on their reputation as women, they aim to succeed as Bauls—as performers earning an income, as human beings with rights like men, as Baul *śilpīs* with a message to spread. Kangalini and Phulmala share some similarities in that both went through a period when they were poor mothers alone and thus had little to lose in trying to get their due from others. And in experiencing various degrees of fame, traveling abroad and earning money and recognition, they have received different treatment, and their gutsy Baul ways have often been encouraged. Siuli, on the other hand, claims to have left her first husband because he did not approve of her decision to perform Baul songs publicly. Perhaps unlike Kangalini and Phulmala who have chosen the Baul path in part because it offered them a way to deal with their situation, Siuli seems driven by her commitment to music. But whatever the initial motivation, all three appear to have a strong conviction that being a woman should not prevent them from living a meaningful live and even pursuing a public music career.

The above examples reveal women who embrace being Bauls and find much to gain in being identified as Bauls. In contrast to this, however, is what women have to lose in being Bauls. The challenges that being a Baul pose to one's reputation as a woman are most evident among those who feel their status as respectable wife is particularly precarious. This is especially true in certain areas, such as Birbhum and especially around Santiniketan, where several Bauls have loose, unstable marriages. Baul women aware of the possibility of being abandoned by their husbands cautiously negotiate their situation so that they do not get abandoned or at least have something to fall back on should their husband leave. For this reason, women—even if they go out to perform at programs or to sing for alms—try to maintain a good reputation within the community.

This concern for feminine respectability among performing women is not unique to Baul women. The Tamil actresses studied by Susan Seizer (2005) create semiprivate spaces as they travel and establish other ways of interacting with the public to counteract the stigma incurred by their mobility and public performances. Similarly, in Donna Wulff's study (2008) of women *kīrtaniya*s in Bengal, she demonstrates that women performers aim to maintain their respectability by modifying their behavior, for instance by sitting during a performance instead of assuming what seems to be the more male posture of standing (and gesturing expressively) and by performing only at certain types of settings. Women performers in South Asia are well versed in ways that might minimize criticism of their public behavior.

So while both men and women Bauls talked about the value of women and the high status women have among Bauls, women stressed that their position in society is still limited and circumscribed by local expectations of women. In particular, women often told me that their happiness and well-being depend on the presence of a man, such as a husband or brother, and his care for her. However to say that women are merely succumbing to societal pressure would miss the point, which is illustrated in the following discussion on Madhabi and Jaya, that for some women, appearing as a respectable Bengali wife is a strategy for responding to the conflicting expectations and lifestyles of Bauls and of women living in Bengali society.

Despite the challenges that being abandoned pose to her image, Madhabi draws on the limited pool of options available to her in order to create an image of respectability while simultaneously gaining some mobility. As a young woman, she is especially vulnerable to exploitation by men. It is due to concerns about both safety and respectability that Madhabi now lives with a man she refers to as her *dādā*, a term that means older brother but in this case is used to establish a fictive kinship relationship, and his wife, whom she calls *baudi*, or brother's wife. Fictive kin are common in South Asia, and a young girl or boy may call a number of unrelated neighbors uncle or aunt. For a woman to call a man older brother or uncle is often an effective way to establish a nonsexual relationship among strangers or non-kin and is a strategy sometimes used by women traveling alone. This also serves to draw a person into a protective role, as would be fulfilled by an actual older brother or uncle. Madhabi's use of the term *dādā* for the person she is living with suggests that he is both not her husband and also not in a sexual relationship with her. Such terms are only effective to a degree, however. When I had been using *dādā* to address men with whom I wished to have no ambiguous or intimate relationship, a few Bengali women told me that it does not necessarily give the clear message I had hoped to convey. Also another woman living with a Baul couple referred to the couple as "*mā*" and "*bābā*," or mother and father, but others were more inclined to think of her as the man's second wife. Thus while fictive terms may be helpful in establishing a particular kind of relationship, such as a protective one, they are no guarantees that others will not arrive at their own conclusions about the actual nature of that relationship.

Nonetheless, Madhabi's *dādā* plays an important role for her as he provides her a degree of protection when they travel together to beg for alms or to sing at programs. As she explained, "[When] I went to some places to perform, [some men] said, 'Who came [with you]?' I say my brother came. Then they wouldn't say anything else. They wouldn't stay. They left." Madhabi wears either a white or ocher-colored sari, both colors that are worn by renouncers, and this also functions as a defense against harassment because of the message it gives people of her renunciant status, ideally entitling her to more respect from strangers.

Nonetheless, Madhabi is quick to clarify that these actions do not in themselves prevent men from trying to take advantage of her. In the end, only the presence of a husband would be effective, and because her *dādā* ultimately has no responsibility to her, his presence is a less than adequate solution. This is even further compounded by the fact that she is a guest in his house and that if he no longer wanted her around, she would have to leave. "I am now staying in someone else's house (*parer*[5] *bārite ācchi*). If they tell me I have to leave, then I have to leave. [We're] not related." Any freedom of movement she might have as a single woman is curtailed not only by her concerns for her own safety but also by a sense of obligation to the person on whom she now depends. "I'm independent now. I'm not a wife, I'm independent. [Yet] still dependent. If [someone] calls, I don't have to go. If I go anywhere, then *dādā* and I go. Somewhere. I have to ask though [for permission]." Although in some ways she is not obligated to go anywhere if someone asks her to go, she still recognizes that she needs to ask her *dādā* for permission to go somewhere. As she explains,

> I have to. If I leave suddenly, *dādā* will search for me, "Where'd she go?" In the family, there's a *khuṅṭi* (post or pillar, figuratively a patron). Do you understand? If the *khuṅṭi* is fine, then everything's fine. [So I say:] "Tell *dādā* I went to such and such place." [And they tell him,] "She went out somewhere." If she [anyone] fell into the hands of a husband, then the husband will say, "go." Then you [can] go. So I tell my brother and then go.

Madhabi feels the need to not only manage her travels outside the home but also to keep her status within the home secure. Thus she aims to make sure that her fictive brother remains pleased with her actions so he will not kick her out. Madhabi is keenly aware of the precariousness of her situation.

Jaya, a young attractive woman like Madhabi, is also concerned about maintaining a respectable reputation within her community. The daughter of a well-known Baul in the area, she grew up learning quite a bit about Bauls and had significant doubts about the Baul path before marriage. As the time for her marriage approached, her father considered one of the young Bauls, Niranjan, who frequented their home. Niranjan's parents had died when he was a young boy, and he had been taken into the home of a Baul. It was there that he began to learn Baul songs. As he gained his independence, he had decided to pursue the Baul path. Jaya's father believed Niranjan to be a good, young man, without family himself and without large demands of a dowry. Despite protests from Jaya and her sympathetic mother, her father arranged Jaya's marriage with Niranjan.

Jaya's feelings about her marriage to a Baul came out in a conversation I had with her and Niranjan one day. Toward the end of my stay with them in the summer of 2000, I brought out the tape recorder I had not used since my first interview with them in 1998. I had felt that time was running short, and conversations had become very interesting and informative and I wanted to be sure that, in all the activity before departing, I retained them. Since Jaya and Niranjan had both become interested in my work, they were willing to turn our conversations into ever so slightly more formal interviews. Often, however, we would just let the tape recorder run as our interviews turned into conversations about topics we were all interested in. On one of these days they had been telling me in more detail how they got started on this Baul path. Niranjan told me that Jaya had had absolutely no interest in being a Baul or marrying one. I quote the conversation at some length because the dynamics evident in this dialogue are also interesting. When compared with statements in the previous chapter about the expectation that Bengali women should be silent or demur, especially in front of their husbands and in-laws, Jaya emerges as particularly outspoken and even at times argumentative with her husband.

> LISA: So, when you heard that Niranjan was a Baul, you didn't want to marry.
> JAYA: No, I didn't want to marry! No, because the Baul situation is very bad.
> NIRANJAN: (tries to say something)
> J: (Interrupting) I can't say now what he—now things are fine. What he'll do to me later, I'm not able to say. Because now things are fine. Perhaps now he likes me. Later he may not like me. . . .
>
> It's true. I will not be able to go anywhere else because I have a daughter. Later if something happens again, then I—I'll have a family alone. Then I'll have to keep it together. Men don't understand this. Usually.
> L: Right, right.
> J: I'm not able to be completely confident. Because now I know things are fine. But if he doesn't love me later. . . . Or if something like this happens, then he'll abandon me. That's it.
>
> L: Did you say anything to your father before marrying?
> J: Yes. I said many times, I won't marry a Baul boy. Just give me in marriage [to anyone else]. I don't want to marry a Baul boy.
> N: Her mother also—
> J: Mother also didn't want it.
> L: Only your father said that—
> J: Father then agreed. Father didn't want to arrange the marriage, but there wasn't any abundance at my father's so that he could give a lot of money for my marriage. There wasn't anything like that. That's why a special arrangement had to be made for my marriage. If it wasn't for that, no one would have agreed to have me married into the Baul line.

It is not unusual for poor rural families to marry off their daughter to a Baul or a Vaishnava who will not ask for much of a dowry. Still, her parents gave two bicycles as well as their own house for the young couple to live in. Although the plot of land the house is built on is owned by the West Bengal government, it is unlikely, thanks to squatter's rights, that the government will take such property away from families already settled on it any time soon. Still, the house is old, and signs of its age are showing in cracks in the walls. But as Niranjan had no natal house and family to whom he could bring the bride, he welcomed the house as part of the dowry. Her family has since built another one on another piece of unclaimed land nearby.

Niranjan, protesting her complaints, interjected that Jaya's situation is much better than her neighbors' who live in ordinary households:

> NIRANJAN: But now she understands, because her sisters [neighboring friends] have all been given away in marriage. Their situations are bad. Good homes/ families [were picked for them].
>
> JAYA: Their situations are bad, that's a fact. But what my subsequent situation will be like, I myself don't know. Right?
>
>   Now their situation is just fine. Because their *family*—no one will ever leave them. But our Baul line is a disgusting line. *That's* [my] situation.
>
> N: The Bauls—some of the Bauls—
>
> J: (interrupting) Because they have such a bad reputation that I—I can't trust him—that he might do something.
>
> N: Because she's seeing—
>
> J: I'm seeing everyone—
>
> N: —She's seen, with me. She listens to songs. She hears men's names, hears songs... hears Nityananda's [name], hears other names... she sees all this.

When Jaya states that the marriage situations of her neighboring friends are both bad and fine, she is making an important distinction. As is clear from other conversations quoted in the previous chapter, Jaya does not think ordinary women have many rights in the family. At the same time, however, they do have a degree of protection that she does not have. Niranjan agrees with Jaya that the behavior of many Baul men is bad. Since he has taken her out to performances, she has been able to see men mixing with other women, sometimes eventually leaving their wives or partners for these women. Niranjan cannot—and does not—deny this. But as Jaya states above, men do not understand fully what this means to women. Since she has a child already, she sees herself as being in a vulnerable situation. If he were to leave her, she would be left taking care of that child. At this point in the conversation, both talk at the same time, and there is disgust in Jaya's voice.

> JAYA: I see everyone. And hearing songs... I go and mix with everyone and see their behavior with my own eyes. [I see] that this kind of stuff is happening. That's why I am not able to completely trust a Baul.
>
>   [But] now I'm fine. We're now—I'm fine now, I think. Later, when my youthful image/beauty goes away, then maybe he won't love me anymore.

[Pause] Now, I don't know. But now it's fine. What he'll do is his matter. (She turns to her husband and asks him,) Tell me a little. What will you do?

NIRANJAN: Ask me.

[Silence as Jaya and I look at Niranjan, waiting for him to say something.]

LISA: Will you say something?

N: Yes!

L: What do you think?

N: I don't worry much about it. I think that the happiness we have in the Baul world—I have my doubts that anywhere else is there peace like ours. Peace. We're doing really well. I have taken it upon myself to teach her like this. Now we're hoping that we'll remain like this. I believe [we will]. I believe we'll stay like this. We have to stay like this.

L: And when the hair grays...?

N: *That* I know [for sure], I'm saying!

[JAYA LAUGHS HARD.]

N: That's nothing. Now maybe I have my youth. I have all this. But one day my hair will also fall. I'll get old. Then what she'll do, I don't know.

J: When we get old, then we'll have to stay in one place. That's no problem. The problem is now. If we're able to stay right now, then nothing will happen in our old age. Because then we'll be in one place. But in this "moment" if he does something backwards, then it won't be possible to stay fine. I'm talking about this time now.

N: That we won't do. Because this is the "main" time. Because not everyone can keep it together during this time. We never quarrel. You've seen in other Baul homes. We have nothing in common with anyone. There are all kinds of worries [there]. There's plenty of money. There's everything. But there's no *peace*.

But let there not be much money for us! Happiness, meaning peace, joy, can't be found in money. The peace we have—if we had money, perhaps we wouldn't be able to stay so happy. That's what I think. We're very happy. Whatever we have, we eat. And what we don't have, we don't eat. We're in this happiness. [We're] very happy.

From what I have seen, I tend to agree with Niranjan that their situation is not like that of many other Bauls in the area. Niranjan did say in another conversation, when Jaya was not around, that if he had known earlier how difficult family life was, he would have stayed alone. Whether or not Niranjan will ever leave Jaya is something I cannnot venture to guess any better than Jaya can. But if the way he was acting with me is any indication, I would say Niranjan is very careful not to give people reasons to imagine scandals. When I bicycled home late at night, it was only when Jaya would say it was okay that Niranjan would accompany me on his bicycle, and we would part ways in the middle of a well-traversed street. If we ever met anyone when Jaya was not around, he always introduced me as Jaya's friend. This is in contrast with other Baul men I know who would flaunt their associations with foreign women, hoping to enhance their reputation among other Bengali men in the process. Jaya speculates that even though she has noticed women paying attention to him at programs, Niranjan has probably thus far not strayed.

That Jaya asked Niranjan if he will abandon her in my presence (and with the tape recorder running!) is significant. Jaya and I had had similar conversations before, and she knew I was interested in and understood her concerns. Furthermore, I believe she knew I was not a threat to her marriage. Despite the research agenda, we had established a friendship and spoke openly about both of our lives, and so she probably felt I was on her side. But more than that, she was drawing on a resource of protection. According to Jaya, even though her neighbors' situations were bad, what they had that she did not was the protection of having been married in a socially appropriate way with a family that would adhere to that marriage. As a Baul she believed she did not have that protection. Confronting Niranjan about the possibility of abandonment in my presence was a powerful act on her part. It made him listen to her concerns. It made him aware that I understood the reasons why Jaya worries. I believe also she feels I would help defend her or even support her if Niranjan did ever leave her. Since my friendship with Niranjan has largely been mediated through Jaya, I suspect Niranjan believes that he would lose his connection with me should he stray.

Niranjan is also right in saying that their situation is very different from their neighbors.' As Jaya has told me on a number of occasions, her "sisters" have no independence and no rights within the household. Unlike Jaya, they are not able to travel about. Also unlike Jaya, they are not able to speak freely in their conjugal home. As is evident in the above dialogue, Jaya speaks her mind freely with Niranjan, often cutting him off and even confronting him with a difficult question.

But despite these differences between Jaya's life and those of her neighbors, Jaya attempts to maintain an image of a respectable housewife, thereby drawing on—and sometimes fabricating—similarities between her and her neighbors. She was aware of her difference and was concerned with how others viewed her as soon as she married a Baul. She was still in school when she was married to Niranjan, and at his insistence, she remained in school. Since Niranjan had not been able to earn an education, he was eager for Jaya to be competent in reading and writing so that she would be able to read documents and write letters when needed. Jaya, however, described being embarrassed to go to school wearing a sari and *śaṅkh-sindūr* (conch bracelets and vermillion), all signs of marriage, which her schoolmates, unmarried, did not yet wear (those who had gotten married had stopped attending school). In a different conversation, she told me that Niranjan had encouraged her to wear a *salwar khamiz* so that she would not stand out in school. In fact, he still encourages her to wear this, arguing that while a sari is much more attractive, it is often impractical and cumbersome. Though Jaya explained that she would prefer to wear a *salwar khamiz*, she refuses to on the grounds that it would give people the impression that she had the status of an unmarried and available girl or that she was sexually loose. Niranjan claimed he did not care what others thought, but for Jaya it was more difficult to ignore gossip.

There are several other ways in which Jaya attempts to maintain a reputation as a good housewife in her village. When I would arrive at her home in mid or even late morning, Jaya often looked tired after a late night of performing. She explained that even though she had been up late, she would rise before dawn in order to begin her household chores of cleaning and preparing food because it would look bad in the eyes of her neighbors if she slept in. Since Jaya is often out late or all night with Niranjan at performances, she does not always manage to get up early enough, and on such days Jaya says her neighbors will speak ill of her.

In Bengali households, it is typical that women prepare and serve meals to the men of the household (and any guests) and wait until the men are finished before they eat themselves. If a husband stays out late, the wife is expected to refrain from eating until he returns to have his meal. Jaya and Niranjan, however, would sit together and eat their meals; on the many days that I ate with them, we all sat and ate together. If Niranjan was out late, Jaya, on his insistence, would eat before he returned. As this kind of behavior would be interpreted as disrespectful to the husband and again cast aspersions on her reputation as a good wife, Jaya would try to hide their eating arrangements by eating indoors and out of sight, especially if she was eating alone before Niranjan returned home. It was with pride that Niranjan also told me he taught Jaya to cook. Some of the meals I ate with them were prepared by him, and if Jaya was not feeling well, Niranjan would step in to take care of this gendered responsibility.[6]

Finally, Jaya claims that she conducts household rituals (*mūrti pūjā*) primarily because it is expected of her in her village. When I first met Jaya it was in part the evidence of such household rituals[7] that made me suspect Jaya was just an ordinary housewife. As I learned later, however, this image was intentional: she wants to appear like an ordinary housewife. After I had gotten to know Jaya much better, she whispered to me that she really did not believe in all these images of deities and their worship but that her neighbors would think her a bad wife if she did not engage in what was locally a very common practice in Hindu households.

The other side to this, of course, is that Niranjan also does not fully meet expectations for masculine behavior. While women are expected to behave in modest ways, putting forth the care of their husbands and children before themselves, men too are expected to make sure their wives maintain that modesty and appropriate feminine (motherly, wifely) behavior. Because women's modesty reflects on men's honor, a man will often enforce appropriately modest behavior by the women under his care in order to maintain his (and his family's) honor. Niranjan's actions do not follow these gendered roles. In fact, it would seem he does everything wrong: he encourages Jaya to go out and perform music, to wear a *salwar khamiz* instead of the sari traditionally worn by married women, and he insists that she eat before him if he is late coming home. Even his interest that Jaya continue her studies after marriage is interesting in light of the fact that Niranjan himself is illiterate. In South Asia, like elsewhere (including America), masculinity is often seen as threatened when a woman is more accomplished than a man. South Asian women with a high academic degree frequently have a difficult time finding marriageable partners, as few men would agree to marry a more educated woman, and for this reason it is not uncommon for parents to hold back their daughters. But as Niranjan points out, their marriage is not like those of their neighbors. Nor is he like his male neighbors. Niranjan supports and encourages behavior in Jaya that could reflect poorly on his honor. But, as he also states, he does not care what others think. As a man, he has more freedom not to care about his reputation in the community (though I have no evidence that he is maligned by any of his neighbors, and the *bhadralok* I met in Kolkata and Santiniketan who know him generally praise his character and honesty). But Jaya feels that she does have to care, even if she does not agree with the expectations her neighboring community have of her as a woman. And given that she, unlike Niranjan, would have to depend on the kindness of her neighbors for her own well-being, especially after her parents have died, she probably does need to care about their opinions of her.

Despite her aberrant behavior as a Baul woman who travels often to sing publicly, Jaya consciously and deliberately attempts to fashion herself as an otherwise ordinary housewife. She tries to mediate between her position as a Baul who engages in activities that challenge gendered norms of modesty and her image as a Bengali woman who is doing everything appropriately as a wife and mother. The challenges to this respectable feminine image are many, and Jaya responds by hiding many of her activities and beliefs from the watchful eyes of neighbors.

But is Jaya merely supporting the status quo, enforcing through her acquiescence the patriarchal society she secretly criticizes? I suggest that Jaya is both challenging the status quo and ensuring her protection within it. Both she does cautiously, deliberately, and consciously. Jaya knows that she cannot turn society on its head, changing social structures and beliefs that are engrained and enforced by most of those around her. But she does try to raise the consciousness of some. She tries to discuss with other rural Bengali women the treatment of young girls in the home, as discussed in chapter 3, and points out to them that while girls are not fed or educated to the same degree as boys, they should be. By performing and carefully negotiating her travels, Jaya also tries to show that women can contribute financially to the household and still be respectable women. In South Asia poor women often do have to help support the family by working outside of the home, and they are the ones who are less likely to have the luxury to care about modesty.[8] But Jaya wants to convey that even respectable women can do this.

There is another way in which Jaya both challenges and appears to acquiesce to the status quo that deserves further discussion, as it is applicable to other women I interviewed: the telling of her story is, I believe, best read as an act of agency in which she re-creates her image as a respectable wife.

Refashioning Lives

In telling their stories, Jaya and other women I interviewed chose what to reveal (and not reveal) and how to represent themselves. Jaya and I had numerous long conversations without the tape recorder over a period of several months, so I had gained a good idea about her concerns and views on a number of issues. That Jaya discussed different things when she and I were alone as compared to when Niranjan was present is not surprising. For instance, it was during some of these private conversations that she first began to reveal her concerns about being abandoned by Niranjan. Also in these conversations without Niranjan she openly praised Baul ideology and her freedom while criticizing the status of other Bengali women. But what she chose to discuss when the tape recorder was running and with Niranjan present was not praise for the Baul path but criticism and concern about where it might lead her. These statements were, I believe, largely directed at Niranjan, and I with the tape recorder was the witness.

Jaya is actively engaged in creating her life and image as she talks about it. Here I believe that the telling of her story and the voicing of her complaints are important. Although she agrees with Baul ideology, she criticizes what she sees as aberrant male behavior among Bauls. She believes that women should be treated the same as men, yet she knows that without a husband she will not be treated well by society. For this reason, she believes men should protect women from scandal by behaving appropriately and, particularly, by not abandoning them. In the dialogue above, she blames Niranjan in advance for something he may or may not do: leave her, like many Baul men leave their wives. Lamb (2001) argues that a life story is in itself an act of agency, and I contend that this is certainly the case here. By stating in front of Niranjan, me, and the tape recorder that she never wanted to marry a Baul, that she did so against her own wishes, and that she knows how poorly Baul men can treat their wives, she fashions herself into a wife and mother who has concerns and *should* be supported by her husband. These concerns are legitimized by society's norms, which in this conversation she appears to value (to some degree). Jaya did not want this Baul life; her father and Niranjan dragged her into it. I know from other conversations that Jaya also likes being a Baul because of the freedom it gives her outside and inside the home, but this is not what she chose to focus on during this taped interview, though Niranjan tried to draw her into the direction of praising all that was good about her—and their—Baul life.

People are complicated, and many truths that seem to contradict each other can actually coexist in a person's life, beliefs, words, and actions. Thus the question is not whether or not someone is telling the truth but how that person chooses to represent her or himself at a particular moment. Tracing these shifts can reveal a great deal about a person's multiple concerns and how that person may juggle them. As evident in the above dialogue, what Jaya chooses to discuss during one of our few and last tape recorded interviews was something she deliberately wanted Niranjan to hear in my presence. Thus the audience plays a significant role in what one chooses to reveal at particular times. This is nothing new in anthropology, of course. Self-reflective scholars have raised our awareness of our own role as ethnographers whose mere presence in the field, never mind our choice of questions, influence not only the data collected but also the "subjects" themselves. Talking to me alone and at times with

Niranjan, Jaya does present seemingly contradictory views. But these seemingly contradictory views make sense when considered in context. On the one hand, she
reveals the complexity of her situation: being a Baul may offer her freedoms and
opportunities she enjoys, but it also challenges her status in the non-Baul community
in which she lives. On the other hand, what she chooses to focus on in the taped interview is a concern she wanted to make certain Niranjan was aware of.

In choosing what to discuss and how to represent oneself, other women also
fashioned themselves deliberately and consciously. Kangalini, who has been interviewed by many reporters and scholars, launched into a life story that appeared well
rehearsed. "My Baul life is a life of pain," she began. In our early interviews she
also claimed that her first husband had died, but later on she modified that statement to explain that he was actually still alive and had remarried. Rajani, a woman
in Birbhum (discussed more in chapter 6), also had first presented herself as a
widow but later stated that she had actually left her husband in order to pursue her
Vaishnava path. Although being a widow does not necessarily free a woman from
guilt in the eyes of Hindus who may argue that a woman's karma caused her own
misfortune, widowhood is still more socially acceptable and understandable among
many Hindus than leaving one's husband for any reason. At the beginning of
chapter 3, Kangalini and Madhabi both claim that they have done everything right
as women. Verifying this claim is not the point; what is clear is that they both want
to establish themselves as guilt-free in a society that values appropriate behavior for
women. In so doing, they also proclaim that society failed them, particularly their
husbands and those who should have enforced appropriate behavior by these men.

Women know that the responsibility for appropriate behavior is not only on
their heads. While women may be expected to adhere to gendered codes of behavior
by exhibiting, for instance, *lajjā,* men are also expected to help protect them. In fact,
women's demonstration of proper conduct often solicits proper conduct by men, as
I address further below.

Turning the Tables

THE SHAMING OF MEN

Like women's good or bad behavior, the behavior of men also influences the reputation of the family, including that of women, though to a lesser degree than the
behavior of women. Lamb suggests that although men can be seen as having bad
character, "the merit or demerit resulting from a man's sexual behavior affected
mostly himself, not his household, ancestors, or the continuity of his family line"
(2000:191). While it may be true that a man's poor behavior does not have such a
lasting effect, it is my impression that his reputation does have consequences for his
wife, who will at least have to endure the rumors and gossip. Baul men may engage
in a variety of activities that call into question the integrity of the family, from
smoking ganja or drinking alcohol to promiscuous behavior or abandoning their

wives. Abandonment, however, is by far considered the worst, as several women, a few with husbands who were having affairs, told me that affairs were not as significant a problem as being left.

When a woman's reputation and situation are threatened by the actions of her husband, sometimes she will draw on feminine codes of behavior in order to show how her husband did not abide by the codes that serve to protect women. Oftentimes this is embedded in conversations, in complaints listing how proper she herself is—like Kangalini saying she used to feed and obey her husband and keep her head covered—the implication being that her husband did not treat her right. Another woman, whose Baul husband has taken on a European disciple whom most villagers claim is also his second wife, responds to her difficult home life by attempting to prove herself as a proper Bengali housewife. Although she, like other Baul women, does go out to some festivals, she tries to distance herself from being a Baul by not singing or learning yoga, both of which her husband and his disciple do regularly. Criticisms of her husband's behavior are situated in her own self-denial, often more verbal than actual. While her husband and his European disciple eat rich foods, drink plenty of milk tea and gin, and smoke ganja, she announces that she needs nothing more than rice and water, refusing even tea during my visits. Nothing much will probably change in her situation at home through her actions and words, but the message she conveys to her non-Baul neighbors is that she is trying to do things right as a wife and that he is not holding up his end by protecting her from criticism. If he were ever to leave her, she might be able to find some support in the community in which she lives, as her neighbors will likely have observed her good behavior despite her husband. Whether believable or not, her words are offered as witness to her good behavior and the failings of his.

Baul women are not always able to get their husbands to behave properly and in ways that shield their wives from criticism, but implicit in their complaints is the expectation that men too are responsible for maintaining wives' *lajjā* and protecting them. This extends also to other men whom Baul women encounter. Even though Baul women may be engaging in activities not considered *lājuk*, they may portray themselves as modest and shy in order to elicit a proper response from men. I have watched Jaya switch quickly into a different manner of behaving and talking when dealing with a man who does not address her with respect. After she became reserved, cautious, and respectful, he in turn treated her with more respect.

Because of their reputation as Bauls who perform publicly and whose marriages are sometimes unstable, these women are doubly challenged when they wish to convince others of their respectability. However, the same two qualities that go against them—being women and being Bauls—can also be used to their benefit. On the one hand, they are vulnerable because of their gender and because being a Baul often necessitates questionable behavior for women. On the other hand, they know that if they can convince people that they are *lājuk* women, good Bauls, or—better yet—good *sannyāsinī*s, they are more likely to be safe. *Lājuk* women are viewed as worthy of protection, and Bengali women are well versed in the ways of eliciting guardianship in men unknown to them. Furthermore, *sannyāsīs*, which some Bauls are seen as being, are entitled to respect and support from householders. Many Bengalis view giving alms and other needed assistance to those who have fully devoted themselves to a religious path as a duty of householders and believe that doing so will bring merit to the donors. Evoking this responsibility in men may secure more than just a donation; a woman's honor and dignity may also be maintained.

A story Jaya's husband, Niranjan, told me seems appropriate here. In the region of Birbhum where he and Jaya lived, there is a large community of Santals (so-called tribals). He explained that Santals do not know much Bengali, or rather they *pretend* not to know Bengali well. They also have a general disregard for Bengalis, even the *bhadralok* for whom some of them work, especially not caring for their hierarchical caste system. The story is this: One day a Santal was walking down the path, and he was about to pass a Bengali *bhadralok*. Before he passed the *bhadralok*, he stopped to give him a warning of what lay ahead: *okhāne jās nā; pāikhānā āchen*—which (using the conjugation of "to go" usually reserved for children and servants) means: don't go over there; there's a pile of shit (using the respectful conjugation of "to be" to refer to shit). Niranjan and Jaya, laughing freely, were delighted with the insult that was inflicted on the *bhadralok* while the Santal feigned ignorance. Such hidden and powerfully ambiguous forms of resistance are not uncommon among people considered powerless (see for instance, Scott 1985, Abrahams 1992). With a simple linguistic reversal of verb forms, the Santal had insulted the *bhadralok*. Moreover, because Santals often claim to be ignorant of Bengali, the Santal in this story—who knew very well what he was saying—got away with it.

Jaya told me several stories of confrontations with powerful men in which she too fashioned a reversal and relied on her powerless status to protect her. Two of them she told in the context of explaining to another woman that she had to learn to fend for herself whenever she goes out—she had to learn, essentially, street smarts. Both involved ticket collectors on trains. In the first story, she was traveling with some Baul men, and Niranjan had gone ahead with the tickets to find their seat. She was behind with another young Baul man, and a ticket collector approached them, insisting on seeing her ticket. She explained the ticket was with her husband up ahead. Disregarding her explanation, he continued to insist that he see it, all the while calling her *tui*—a term considered disrespectful when applied to strangers. While elite Bengalis often call Bauls and servants *tui*, Jaya thought he was extremely disrespectful and perhaps a bit threatening. With a mischievous gleam in her eye, Jaya told us that she then grabbed the ticket collector by the collar and said she would throw him down on the tracks. As one would expect from any skirmish, people quickly gathered around them to see what was going on. She gained their sympathy when she explained that the ticket collector was harassing her for the tickets that her husband, who had gone ahead to secure a seat, had in his possession. The ticket collector disappeared. When I asked if the young Baul man accompanying her had helped out, she answered that he is a man; if he had tried to protest, there would have been a big fight.

In the second story, she and Niranjan had finished an all-night program and were returning home on the train. They had not received any money for the program, only an ocher-colored sari and a *pānjābī*. They were about halfway home when the ticket collector came by, asking for their tickets. She explained that they were Bauls and therefore did not have money to buy tickets. He told her that they should then sing, as alms seekers and hawkers are entitled to ride for free only while they are performing. She tried to explain that they were not singing because they were extremely tired, having been to an all-night performance, but he continued to insist. Finally she suggested that he take the ocher-colored sari and *pānjābī*. Laughing at her own cleverness, she told me she had known that if he took the ocher-colored clothes, recognizable as Baul clothing, then he would be shamed by passengers. The ticket collector became quiet at her offer of payment and left them alone after that. Again, the man accompanying her, this time her husband, said nothing.

In these stories, Jaya asserts her dignity by drawing on two responsibilities powerful Bengali men have vis-à-vis Baul women. One of the duties of men of householder status is to offer respect and alms to those who have devoted their lives to religious pursuits. This duty usually extends to Bauls, though because some Bauls are professional singers without immersion into a spiritual life, their status as holy is sometimes perceived of as ambiguous. Whether or not this was going on in the minds of either ticket collector is hard to say and perhaps beside the current point. What appears clear is that Jaya predicted the outcome of her otherwise outrageous behavior. She knew that any self-respecting and honorable man would not take advantage of a vulnerable woman but would ensure her safety and protection; nor would he deny the alms given to Bauls. She also knew that even if these ticket collectors had no respect for her as a woman or as a Baul, they would wager that others present would, and the ticket collectors would at least feel shamed by their scorn.

As these examples suggest, *lajjā* is a multifaceted cultural expression that is also a response to complex power relations and can be experienced and enacted by men as well as women, high caste and upper-class individuals as well as low. So, on the one hand, there is the shame that women feel and enact in order to save their—and their families'—reputation. In this sense shame is like a shield, not unlike a veil, to protect them from scandal or criticism. But, as I have shown, women are not the only ones who feel and enact shame. Men too are subjected to the emotional and social conditioning effects of shame, which arise from evaluations of their particular social responsibilities. Furthermore, as the stories suggest, women can also cause men to feel shame by reminding them of the responsibility that goes with their relative privilege and power.

SHAMING THE RESEARCHER

Phulmala, with whom I began this chapter, often subjected me to a similar kind of shame. This was one person who made me very aware of the power dynamics between us. Although I rarely could forget issues of power in the other relationships

I made in the field, Phulmala seemed to remind me regularly that as a foreigner visiting her country I had considerably more power than she would ever have. This was particularly evident in the form of opportunities, connections, education, and wealth—even the mere fact that I was there researching Bauls like her. By reminding me of my position of privilege, Phulmala exerted a power of her own. Moreover, I never felt I had any control in the situation, and despite various attempts at arriving at a compromise between our personal objectives, I felt I was never able to meet up to her expectations.

In fact, I usually had a difficult time with Phulmala. I really liked her, and I found her interesting, but she was unpredictable. Some days she was very warm and welcoming; other days she was demanding and controlling. Because she so often asked me for money (to help repair a roof or simply because it was my responsibility to give to her), I toyed with the idea of hiring her as a research assistant. My hope was that she would take me to meet other Baul women and that in the process I could help her out with some payment without setting a precedent of financially supporting interviewees. I also hoped that she would take an interest in my research and that I would learn more about her as well. I finally suggested this arrangement before Joydeb Mela, and on one of the days we were at the festival, we did go around together to meet other Baul women.

However, I found it a very frustrating experience. While I fully expected her to direct me and my questions in some ways that she preferred, I found I actually had absolutely no say in our interviews. She took me to meet about five women that day, and after I got through only a few questions (age, marital status, home, and whether or not they sing Baul songs), I found her concluding our "interview" and leading me away. As we stepped away from the woman being interviewed, Phulmala would tell me if she thought I should pay her anything, and if so, how much I should give (usually around 10 or 20 rupees). On the last interview, which lasted longer than the others, I told Phulmala that I was not ready to leave and had more to ask. Phulmala told me, "No, you won't," and that was clearly final.

I spent a lot of time trying to figure out how and if I could work further with Phulmala. I had met Phulmala very early on in my research; a Bengali friend in Santiniketan took me to her place so that I could meet her during my preliminary research in 1997. I quickly became interested in her because of her forthright manner and her clear appreciation of her own efforts and value. Although I did spend time with her, interviewing her formally a few times and chatting with her many other times, I never felt I learned just how to behave around her. What was particularly troubling was that she kept asking me for money, and as an inexperienced and naive anthropologist, I was unsure about how to respond. Do I pay her for interviews? Do I just give her money, if I can, when she asks for help? And what about others who may ask? Or those who don't ask? To be fair, should I be paying everyone I worked with or paying for formal interviews as opposed to engaging in more casual interviews? (These lines were often blurred in my mind and work.) I began asking others for ideas on how best to respond. Most Bengalis I asked insisted that I not pay Bauls for interviews, arguing that this would "spoil" Bauls and taint the data. Others, though, felt equally strongly that I should pay them for their time and knowledge. I finally developed a policy that worked okay for me: I gave money to ashrams whenever I came across them, brought foodstuffs or useful household items to those I visited on a frequent basis or for an extended period, and to those households I visited the most, I gave a donation before leaving for America. Unfortunately, this policy did not help me much with Phulmala, who would accost me on the street to demand 300 rupees to repair her roof.

But I soon discovered I was not the only person Phulmala was asking for financial assistance. Several of the *bhadralok* I knew in Santiniketan said she frequently asked them for money. But although I felt some comfort in knowing I was not being singled out, it did not help me figure out how to respond to Phulmala. I was perpetually uneasy about my relationship with her and ashamed of my position of privilege as well as my own hopes to gain something from her. I realized through my own discomfort that Phulmala was in many ways right in expecting support from those of us who appreciated her, her music, and her path. We were all gaining something from her hardships—from her long, grueling hours singing over the noise of the engine in the trains, from her knowledge of numerous songs and their meanings, from her part in preserving a traditional form of Bengali art and philosophy, and from her willingness to share her knowledge or sing into a microphone. Although we might have more money, security, and social standing than Phulmala did, Phulmala knew she was doing something we all valued dearly. By reminding me and *bhadralok* in Santiniketan who admired her work and effort that it was our responsibility to support her, she would shame us, much like Jaya shamed the ticket collector. The discomfort I felt resulted in large part from realizing that Phulmala had every right to demand that I contribute to her financial support.

Conclusion

As the examples in this chapter suggest, age and marital status often play a role in how willing a Baul woman may be in openly challenging the societal norms that restrict and sometimes denigrate her. Jaya, a young married woman with a child, chooses her battles carefully. Although she is very critical of local Bengali expectations and social structures, she is also aware of her position within—and her dependence upon—those structures. Thus, although as a Baul she could ignore gendered expectations, she feels dependent on the society in which she lives because of the vulnerability she feels in a Baul marriage. Madhabi, a young mother abandoned by her Baul husband, is similarly concerned with her reputation in the communities in which she lives. But because of both her financial need and lack of marital security, she negotiates her image within the less than ideal parameters of residing and traveling with her fictive brother and as a *sannyāsinī*. Perhaps at the other end of the spectrum of marital status and age is Phulmala, who pays little heed to local expectations of women and instead demands the respect she believes she deserves as a human being and a Baul artist.

This is not to say that challenging dominant gender ideology is necessarily at the forefront of these women's lives. While it may be the case that some women, like Jaya, like the Baul path precisely because of the equality espoused by Bauls and the personal freedom they gain, oftentimes they have goals and objectives that have more to do with their own lives than with the general enlightenment of society. So, for instance, though Jaya does attempt to talk to her neighbors about gender restrictions and equality, she also uses those very gendered restrictions and norms that encumber her to her own benefit. Jaya thinks that being able to move out of the village, earn her own income, and eat when she is hungry (as opposed to after her husband has returned home) are her rights as a human being. But because she is also acutely aware that these are privileges that are characteristic of her own marriage and not favored by many other rural Bengalis, she also tries to reconcile her own liberties with the social structures around her.

Returning to the question of resisting or acquiescing to gendered expectations, we can also see that Baul women sometimes use gendered norms to insist that they be treated with respect. Arlene MacLeod (1992) makes a compelling argument that provides further help in interpreting the behavior of some Baul women, like Madhabi and Jaya, which at least somewhat appears to support normative gender roles. In MacLeod's study of the recent tendency among young working women in Cairo to veil themselves, she shows that women use the veil in a way that both "conveys women's desire to accommodate as well as resist" (1992:552) normative expectations of women and men. For women who are not expected by their husbands or families to veil, using the veil communicates a message that these women, by behaving modestly, should not only be valued for their economic contribution but also be treated with the dignity due to respectable, traditional women. Jaya and Madhabi are both attempting to convey this message when they insist that they are doing everything right and when they try to behave like respectable women. In the above dialogue, Jaya tells Niranjan that she also should be treated with respect, that is, that he should not abandon her. Madhabi, by going around with her fictive brother or drawing on her status as a *sannyāsī*, attempts to convey that she is protected by her *dādā* or her religious status as a renouncer. Kangalini, when she states that she did everything right as a young married woman, is blaming her first husband for not fulfilling his duties.

MacLeod further suggests that "[r]ather than charging men with the responsibility for changing their unwelcome behavior, women accommodate by altering their dress to fit the prevailing norm that men cannot help responding to women as temptations" (1992:552). By altering their behavior, especially in certain situations, Jaya and Madhabi do suggest that men cannot control themselves.

Rather than viewing these women as complicit in the very patriarchal structure they critique, I see their adherence to select norms as key moments of agency. However, reading their accommodations as subtle or covert resistance should not be taken to mean that their goals are focused exclusively on gender equality. Even to the extent that these women embrace Baul ideals, multiple overlapping goals coexist that coalesce on the value of each human being. Feminist scholarship has sometimes struggled to make room for other goals, especially if they relegate gender concerns to secondary status. Here Saba Mahmood's recent work (2005), also on women in Egypt, is instructive. Mahmood has demonstrated that the central concern of women in the mosque movement is increasing their piety. In fact, in order to realize that piety, these women confronted and overcame several obstacles, including aspects of Islamic orthodoxy and the authority of men and family. Their performance of Islamic femininity, including veiling and modesty, is therefore not reflective of passivity but, rather, represents a constructive project toward a different goal.

There is much that is very different between the women in the mosque movement studied by Mahmood and the Baul women in this book. Most obviously is the liberation agenda espoused by Bauls who seek to challenge discrimination in its various forms. What is instructive about Mahmood's work in this context, however, is that the goals behind actions that seem to support gendered norms and a patriarchal system may have little to do with gender power struggles. Mahmood's examples reveal that the subservience/resistance or acquiescence/rejection dichotomies are limited to power struggles that may not be the central motivating principles in people's lives.

As the examples in this chapter suggest, Baul women are not merely succumbing to pressures from and within the dominant social structures when they appear to accommodate norms; these women also challenge those structures, attempt to raise consciousness among others, and draw on some gendered norms in order to evoke certain behavior in men and potential sponsors. In these various ways, they navigate their everyday realities to construct meaningful lives. My observations have led me to conclude that these women may be aware of and concerned about gendered norms in their communities, but overturning those norms is not their only or primary goal. The following chapter takes this issue further by looking at the ways in which Baul women utilize songs to transform both themselves and society, suggesting that a central guiding principle for these women is the experiential realization of the value of human beings.

"Do Not Neglect This Golden Body of Yours"
PERSONAL AND SOCIAL TRANSFORMATIONS
THROUGH BAUL SONGS

Prelude

O mind, the Baul is my dress and ornament.
If you want to recognize her,
you'll have to become a Baul yourself.

Rina Das Baul

The sun was starting to set as a man ran over to where we had been sitting, drinking a little tea after our journey to the village. "Where are you? People have come from all over and are waiting. Hurry up!" he said to the Bauls. Dibakar turned to me and said that they were going to change. Not knowing what was expected of me, I said fine, and remained where I was, thinking that they would leave to change somewhere else. But instead of leaving, the Baul men and women pulled out their clothes from their bags and changed on the verandah in front of me and the household, not exposing much more than an occasional stomach. Dibakar had an elaborate set of clothes: an orange *lungi* over which he put an orange *pānjābī*, over which he pulled on a longer *pānjābī*. Then he tied an orange sash around his waist. He looked down at his clothes and expressed disapproval that one of his layers was wrinkled, and a couple of the men agreed that it hadn't been ironed right. One Baul man attempted to smooth out the wrinkles in Dibakar's clothes without much success.

An older Baul man put on a white *lungi* with an orange border and a long *pānjābī*. He then tied a light orange cloth around his head like a turban with a long tail in the back. He took another similarly colored cloth and draped it over one shoulder and tied it at the waist on the opposite side. He tied a red cloth around his waist. He added a few strands of beads around his neck: crystal, seeds, and *tulsī*.

The other men dressed more simply in orange *pānjābī*s and *lungi*s or *pājāmā*s. But it was clear they were all taking great care in their appearance. They fixed up their hair, checked themselves in the mirror, and inspected each other to make sure they approved of each others' attire. Dibakar made up a mixture of sandalwood paste from a little jar, adding some water to it in the palm of his hand. He then put a sandalwood paste *tilak* on the men's forehead.

The women began dressing in front of everyone else. Rina combed her hair and pulled it into a bun on the side of her head. But they ducked into a dark room to put on their bright orange saris and blouses. I left with the men to go to the stage area, and on the way they were fed a snack of puffed rice. After a while, the women arrived, dressed brightly in orange. Rina had an elaborate sandalwood paste *tilak*: it extended down to the tip of her nose, and, near the bridge, comprised three sets of three dots on either side and in the middle. She also placed the typical Hindu woman's red *bindi* on her forehead and red in the parting of her hair. The other woman's *tilak* was simple, with two lines going up from the bridge of her nose up to her hair like a V, and a red dot in the middle.

Baul *śilpīs* take great care to dress in a way that pleases their sponsors and audience. Simultaneously, Bengalis claim they recognize Bauls by their appearance or, for those who are more discerning, by that "something" in their eyes. But Rina warns that sartorial claims of authenticity can be misleading and that Bauls and Bengalis alike easily fall into the trap of relying on superficial markers of identity, whether those markers are certain clothing, Baul songs, or carefree behavior. Bauls like Rina argue that the only way to really understand what Baul means is to find a guru, to enter the Baul path, and to *experience* the meanings found in songs and ritual.

Scene One

Earlier in 2007, Phulmala had moved to a small mud house on the outskirts of Bolpur. She shared the space with a younger woman, and they had their beddings stacked up on narrow cots along the side of the room. Clothes were draped over ropes against a wall, and our empty tea cups were stacked up by the door. Although a small window allowed some of the early afternoon light into the room, the darkness sheltered several hungry mosquitoes. We sat on mats on the ground, trying to keep the cold floor from giving us a chill. Three weeks before when I visited Phulmala with Rina, Phulmala had been too ill for lengthy conversations. She had shown me slips of paper on which doctors had written, in English, "bronchitis," "infection," and "mouth ulcer." Phulmala had improved with treatment, and on this visit she was her regular spunky self—more like the person I had come to know seven years earlier. Nonetheless, there was an air of somberness to her that I hadn't seen previously, though she had always been capable of being serious and stern.

We had been talking about the role of singing in her life, and Phulmala explained the realizations that can come from meditating on songs. She described the stages leading up to realization and emphasized the distractions that consume a person while involved with family life. It seemed those distractions consumed her mind still, even as she tries to distance herself from them:

> I heard these ideas [about spiritual realization] in the songs [when I was young], but I did not realize their importance. At that time, the urge I felt was that I must earn money, bring up my children, teach them reading and writing, get them a home and car. This is an addiction *(neśā)*. A *rubbish* addiction [*bāje neśā*]!
>
> See, here I am, out, leaving behind my family—everything! There is no lack of anything in my home [there]. You can go and check in this address. I have my son, daughter, grandchildren. There's everything [there]. I am not interested anymore. I like to have a solitary place so that I can sing His name, so that I can become blissful to my heart's content. I do not like to bear the pain of family troubles anymore. Many *sādhak*s like me have gradually gained detachment [*tyāg*] in this way.

Phulmala's interpretation of her current situation reflects Hindu ideas about life stages (*āśrama*) in which individuals gradually distance themselves from family life and responsibilities to focus more on religious matters. In this light, she is exactly where she should be. In the past few months, she has also distanced herself further from ordinary householder life by becoming a strict vegetarian, refusing to eat onions and garlic and other foods that, like meat, are considered to be heat-producing and therefore more appropriate for householders.

Phulmala spoke for close to twenty minutes about the tensions between family and spiritual work and the goals of *sādhak*s while a young Baul man she had invited to perform with her sat quietly. Finding a brief moment to jump into the conversation, he said: "Let's do a song!" Without hesitating, Phulmala tuned her *ektārā* to his *khamak* (stringed percussion instrument), hummed a few notes to find the right pitch, and then began to sing. The song she chose was by Pitambar Das and emphasized what she had just been discussing, detachment from family, as if the music merely became a different medium for her to articulate her views and experiences. Perhaps she did not have as great control of her voice as she did in her youth, but she was able to convey steely determination as well as pain through her singing. These songs clearly resonated with her, and she felt every description of misguided dreams and inevitable separation.

Jāno nā man she din kabe habe[1]
by Pitambar Das

> Mind, you have no idea when that day will come.
> Realizing your time is up,
> the King of Death will assign you the time of departure.
> His authority is strict:
> You shall have to leave then and there.

Your elephant, horse, bundle of notes
will lie there left behind.

Those who are your wife and children
are nothing but a trick of magic.
Being wealthy with your wealth,
[they] will forget you.

With torn pieces of jute sheet, on a cot made of bamboo,
tied tightly with straw,
you are carried to the burning ghat,
and they put you on open fire.

Running after wealth and money
[you] show off for no reason at all.
When you are departing, only Krishna is your companion.
Pitambar Das wonders.

Scene Two

Sitting alone on a large cot in the downstairs room of Rina's recently completed two-story *pākā* (cement) house, she and I talked about the stages leading up to realization. The terminology she used was basically the same as Phulmala's, though Phulmala's explanations were colored by distinctly Vaishnava interpretations. Rina also expressed concern about the passing of life, and her songs and speech articulated a sense of urgency. The first song Rina sang that day described the stages of life from her perspective. It was as if Phulmala and Rina were looking at the same page but from different angles. Rina played the *dotārā* (stringed lute) and kept rhythm by tapping bells wrapped around her foot. During some parts of the song, her *dotārā* followed the melody; other times, it played a drone that seemed to draw out and emphasize the heartfelt message of the lyrics as her clear voice filled the room with sadness. Even without understanding the words, a listener would feel the weight of this song.

Mana śikṣā (Teachings of the Heart) (traditional lyrics and melody)

The day has passed and you haven't called on "Dinabandhu" [guru known as friend of the lowly].

You've not given a thought about the day when your *paramātmā* (Supreme Being; manifestation of God in one's heart) will leave your body.

First you were in your mother's womb and your hands and feet were bound with your umbilical cord. On that day when you were suffering greatly you said: "O Guru, I will perform your *sādhanā*"—the day went by and you didn't call out to Dinabandhu.

In the second instance you were born and drank your mother's milk, and now
   you've grown up—the day went by and you didn't call out to Dinabandhu.
In the third time period you married, and falling under the influence of that
   beautiful woman, you have now forgotten everything. You have become
   involved with children and family and not called on the guru even once—the
   day went by and you didn't call out to Dinabandhu.
During the fourth part of your life you've become old. Your skin is loose and
   hangs down, and you need help getting up. Now you've given up on both Hari
   (Krishna) and guru and just lie in your bed—the day went by and you didn't call
   out to Dinabandhu.
In the fifth part of your life you are now dying. Four people take hold of your
   funeral bier and yell out, "Say the name of Hari!" Now they take you to the
   cremation grounds and place you on the funeral pyre. They break your head open
   with a knot of bamboo—but the day went by and you didn't call out to
   Dinabandhu.

Both Rina's and Phulmala's songs highlight the challenges that having a family
pose to fulfilling a spiritual goal. Both list distractions of everyday life: beautiful
women, wife, children, money, elephants, and infirmity. Both also convey a sense of
urgency as life marches to an inevitable end on a funeral pyre. But their songs differ
in their perspectives and how they present alternatives to the typical life trajectory.
Both songs, though composed by other people, are uncanny in the way they reveal
the differences in these two women's lives. The song by Pitambar, sung by Phulmala,
seems to address wealthy men—perhaps even kings—for no one else would be accu-
mulating horses, elephants, and bundles of notes! Phulmala sees herself as having
acquired all sorts of items considered luxuries for rural Bengal: a house, television,
radio, mobile phone (though she would claim all the while that she has not been
properly remunerated for her efforts). Providing a good home for her family has
occupied her entire life, and she has accomplished quite a great deal on her voice
alone. But what, she emphatically argues, have these possessions given her in the
end? Now she is living away from her house and family, and they are enjoying her
wealth. When she is dead and gone, she knows, they will still be living off her
contributions.

   The way these distractions and obsessions are described in the song sung by
Phulmala make it clear that they fall into the Hindu category of illusion, or *māyā*,
and really do not constitute ultimate reality. In fact, in this song, Krishna is the only
true companion, the only one who will accompany an individual after death.
Implied in the song chosen by Phulmala—but certainly not explicitly stated—is the
Vaishnava view that one should offer devotion to Krishna. After all, if Krishna is
one's only companion after death, would it not be a good idea to pay attention to
him now?

   The song Rina performed takes the perspective of a more average and probably
lower-class individual, as suggested by the term Dinabandhu, or, friend of the lowly.

Life looks more ordinary: suckling at the mother's breast, falling for a beautiful woman, having a family, becoming old and frail, and finally dying. And what is the alternative? As sad and urgent as Rina's song is, there is great hope: find a guru and do *sādhanā*. Rina's song begins before birth, when babies in the womb are said to be able to remember previous lives and to be conscious of their current situation. While in the womb, explains Rina, the baby is in great discomfort and as a result makes a promise that it will get a guru and perform *sādhanā* in order to achieve the kind of spiritual realization that can prevent endless rebirth. (Most Hindus view reincarnation as undesirable and unavoidable unless deliberate action is taken.)

> [The baby] says, "Get me out of here quickly, and I'll do the right thing!" After that, it said it would do this, but didn't. After that, when you come here [into this world], you are drinking milk, eating everything, seeing everything, but then you forget. [The promise made in the womb] is just not on your mind anymore. When you become young, then you don't remember. When you're married, then what can you do?—you have all these children, many kinds of distractions; for that reason [you don't get a guru]. But, it is at *this* time that we need the guidance from a guru, have to take a guru; we have to learn what's going on in our bodies, and all that.

Rina's emphasis on the need for a guru also reflects her current perspective. She knows very well the challenges that people face while in family life: she has a young son who has just started school and a daughter who is approaching the age of marriage. She is in the prime of her life: active, beautiful, and healthy. But, she argues, this is exactly the right time to find a guru, even despite the numerous conflicting demands on her time and energy. She is not looking back on her life, counting her missteps; she is right in the middle of it and full of passion, hope, and a sense of purpose.

Many of the conversations and interviews in previous chapters have been peppered with statements expressing Baul women's love—often all-consuming—for the Baul songs they sing or hear. But to this point, music has been discussed primarily in the context of describing how Baul women's lives differ from those of other Bengali women or of illustrating their determination. In this chapter, I focus on songs that women sing and compose as well as messages about women in Baul songs. Although there is excellent scholarly work that compiles and analyzes Baul songs, my objective here is to contextualize Baul songs in everyday life. Even more important for the aims of this book, I focus on the ways in which Baul women seek to share their experiences and ideology with others and to utilize songs as a transformative medium, whether for themselves or for others. There are hundreds of songs called *bāul-gān*. Certainly many songs are sung because their melodies and lyrics are beautiful. But Baul songs are generally recognized to be instructive, and many of the songs chosen by individuals speak to the concerns, interests, and level of knowledge of those who sing them. The Baul women in this chapter not only sing

Baul songs that resonate with their own interests and experiences; they also select
or compose songs they believe might help contribute to a more meaningful life and
a better society. As they select songs to sing, they assert their authority over which
ideas to prioritize and in which context (Kelting 2001), thereby choosing how to
represent their own concerns and influence others.

"Why Are You Sleeping in That Dark Room, O Mind? Wake Up, Wake Up!" (excerpt of song composed by Rina Das Baul)

From the perspective of Bauls, questions of authenticity concern not only the views
others have of them but also their own role in society: Do they merely entertain
their audience? Or do they attempt to instruct others, whether through their words
or through their own life examples? Almost all Bauls I met distinguish between *śilpī*
Bauls and authentic or *sādhak* Bauls, and I cannot recall one time when they placed
themselves in the former category, even when others did. Bauls who sing instructive
songs, like Rina, have to navigate between views that Baul songs are for entertainment and views that Baul songs should be used for spiritual and/or societal transformation. I begin by situating instructive songs—and the desire to sing them—into
a larger context of audiences and Bauls that often seems to prefer light, fun songs.

I recorded some songs during my 1998–2000 fieldwork, but in the fall of 2007,
having been away for several years, I returned to Birbhum to visit old friends and
specifically to record Baul women's songs. The weather was beginning to cool, and
musical events were starting to pick up again as the music season for Bauls coincides with the milder weather. Paus Mela was still two months away, though on this
trip I was not staying for that event. With my three-year old son, Stefan, in tow,
I split most of my time between Rina and Dibakar's household and Phulmala.

Shortly after arriving in Bengal, I went to visit Rina and Dibakar, a couple I had
begun to spend more time with during the tail end of my earlier fieldwork. Since my
previous visit, they had built a two-story, cement house with a gated door and win-
dows. Attached to one side of the house were two small rooms, one for bathing and
another for the toilet. On my way to their house, I had noticed that there were several other new cement houses in the village, and I barely recognized the area. While
Rina and Dibakar had clearly improved their situation, they were not the only ones
in their village to have done so. Inside their house were a television and a VCD/
DVD player, which Rina said she won through a lottery. It was Bhai Phota, and
Rina persuaded us to watch—and participate in—the annual ritual celebration of
the bond between sister and brother. Stefan participated only long enough to gain
a rupee coin, which he held onto for the next two hours, as if it gave him the stability
he needed to stay among people he did not know who were speaking in a language
he could not understand. Later, Stefan became fond enough of Rina's young son to
allow us to have fruitful discussions, and we often took both boys when we went to
visit other Bauls.

Rina had become a confident singer and Baul since I had last seen her. Having a clear idea of her own role in society, she is not afraid to confront people and readily speaks her mind. She has also begun composing her own songs, though so far she has only performed a few in front of other Bauls. Her husband, Dibakar, who does not write songs, has sung several of her compositions. Most of the songs she chose to sing for me, including her own compositions, were instructive. Broadly, I discerned two types of songs:[2] those that described the need to pursue a path, find a good guru, and attempt to gain spiritual realization and those that addressed problematic societal assumptions and practices. What ties these two types together is a desire for transformation—of oneself as well as society.

What her songs are *not* about is fun and entertainment—something she discussed at length. Although she recognizes that the audience may prefer light songs, she is determined to sing primarily serious songs. After explaining the meanings of the song quoted in full above (scene two), she elaborated, thoughtfully strumming a few notes on the *dotārā* as she talked:

> The song is very beautiful. The words are very beautiful. The song…it has a good message. If people listen very closely, then they'll feel it here [hand on chest], and they'll ask themselves: 'Why am I like this?' But people don't want to do this now. People just want to "enjoy," to have pleasure, to consume a lot—this is their thought. They believe they need to have a lot of money. This is their worry. But no; there's no peace in that.

Rina's worry that audiences prefer not to be moved by songs extends to her observation that many Baul performers also sing primarily light, inconsequential songs:

> A lot of Bauls want to sing very good songs, with good words; they want to sing lyrics with a good message. But now there are some Bauls who [sing] light songs. . . . Generally people will say, 'Oh yes, a Baul came here and sang.' But [what many Bauls are singing] is all mostly banal stuff. They sing songs just to entertain folks and have fun.

Rina described being very disappointed when she learned that women from Baul families she knew do not sing good Baul songs but rather sing to please a crowd. "If a Baul's daughter doesn't do Baul songs, it is very painful." Her concern is all the more tangible because she is raising a daughter herself, and as that daughter approaches marriageable age, Rina is worried about finding a good Baul man who will encourage and support her daughter as a Baul. Rina sees the problem as two-fold: first, these Baul women are succumbing to the demands of the audience and producers who want to capitalize on the popularity of Baul songs for purposes of entertainment and profit; second, many of these women are also compromising their own dignity. When I mentioned that a Baul woman we both knew had been included in a recent Kolkata newspaper article on Baul women, Rina emphatically stated that the woman had lost her way. "She's just like the others! She sings a *filmi* song, light entertainment, and gets on the TV and dances like this [imitating a Bollywood dancer and making suggestive moves]. Why does she do this? *Why* does she do this?!" Since Rina is very critical of local normative views of women and believes that women are as capable as men, her low opinion of suggestive dance moves does not arise merely out of an acceptance of societal expectations of modesty by women. Instead, she recognizes that this woman is not (or is no longer) committed to Baul ideology enough to present it in a serious manner and to utilize her stage to communicate the value of the Baul path. Her dance moves, though they may increase her popularity, are distracting. For Rina, this Baul woman is sacrificing her own social and spiritual integrity in order to increase her own fame, belittling herself and the path in the process. Another day, Rina added that this woman, along with her well-known Baul husband, was no longer progressing on the Baul path. Her evidence for this was not only the Baul woman's choice of songs and dance moves; it was reflected also in the couple's health and general appearance. "They're not doing anything [i.e., *sādhanā*]. If you look at them, you can tell that they don't know anything. Her complexion is no longer good. He has become thin. You can tell by looking at them. If you do *sādhanā*, then what's inside shines through to your face. They have lost their way."

Most Bauls are willing, if not eager, to have their songs recorded professionally. Through recordings, their songs and voice endure. Phulmala, for instance, feels that recordings would contribute to her mark on society and might elevate her and her family to a higher status. Many Bauls, however, are simultaneously wary that they might be taken advantage of, having others make a profit from their skills while they remain in economic obscurity. But Rina's concerns about recordings are different and reflect her own particular motivations for being a Baul. She is in fact willing to risk economic success in order to remain focused on Baul ideology. Explaining that many people have asked her why she does not have any recordings to sell, she makes a distinction between the real-life performative context and the static nature of recordings. She says:

> I don't want light songs. If I do one or two light songs on the stage, then fine. But I will not record them. If I recorded them, then everyone would know that I do those kinds of songs. I don't want that. I'll do light songs, sure. But I won't record them. On the stage the songs take just a little bit of time, and then people forget them. But if these songs are played over and over [like they would be on cassettes], then people will think bad things. I don't want that. I don't have the need for a hundred people. If just one person listens to our songs, then that is good with me. I don't have any need for them to dance around and make noise. I won't make cassettes for them to play here or there.

When producers and listeners prefer songs for entertainment, what Rina calls dead songs, then the problem is compounded: recordings will reflect that demand, and any songs with meaningful messages will be overlooked or overplayed to the point of inoculation. Just as Rina criticizes Baul women for dressing up their songs with extraneous dance and frivolity, songs that are played over and over again on cassettes and CDs lose their vibrancy and relevance. In actuality, I think plenty of people like to hear recordings of Baul songs on philosophy and *deha-tattva*, but I suspect that is not the point. For Rina, Baul songs, along with Baul rituals, should be transformative. In fact, ideally interest in and knowledge of songs and rituals are developed together. The songs should be felt inside and should move people to embark upon a path for spiritual realization. As Rina explains:

> Today [typically] songs are sung, and then it's over; that's it. But a real Baul song will give you real pleasure for a whole lifetime, that is, if you take it seriously and be mindful [of the message]. This song that I just sang, it's an old song. It was here before, it remains, and it will always be here. It won't die. It is always new. That's why we say this is the path of the great ones [*mahajaner path*]. Those who have written very well, they have thought really hard. It's not a song that will die; it will always remain. If people will listen, then that's really good. Really good.

Like other Bauls, Rina utilizes her position as a Baul singer to teach people. Even though she believes that most ordinary people are not going to take her serious songs to heart, she feels strongly that performing some of these in public is part of her role in society. After singing for me the song quoted above that describes the futile passing of one's life for those who do not seek out a guru, I asked her when she sings such songs. She responded that she sings them often and particularly enjoys singing them at an *ākhṛā* or ashram where there are many *sādhu*s who actually understand the songs. "But if we go to a village where there are all sorts of people, then I'll want to sing a little of this type of song [by way of instructing them]. I want to tell them that this [how they're living] is not right; don't do that, that is bad; that will destroy your life. This is something we do [to teach]. If Bauls say this, then people listen. A lot of people will listen." Rina takes what she considers her responsibility to society seriously.

Taking Shelter at the Feet of a Guru

As suggested above, Rina expects songs to do something. She knows that not all performances of songs will fulfill that goal because most people will not be moved by the messages. However, she and other Bauls understand Baul songs as a means of personal and social transformation. One of the main reasons Baul songs need to be performed in public, rather than repetitively played on CDs, is that many of them tend to raise more questions than they answer. Although common imagery may be used, the meanings are not at all obvious. Baul songs typically have several meanings, most of which actually need to be learned from a guru. Thus if Baul songs are to be truly transformative, it is the guru who has the key.

Rina told two stories to emphasize the importance she places on the role of the guru. She is particularly alarmed by what she views as casual interest on the part of people who dabble in Baul philosophy but do not commit themselves.

Many people come to Bauls to ask questions; they want to know a little bit, but they don't really take it seriously. This is a big problem. If serious research is being done, that's fine, but if people are writing for a magazine or just want to know a little bit, that's not okay. At Joydeb Mela, there was a conch bangle seller; he had a store. He asked Dibakar who I was. Dibakar said I was his *bāulinī*. Then the man asked me, "What does Baul mean?" I said, "You want to know what Baul is? Fine, then throw all your conch bangles into the river and come with me. Then I'll tell you. But not until you throw away all your bangles." He then put his head down and didn't look at me. I don't think he'll ever ask another Baul what Baul is!

Rina laughed as she concluded this story, convinced she had taught this man a lesson. Implied in her story was her offer to initiate this conch seller, to become his guru, and to teach him what it really means to be a Baul. Although the conch seller began by addressing Dibakar first, he posed the difficult question to Rina. In a society that emphasizes women's modesty, a direct question about the nature of the Baul path could be viewed as provocative. Yet Rina challenged him to follow through with his interest, knowing full well that he would not. Rina's story also emphasizes the seriousness of the Baul path by suggesting that the man would only fully understand it if he abandoned his current trade (and all the benefits and responsibilities that come with it). When she tells him to throw away the conch bangles (worn by traditionally married women), she is also making light of a pervasive symbol of normative society. Rina wears conch bangles herself (primarily because she has not taken renunciation), but not all married Baul women do.

The second story followed.

Another time, a couple came; one was a college student. He was with a woman. They came up to me to ask some questions, and I said go ahead. I asked him if the woman was his wife; he said no, his friend. They had a video camera pointing at me. They asked, "What is Baul *sādhanā*?" I said, "That's not for telling. That's an important matter and not for magazines." [To me] Right, Lisa? If it's in magazines, then anyone can read it. If that's the case, then what value is *bāul*? Everyone will know, and they won't really understand. These things need to remain secret. If you go to a guru, take mantra, then that's one thing. But you have to really practice. It's a hard thing, Baul *sādhanā*. It's not really difficult if you're practicing and practicing, but it's not something to take lightly. One can really gain bliss by doing *sādhanā*. True *ānanda*. I sent the couple to a senior Baul. I don't think they got anything.

This story did not make Rina laugh in the telling; it concerned her. She knows there are Bauls who will tell uninitiated people (Bengalis and foreigners) about Baul *sādhanā* and other matters she strongly believes should be revealed only when someone is ready. Some of this concern comes out in a song she composed, though the lyrics mostly underscore the need to find a good guru.

Bāul khujte giya koro nā ko bhul
by Rina Das Baul

> When searching for a Baul be sure not to err!
> What a blunder
> I made when searching for a Baul.
> A Baul is so crazy that you'll never find a limit [to the craziness].
> When searching for a Baul be sure not to err!
> Bauls never call themselves a Baul.
> So mind, don't make any mistakes.
> If you want to recognize a Baul,
> then take shelter at the feet of a guru.
> The Bauls are crazy and won't reveal themselves to just anybody.
> That *sādhanā* performed for the thief of the heart
> gets to the root of it all.
> The Baul is the king of the mind,
> and her job is to search for the "person of the heart/mind"
> She doesn't care for the opinions of others
> and always stays in a heightened state of awareness.
> O mind, the Baul is my dress and ornament.
> If you want to recognize her
> you'll have to become a Baul yourself.

Several messages are communicated in this song. First, Rina warns that it is not easy to find a "true" Baul, one who has genuine knowledge, performs *sādhanā*, and has gained spiritual awareness. She asserts that real Bauls do not identify themselves as Bauls, or at least they do not advertise their identity, and will not blurt out Baul secrets to just anyone. Baul practices and beliefs can be truly understood only by those who take initiation with a guru and do the work of becoming a Baul. For Rina, and other Bauls, the guru is the link to learning about *sādhanā*, which she describes in broad terms: It is an internal activity involving the search for the Divine within. It is all-consuming, such that an individual who enters this practice ideally remains affected by its benefit at all times. Furthermore, according to Rina, Bauls do not care what others think of them; they have reached a place beyond differentiation, where the opinions of others lose their potency. In other conversations, Rina explains that many of society's assumptions (about caste, gender, and so on) are actually constructions not based on truth and therefore concludes that it is only after someone has become a Baul that the person can recognize truth.

An interesting line, within the context of Rina's life, in this song is the third to last: "O mind, the Baul is my dress and ornament." Through sarcasm, Rina dismisses sartorial markers of identity; the Baul that is her ornament and dress is really her *sādhanā*. Rina is very concerned about what she views as the problematic reputation of Bauls in the Santiniketan area. One day when I visited Rina in 2000, she had just learned that a member in her musical group had become involved with a white European woman. Rina was devastated. What was most disturbing to her was that the Baul man was already married, and Rina was good friends with his wife. After seeing several married Baul men start relationships with other women, she felt very uncertain about the company she kept. At that time, she was ashamed and, pointing to the ocher-colored sari she was wearing, told me: "How can I wear these clothes? How can I show that I am a Baul when Bauls do these [kinds of] things?" In this song, she asserts that the Baul dress is not actually indicative of any internal state and that becoming a Baul comes only through personal transformation.

Rina's concern about the actions and reputation of Bauls is well-founded, as shown in previous chapters. Witnessing the promiscuity of a number of Bauls, she worries that their behavior detracts from what she now believes is the true value of this path. But she does not take that sitting down; through composing songs (and singing them), Rina has found a way to respond. As we sat together in her house, Rina updated me on Bauls in the area and, knowing I would remember the context of our conversation seven years ago when she complained about the promiscuous behavior of some Bauls, pulled out the notebook of songs she has learned since then—as well as an increasing number of songs she has composed—and read the following out loud:

Āmi bāul haechi
by Rina Das Baul

I have become a Baul.
I dance well, sing well.
I have even gotten a few disciples.
I have become a Baul.

I don't do Baul *dharma-karma*.
Never gone to a guru.
I don't like the *sādhu* community.
Why? I am my own guru.

In my house is my *sādhan-saṅginī*,
but that didn't satisfy my heart.
That's why black, white, whoever came my way.
I perform my *sādhanā* with them.

I have become a Baul.
What's more, I have a secret *sādhanā*,
which none of you know about.
I drink nothing but sweet liquor;
that's why my body has such a glow.

I have become a Baul.
I dance well, sing well.
I have even gotten a few disciples.
I have become a Baul.

Rina says to this guru-ji:
After seeing and thinking about all this I could die!
What is the situation of these Bauls?

As Rina read, she occasionally interrupted herself to make sure I was following the points she was making: "He didn't have a guru, you know?" "He puts on all these clothes and acts the part; sings a few songs; even gets a few disciples—but what does he know?!" She laughs. Meanwhile, Dibakar returned home and, raising his eyebrows and shaking his head sideways, affirmed Rina's words, as if to say, "You see? The situation with Bauls is like this."

The Baul described in this song is male, and he exhibits the indiscriminate promiscuity of Baul men Rina personally knows. He is not satisfied with his own partner (probably wife) and utilizes his Baul status to attract other women, both Bengali and white. Rather than complaining about the situation of Bauls, Rina is

FIGURE 5.1. *Dibakar and Rina, 2007*

able to utilize her newly developed skill of composing songs to publicly denounce this type of behavior. Such words are powerful. Without naming particular individuals, she is able to draw attention to the hypocrisy of some Bauls by articulating exactly the ways in which they do not live up to ideal expectations for Bauls. After stating that this Baul has never actually taken initiation with a guru, she mockingly calls him "guru-ji," emphasizing the falseness of his claim with the honorific "-ji" ending. This song, however, does not merely condemn people who make false claims of being Baul for their own advantage (i.e., to gain disciples and women and to justify their desire for strong drink); it also suggests contrasting claims for "real" Bauls. In other words, according to Rina, legitimate Bauls have gurus, belong to the *sādhu* community, do not leave their wives, and glow because they practice a *sādhanā* that is in fact known by other Bauls.

Since I saw in Rina in 2000, when she had some strong but perhaps momentary misgivings about Baul identity, she has fully thrown herself into this path. She believes very strongly that this Baul path is fundamentally good. And now when she thinks about her future, she sees ocher: "My gurudeb says he wants us to leave all this behind some time, to wear white. I think we'll leave this kind of [householder] life, but I want to wear *geruyā*. I want to stay a Baul. He's a *baishṇab*, and that's fine, but I want to be a Baul."

There Are Only Two *Jāt*s

When I asked Rina to tell me what she thought of as the difference between a Baul and a *baishṇab*, she stated succinctly: "*Baishṇabs* do *pūjā* [worship images of Vishnu in one of his forms, in Bengal usually as Krishna]; Bauls do not do *pūjā*. But the *sādhanā* is the same. The main thing is the same." Another time she explained her views further, adding that she has never experienced or witnessed God, so why should she worship something she has never seen? Moreover, "Thakur [God] is a human being. Nothing else. Shiva, he was a human being. He became a Thakur by doing *sādhanā*. There are different paths, but they became Thakur by doing *sādhanā*. But really, they're human beings." Rina argues that God was originally just an ordinary human being but that God achieved her or his status by practicing rituals. Therefore, anyone who is devoted to doing rituals properly can achieve a similar state of awareness. At another point, she suggested that there might be a creator God but that that God is now distant and probably not involved with human affairs. So, for her, spending energy worshiping a God who is remote or a God who is really just a human being whom she cannot see is a waste of time. Instead, she argues that one should realize that all human beings have the potential to become realized. *Sādhanā* can transform an individual into someone with a heightened sense of awareness about reality: someone who realizes that the Divine resides within all human beings. What Rina highlights as the main difference between *baishṇabs* and Bauls is not the *sādhanā*, but the *pūjā* practiced by *baishṇabs*, including her guru, which effectively elevates God above humans.

Rina states that as a Baul she believes all humans to be equal. She is determined to convince others that inequality is "just something people made up." Although she believes she will not be able to reach many people with songs that point to some of the more esoteric Baul beliefs and practices, or those that urge them to find a good guru, she feels that it is her duty to try. But she is convinced that she may see more tangible results from songs that clearly address social issues. These songs are motivated by her conviction that as a Baul she needs to help people understand that they need to respect all human beings equally—regardless of caste, religion, or gender. In one of her own songs, which she read from her notebook, she criticizes the *jāt* system.

> Listen my brother-friend.
> Listen my sister-friend.
> *Jāt* doesn't have any form [*akar*].
> If one just considers the nature of *jāt*
> surviving in society becomes impossible.
> You're always talking about *jāt*,
> but does *jāt* have a tangible existence?
> [The concept of] *Jāt* is merely the mind's filth, brother.
> Because of *jāt* the people close to you become distant.
> Why do you care so much about *jāt*?
> Purify your mind first.
> And then consider *jāt*.
> Concentrate on learning the lessons of society,
> and you'll see that *jāt* has no substance [*vastu*].
> Find a teacher—surrender to a guru's teachings.
> Rina says you'll see that *jāt* is nothing but a societal prejudice.
> She'll not give it a place at the heart of society.

This song contradicts one of the most pervasive tenets behind the caste system: many Hindus, especially those in high castes, believe that people are born into the caste system based on previous actions and that degrees of purity or pollution are inherited through birth; they believe that caste (and sometimes religion) has a biological substance, some of which can potentially be transferred to other people through contact. In this song, Rina argues that *jāt* (which can include religion but here probably primarily means caste) has no substance and is merely a filthy construction of society. Like in other songs, she suggests that one way someone can learn to recognize the true nature of reality is by finding a guru and/or purifying the mind (e.g., through *sādhanā*). But even if a person did not seek out a guru, Rina's statements provide an alternative to normative, high caste dominated, and segregated society in West Bengal.

Because of the social consciousness of many Bauls and the evocative melodies of Baul songs, Bauls are regularly invited to perform for government organizations and NGOs to sing about issues like health. Rina says that some of her best programs are those sponsored by the government—and not because she gets paid well. In fact, she says the performance conditions are often not ideal and that the pay is very minimal. She does them, though, because she believes this is part of her duty as a Baul. For these programs, she has written several songs on such socially minded issues as leprosy, AIDS, and mistreatment of daughters. Dibakar sang for me a song he has performed, at the request of government organizations, for many programs. The song was long and repetitive, but using a Baul melody, it was catchy. Dibakar seemed proud to sing his wife's songs in public. I quote a portion of it here:

> Listen, listen my friends.
> Be aware of AIDS.
> Listen my brothers and sisters, friends.
> Be aware of AIDS.
> If you're not then you'll all die before your time.
> (Repeats)
> ....
> If you want to avoid getting AIDS,
> then the use of condoms is absolutely necessary.
> (Repeats)
> If you do you won't die young.
> No one will die before their time.
> Rina says, everyone will remain happy their whole lives.
> So be aware of AIDS.

In Bangladesh, Kangalini also performs for programs that are focused on raising awareness about social issues. When the government or other organizations ask her to sing, they give her a topic, often with a specific line or two to convey the desired message, and she composes a song to perform. As with Rina and Dibakar, this type of work coincides with her own ideology, and Kangalini adds that she is driven to compose songs on subjects she is concerned about. Many of her songs challenge normative society by drawing attention to people she sees as mistreated. Although certainly some of her songs aim to please her audience, she also utilizes her platform as a Baul artist to address social ills. She explains:

Some [of my] songs are [about] my fellow countrymen. For instance, in our villages, farmers, wage laborers work very hard but don't get that much money in return. I sing describing their poor condition. When I go to any program organized by rickshaw pullers, I sing about their lifestyle. [She sings:] "You work hard all day long, but what do you get from rickshaw pulling? Oh, my rickshaw wallahs. Though you work hard for all your life, you don't get recognition in return. Oh, my rickshaw wallahs."

There is a community called Bede that takes snakes out to play. They are floating people. They live on boats. They spend their whole lives on the water. Their lives are floating. I sing for them too. Their lives are to some extent similar to ours. We also float around like water hyacinth. Our Baul life is like that of a water plant.

Being a socially conscious Baul is an extension of the Baul belief that all societal differences and inequalities are merely cultural constructions and that all human beings need to be respected. It is for this reason that they claim they worship humans, not a God they cannot see.

One of the most common sayings attributed to Lalan Shah is that there are only two *jāt*s: man and woman. Many Bauls comment and elaborate on the significance of this view. Niranjan explained, "When Lalan was alive, he wrote that the definition of *jāt* does not agree with how I perceive it in my mind. I can't recognize what *jāt* is." Bauls tend to stress the importance of relying on what one can perceive with one's senses as opposed to what other people, books, or religious traditions claim. They argue, therefore, that they cannot perceive the caste system or the differences between religions. Sometimes they claim there is only one *jāt*: human beings. But at other times they stress the biological difference between men and women, claiming therefore that there are two *jāt*s. To quote Jahangir, who performs with Kangalini, and who says both these in one statement: "Lalan said... 'There is no difference among human beings. There are only two *jāt*s: one of them women, the other men. You may be a Muslim, you may be a Christian, she may be a Hindu, he may be a Dom or Chandal, but we all are human beings." Phulmala added another perspective by counting three *jāt*s: man, woman, and *hijra*. Phulmala's statement was followed by a lively discussion with another Baul on the biological characteristics of *hijra*s, persons considered the "third sex" of South Asia.[3] The point should be obvious: only sexual differences have any grounding in biology or physical form. These different views on the status of women in relation to men pervade much of Baul practice and ideology, even if they are not explicitly addressed: are women the same as or different from men, and how should they relate to each other?

In the summer of 2000, I asked Jaya and Niranjan about Baul songs related to women, and we agreed to record some. Both Jaya and Niranjan took turns singing, though since Niranjan was still teaching Jaya, he knew more songs and provided most of the explanations. Almost all the songs they chose were about *sādhanā*, and these are generally aimed at the initiated Baul. They explained that these songs are sung when they are either alone or among other Bauls or *sādhu*s. These songs are reminders of Baul ideology and practice, and through discussion with a guru or other Bauls, the meanings of these songs are revealed. In this case, they are personally transformative as the initiated singer and/or listener meditates on the meanings.

Although our stated topic was women, women were only sometimes mentioned in the songs recorded with Jaya and Niranjan, and when they were, it was from the perspective of men. The opening section of the first song I discuss follows:

> Oh don't insult women.
> No one [should] insult women.
> Women are very blessed.
> Women are, girls are,
> Ganga, Yamuna, Saraswati.
> Ganga, Yamuna, Saraswati.[4]

It appears that these lines are directed toward anyone, probably men, and serve as reminders of the value of women. By identifying women as goddesses, the listener is reminded that one should respect women. As Niranjan, who sang this song, explained: "...if we insult women, or not do anything for them, or not love them, then we will not be able to attain perfection in our *sādhanā*." Niranjan concludes the song by bringing the topic closer to home:

> A woman is Ganga, Yamuna, Saraswati.
> Which woman? My mother, wife, sister.
> Mother is Ganga, Yamuna, Saraswati.
> My wife is Ganga, Yamuna, Saraswati.
> My daughter is Ganga, Yamuna, Saraswati....

Other than drawing his family members into this song, the woman is abstract and distant: an ideal. The song reminds men to treat women right, but it also stresses the importance of women to *sādhanā*, a theme noted in several other songs as well. The sections between these opening and closing phrases describe *sādhanā* in colorful and slightly veiled language:

> Every month a woman's high tide comes.
> The confluence of the three rivers.
> Women are the Ganga, Yamuna, and Saraswati.
>
> When a woman is excited,
> for three days there is play [*līlā*].
> One day it's white, one day it's black,
> and one day it's reddish.
> Again if you bathe in that river
> the body will become golden.

Another song, this one attributed to Lalan and sung by Jaya, also uses the imagery of a river:

> Oh mind, you don't know that when the canals and lakes dry up,
> the fish don't stay.
> So what's the use of damming it up when there's nothing left?
> When the time passes, *sādhanā* won't happen.
> (Repeat)
> For what reason do they do it?
> And thus uselessly die out in the field.

> Again, if thc tree drops its seed on the ground,
> then it will not bear fruit.

Utilizing rural imagery—a flowing river, a dried-up lake, and seeds that do not bear fruit—these songs describe menstruation as the correct time for doing *sādhanā* and warn that having sexual intercourse any other time and spilling one's seed in general will lead to death. This view of the dangers of spilling one's seed is familiar to *sannyāsī*s who scorn women as temptresses capable of stealing a man's life essence found in semen. However, unlike orthodox *sannyāsī*s, Baul men do not depict women as temptresses out to steal men's life essence but, rather, as gurus who can help guide men in their *sādhanā*.

When Bauls differentiate between men and women, as in the phrase "there are only two *jāt*s," Bauls rank women higher than men. As Jaya said: "All Bauls say that women's power is a lot greater compared to men's." During one interview, after Kangalini stated that "a woman is stronger than a man," she launched into song:

> Don't go to a woman's house
> without knowing what you're doing.
> Practice, practice. . . .

These few lines sung by Kangalini are directed at men also, but her interpretation of those lines is that it is the woman who holds the key to a man's *sādhanā*. In a later interview, Kangalini again explained: "Men have a lot to gain from women spiritually. In our Islam religion, we hear that Ma Fatima has the key to heaven. Otherwise,

FIGURE 5.2. *Kangalini Sufia (singing) with daughter Pushpa, 2000*

if she doesn't give the key, nobody has the power to open that lock. So, now look, whose power is more? Women's is more."

Not only do Bauls extol women; some Baul songs suggest that men, through their practices, aim to become women—or at least more like women. To quote again a section of the song sung by Niranjan on Ganga, Yamuna, Saraswati:

> I'll die this time and become a woman.
> I'll swim in the ocean of a woman's love.
> I'll learn all the rules of love from women.

Three distinct ideas about women are expressed here: man transforming into woman; man having intercourse with woman; and woman as guru. Each of these suggests an elevated status of women and diverges from mainstream Hindu doctrine, which views being born a woman as both a liability and punishment for previous deeds. If there are two *jāt*s, men and women, then perhaps the goal can be said to achieve a state of one *jāt*, and perhaps in a sense that *jāt* is female. Regardless of how many *jāt*s or which gender the *jāt*, Bauls seeking social and personal transformation use songs to challenge what they view as the societal construction of hierarchy and difference. This aim is communicated exoterically and in straightforward language to ordinary Bengalis and esoterically with the guidance of a guru to Bauls seeking to experience the Divine within.

"Burning Suffering at Home": Reflections on One's Own Life

Among the myriad songs one can sing, individual Bauls select songs that in some way resonate with them. Bauls sing these songs on *sādhanā* as daily reminders, as many of them swirl in the whirlpool of domestic life. Other songs address societal issues and convey Baul hopes for a better society. But the songs Bauls sing can also reflect very personal concerns.

Because Kangalini writes her own songs, what she sings can clearly be connected to her life. She is extraordinarily versatile and can even compose songs on the spot. My interviews with her were sprinkled with lines from songs she knew or had composed, and she used these to emphasize or illustrate her discussion.

When we recorded Kangalini's songs, she sang her own compositions in a powerful, moving voice. Her songs reflect some of the sentiments she expressed in interviews: a longing for the simple life before she moved to Dhaka, where she is consumed by performance obligations, even ones that pay little or nothing, and frustration about not having enough support from the government to pay her rent or to get treatment for kidney disease. Recall that on the first day I interviewed Kangalini she told me that "my Baul life is a life of pain." One of the most moving songs we recorded describes an intense desire for love and connection, a very common theme in Baul songs, the object of that longing usually understood to be the Divine within.

> Oh merciful one, I've fallen in darkness, but please look after me.
> You don't think of me even as I'm sitting here in sorrow. . . .
> Oh merciful one, how I love you!
> So why don't you listen to me?
> . . . .
> I've become useless and just lie around.
> And even today I can't have your attention.

The interpretation of longing for the Divine, seen in many Baul songs, applies to this song as well, and the song is probably typically used by Kangalini to convey that message. But it is also likely that while we were recording her she was thinking about her husband. As she sang, accompanied by her daughter and another man in her troop, her young husband was flitting around the room, grooming his long hair, and telling her that there was no profit from having us record her songs. The next song was clearly directed at him, and despite the despair of the lyrics, she sang it almost playfully, stealing glances at her husband.

> Burning suffering at home.
> Burning suffering outside.
> My suffering is everywhere.
> There's suffering in this whole world,
> and I've gained absolutely nothing. . . .

On yet another level, these songs of longing and discontent connect with Kangalini's frustration about her current situation, living in Dhaka city where she is responsible for the income of about eight members of her music group. Speaking of her days wandering with her then young daughter in her arms, she says:

> Those were some great days. Then we loitered here and there. We were as free as birds. I have become impatient now. Now you tell me how I can go to villages. There are many things to see in villages: their sorrows, happiness, desires. We come to know through the villagers. [Now] we live in the city. So how much can we know? It was a life of freedom. I had a daughter. She didn't make any trouble for me. I kept her in one hand and an *ektārā* in another. However, pray for me. I want to get back to that time, the life I led. Those were the good days: days full of all sorts of freedom. I don't want to live this life.

Some of Phulmala's compositions are also clearly autobiographical, as she utilizes everyday imagery coupled with examples from her own life to illuminate life lessons. Most of the songs she sang for me in late 2007 were about separation, a feeling that preoccupied her mind. Separation is also an evocative Vaishnava theme, as it describes the loss that Radha and the *gopi*s felt when their beloved Krishna finally left them. Vaishnavas draw on this story of separation to describe what they view as the ideal type of devotion to God (here, Krishna): an intense longing to be close to

God, who is both intimate and maddeningly elusive. Phulmala's Vaishnava roots permeate her songs.

Man ekbar hari bal din phuralo
by Phulmala Dasi

> Mind, chant Hari [Krishna] once.
> Time is passing away.
> Detach yourself from the play on earth and move on.
> What strange laws came in the country?!
> Young men got disabled.
> All old men and women left home.
>
> What mobile [phone] came in the country?!
> All the swallows left the country.
> Indian mynah birds became disabled.
> Water in the coconuts dried up.
> Hence Phulmala says this genuine message:
> Do not neglect this golden body of yours.
> Say out loud; "Hari, Hari, Hari"
> Lift each one her/his own burden.

This song comments on Phulmala's current separation from family and decries a number of losses in the world around her. As she explained the song afterward, it became evident that she does not see her situation of separation from her family as unique: "What strange laws came in the country?!" She believes that it has recently become more common for families to discard their parents who raised and supported them. As if to emphasize this trend, she argues that Western families do not abandon their parents. Ironically, this view runs counter to the majority opinion of Indians concerning the differences between Indian and Western treatments of parents in old age. Additionally, widows in India have long faced hardships, and their fate is usually determined by whether or not their in-laws are willing to support them. In that sense, Phulmala's situation is really not that unique, or new. What is different about her situation is that Phulmala was the breadwinner of the family, whereas rural widows tend to be economically dependent most, if not all, of their lives. It could be, therefore, that Phulmala identifies herself less with the status of widow than with that of a breadwinner (typically male), in which case her argument is persuasive. Elsewhere I have argued that Phulmala identifies herself more as a mother than a widow. In both cases, widowhood is downplayed, which is not at all surprising given the stigma it carries in South Asia.

When Phulmala says that "young men got disabled," there are two ways to interpret it. On the surface, it recalls her own past: her husband became paralyzed when he was still quite young. But the explanation she offered while we were talking was that young men, that is, her sons, become disabled when they listen to their wives, for example, one daughter-in-law who complained about Phulmala, and then no longer serve their parents. The result: "old men and women left home."

The second part of the song brings the focus to the broader world around her, and here we see another interesting commentary. Newspapers in West Bengal have reported that the cell towers built to enable mobile phone usage in the area have resulted in troubling environmental changes, and they stress the potential and observed impact on the health of humans and animals. Bengalis comment that swallows, mynah birds, and doves have all been affected and that coconuts have lost some of their juice. These observations are included in her song. Interestingly, in other conversations Phulmala emphasized her need for a mobile phone, so I would suggest that she is not aiming to argue that cell towers (and phones) should be eliminated altogether. Rather, it seems she is commenting on the significant changes to the world around her. The world is indeed changing fast, and Phulmala, despite her illiteracy and lack of education, has been able to adjust quite effectively even while experiencing significant losses along the way.

Amid all these changes in Phulmala's personal life and in the world around her, she reminds herself—and her listeners—that her "genuine message" is to focus on spiritual development. That brings the song back full circle, back to what really

FIGURE 5.3. *Phulmala listening to recording of her songs, with Sannyas, 2007*

matters: while attachments to family, wealth (elephants, bundles of notes), prestige, and good health lead to distractions and suffering, the only thing that is constant is the Divine residing inside one's "golden body."

Conclusion

When Bauls talk about "*sādhanā*," they often included singing, playing music, and performing rituals. These all constitute ways in which Bauls progress on their path, different ways in which they practice in order to realize their goals. Like other forms of music and rituals, Baul songs and *sādhanā* generate meaning and are viewed as having the power to lead to moral, social, and emotional transformations. They thus do not merely reflect Baul ideology but, rather, become the means through which Baul ideology becomes experienced and embodied. The Baul women discussed here aim to use their singing to bring about social and personal change. However, although women's public performance may be viewed as contributing to changes in gender roles and expectations, the change celebrated and evoked in songs does not seem to explicitly concern gender equality. In fact, it should be noted that among the songs recorded, while by no means a comprehensive sample of songs performed or composed by women, only songs concerning ritual focused on women in any explicit way. Even though it is clear that Baul women are aware of their gendered positionality, the songs offered by these women focus mostly on other concerns. The kinds of societal and spiritual transformations sought by many of the women here coalesce around the idea of the inherent value of each human being, reflected also in the belief of the Divine within. This belief could certainly be invoked in songs expressing women's experiences of mistreatment. One example of this is Rina's song about the hypocrisy of a Baul man who feigns being a spiritual adept to lure women, a critique clearly expressed from a woman's point of view. However, most songs composed by women do not appear to challenge gender roles. My hunch is that these women are using songs to demonstrate their theological competence (and thus be taken more seriously) and to challenge other forms of discrimination but that they reconfigure gender roles and expectations through other means.

Baul songs tend to be described as lofty, with Bauls longing to reach the heights of the Divine, defy death, and achieve divine union through *sādhanā* with one's partner. But taken in the context of everyday life, they also reflect earthly concerns: family life and responsibilities, quibbles between spouses, and discrimination against low castes, rickshaw wallahs, and women. Whether the ideal is envisioned by Bauls as two *jāt*s or one *jāt*, it is here in the everyday that those ideals get worked out, and Baul women who sing these songs invite listeners to reconsider their own assumptions and life journey.

6

Renouncing Expectations

Madhabi and the Ashram

I had been spending a lot of time with Jaya when one day she suggested I meet a couple of Baul women she knew. I was surprised at her suggestion because up to that point most of the Bauls in the Birbhum area where I had been working usually dissuaded me from meeting others, often dismissing them as unworthy as Bauls or irrelevant to my research. I had gotten used to these dismissals of other Bauls and speculated that these Bauls thought others would be competition for the benefits that my acquaintance was perceived to offer. Jaya, however, had a personal interest in my subject and demonstrated that my questions were ones with which she was also deeply concerned. Jaya, a married Baul woman in her midtwenties who lives with her husband and daughter, is particularly worried about her position in society, and she says she never wants to take renunciation. At the time she suggested I meet these other women, she was trying to explain to me the challenges she faced as a Baul living in her village when much of what she believed as a Baul went against the expectations and views of her neighbors.

One of the women whom Jaya introduced me to was Madhabi, and at an appointed time, Madhabi arrived at Jaya's home sitting on the back of her *dādā's* bicycle. At that first meeting, Madhabi was wearing a bright ocher-colored sari with a string of *tulsī* beads around her neck and a longer beaded necklace; her *dādā* also was clothed in ocher: a long lightly colored ocher *pānjābī* shirt and a white *lungi*. As soon as we sat down on Jaya's veranda, Madhabi launched into her story about her "very difficult" life. I had to scramble to pull out my tape recorder, but as soon as she saw it she appeared eager to tell her story to the machine. Her story,[1] as she told it, began right at what she seemed to think is the crux of the problem:

MADHABI: My husband said [to me], "[Your family] has an ashram. They will have to sign over the ashram." Then my father said, "If I sign it over to you,

then my daughter has no future. My daughter has a future [so] I will not
sign over the ashram [to you]. You are a *ghar jāmāi* [son-in-law who lives
with the in-laws]; you're fine." [But my husband] said, "I will not stay. In this
manner I will not stay here." Father said, "Fine. You know best. If you don't
stay, then go somewhere [else], eat, and stay there. Do whatever makes you
happy. But make an effort." [My husband] said, "I won't stay [here]."

[My] mother and father couldn't just throw [me] out: "Where will we put
our daughter?" Uncle then said, "Stay with me." I then stayed with them.
After that, *dādu* and *didimā* (maternal grandparents) died. In [all] that
unhappiness, [my] husband left.

While staying [at my parent's home]...my mother and father played
music. I watched and learned a little. During this time, when I learned
music, my mind had some peace. As I said from the very beginning that
I—if he leaves, I won't marry again.

LISA: You won't marry again?

M: One time [in one marriage] there was no happiness. So would happiness
come from the next time? It won't happen. My daughter's marriage is
complete now. I said, "Fine, then when the girl's marriage is done, then
father, I'll go stay with *dādā*...with *dādā*."

I went to *dādā* and said, "*Dādā*, give me a little place." *Dādā* said, "Why,
sister?" I said, "I have been hurt and left to come [here]. Do you know, my
husband was not happy? So give me a small place to stay." Then he said,
"Fine. Stay. Since you have suddenly come to me for shelter, then stay."

Baudi [brother's wife] and *dādā* love me a lot. Now *dādā* takes me
with him wherever he goes. He said, "Fine, stay here, eat, be happy."
And I am such a person that wants such happiness [*ānanda*]. Give me a
handful to eat. I will [even] stay without eating, but I want peace/
happiness [*ānanda*].

L: Your parents agreed with your leaving [home] to stay with *dādā*?

M: Yes. He gave me a lot of pain. Beat me up. He drank alcohol, meaning,
whatever he shouldn't do, that's what he did.

L: Who's this? Who?

M: Yes. Drank alcohol and all that.

L: Your husband?

M: And hit me. Such injustice [unwarranted behavior]. Meaning, he gave such
grief, meaning, if I said it, you wouldn't be able to believe it! So much pain
he gave me!

L: How did you marry? A conventional—

M: The wedding was a regular event.

L: Meaning with a priest [*purohit*]...

M: Yes, yes. Everything was done right. Father gave a big fancy wedding
[*dhumdhām kare biye diyeche*]. But happiness wasn't written on the
forehead.[2]...I ran away. Meaning, I will not stay here anymore.

She told me about how her husband used to beat her, drink alcohol, and finally left her and their daughter because her family refused to sign over their ashram to him. Though they both had taken *dīkshā* together when they got married, receiving a *yugal mantra*, she took *bhek*, the formal ritual for the renunciation of householder life, when he left. Now she was staying with her *dādā* and his wife and children in Bolpur, where she was hoping to earn enough money to sustain herself.

It was monsoon season, and the rains forced us inside. During lulls in the storm, she would prompt me to turn my tape recorder back on so that she could tell me more. Never had I been so grateful that I had been bold enough to pull out that tape recorder at the first meeting. Madhabi's manner of speaking was difficult to follow. She jumped around from subject to subject, often seeming to assume that I had previous knowledge of her life, and her verb tenses rarely reflected the actual time that events took place. It was not until later, when I could listen to the tape over and over, that I was able to piece together the layers of her narrative. Madhabi also spoke with such urgency that I felt all the questions I had prepared were wholly inadequate. Even though her husband had left three years before, her voice had the urgency of new pain as she called him *badmāś* (loosely translated as wicked or roguish; sometimes used affectionately but in this case has derogatory implications indicating someone who is up to no good) and described herself as having done everything right as a wife.

I began meeting her at her *dādā*'s, and we continued these conversations. During these meetings, she wore an old white sari and no ornaments except for the *tulsī* beads. Many days she was running behind in her morning duties, so I would sit and wait as she returned from her bath, and I watched as she offered incense to the deities depicted in posters in a corner and to whoever was sitting in the room. As she encircled me with incense, she offered the familiar explanation: "We worship humans. It is important to love humans first." One day she described to me her *bhek* initiation: taking off her marriage bangles and *sindur* (marking on a woman's forehead indicating she is married), placing a loincloth over her head (*ḍorkaupīn*), receiving a begging bag (*jholā*), staff, and water pot from her guru, then begging for alms in the village, and finally also receiving alms from her own parents. "Oh how they cried! They cried so much!" she said. My training told me that the act of begging from one's parents was surely a ritual of severing parental–child ties, demonstrating that she had renounced family life and responsibilities. Assuming that her parents' grief indicated such a dramatic transformation, I offered the next question: "So after you took *bhek*, your relationship with your mother and father changed?" But my question did not lead to the answer I was expecting: "I now have four mothers and fathers. I have one set more than before. When I was given in marriage, I had another set of parents. They [too] were my gurus. First guru . . . second guru. My mother and father were the first parents, then there was second [in-laws], [then] third [*bhek* gurus]." On the one hand, Madhabi was explaining that one's mother and father are also gurus, as parents are for all children. But the reason she dismissed my suggestion that her relationship with her parents had changed became clearer as time went on: except for their increased concern about Madhabi's unhappiness, their relationship had *not* really changed, at least not in any way that I could perceive.

Madhabi frequently punctuated our conversations by saying she would take me to see the ashram that she and her parents had refused to sign over to her husband. One day we made the three-hour bicycle ride to the ashram, accompanied by her *dādā*. Her parents' home was northeast of Bolpur, and since my room was on the way, we met by the rail tracks outside Santiniketan. Madhabi was wearing her white sari, and with an umbrella in her hand she sat sideways on the back of her *dādā*'s bicycle. I followed along on my own, and the three of us talked much of the way. We cycled for some time along the road that follows the railroad track, and then we veered off the main road onto a winding dirt road. On both sides were fields, and villages appeared in clusters of trees scattered along the horizon. The small road we traveled on did not appear to lead to any of these villages but persisted in veering away from them. At one point, however, we stopped, and Madhabi pointed to a cluster of trees in the distance. There, she said, is where her family's ashram is; that is where we were going. The distance would not have been so far except that the road we were on did not lead us in a straight trajectory to our destination. Clouds were beginning to accumulate, giving us some relief from the sun, but rain was imminent.

We reached the trees of Madhabi's natal village shortly after the rains began. Madhabi greeted people running across our path as we hurried to her parents' home, umbrellas in one hand, and leading our bikes with the other. Like many villages in Bengal, this one was lush with vegetation: palm, bamboo, banyan, and small shrubbery. We took a smaller path to an isolated area of the village and arrived at the ashram. There was a small shaded pond on one side, fruit trees near the house, and four *samādhi*s,[3] or graves, made of pressed mud. The mud house had two stories, but it was in need of repair, with portions of walls beginning to crumble. As we approached the house, we saw several people: Madhabi's parents, who live in the house, and her daughter and son-in-law who live in another village and came for the day to visit. They were rushing around, pulling things out of the rain, and unrolling tarps that were attached to the roof of the veranda. When he saw us, Madhabi's father waved us into their home as we abandoned our bicycles and sandals and rushed inside, already soaking wet. Madhabi's daughter handed us dry towels and clothes as her parents attempted to secure the tarps around the veranda against the relentless rain. We sat at first on the veranda, but soon the wind forced the rain through large rips in the tarps, and we all crowded into a tiny dark room shared by small *mūrti*s of Radha and Krishna.

I met her parents only once, but I got a sense of the extent to which their lives were closely entwined with their daughter and granddaughter. These were not people who had renounced family obligations but, rather, had tried to maintain family life alongside their own *sādhanā*. Madhabi's parents told me they had taken *bhek* when they learned that they were going to have a child. They did this because they felt they had to demonstrate publicly their commitment to the Baul path, and *bhek* indicated a vow that they would have no more than this one child, Madhabi. Her parents' commitment to their daughter extended to wanting Madhabi to be a Baul, a path they believed should have given her peace and spiritual growth, which is why they had arranged her marriage to a Baul. Madhabi's marriage failed some years after the birth of their one child, a daughter, so that raising the child, providing her with some education, and arranging for her dowry and marriage fell on Madhabi and her parents. Although they now have some satisfaction knowing that Madhabi is living with her *dādā* and is in a sense protected, they still prefer to find another husband for her because without a partner, they insisted, she could do no *sādhanā* and would therefore never really gain the peace they had hoped for her.

What should be evident from the above descriptions is that Madhabi and her parents took *bhek* for very different reasons. Many Bauls view renunciation as an opportunity to liberate themselves from societal obligations, giving them the space to focus on *sādhanā*, and it is in line with these objectives that her parents took *bhek*. Madhabi took *bhek* alone, and her motivation for doing so was her husband leaving her. When I asked her how she came to the decision of taking *bhek*, she answered: "What else could I do? For that reason." Several times throughout our conversations, she stated that as a woman, she is very limited in what she can do. "There's a need for a man. If you go out alone, things happen . . . It happens, right? So [people say to me], 'You don't have to do all that Baul stuff. Stay at home. Where will you go all by yourself? [You're] a woman. Traveling all over, long distances. Alone, there's danger.' . . . Anything can happen. . . . If you don't have a man, [then as a] woman [you] can be maligned. Won't it happen?"

Renunciation in South Asia

Even with their different circumstances, Madhabi and her parents in many ways represent typical Baul renouncers. However, they—and Baul renouncers in general— differ significantly from most South Asian renouncer traditions. A full discussion of renouncer traditions in South Asia and the literature about them is beyond the scope of the current work, but a few aspects should be mentioned here in order to situate Baul women renouncers into a larger context. As will become clear, Madhabi and her parents, as well as most Bauls, do not share the characteristics that most scholars (and, for that matter, most renouncers) consider essential to renunciation.

The literature on renunciation frequently posits that an opposition between renouncer and householder holds great institutional and conceptual importance in South Asia. The standard and orthodox view, emphasized by Louis Dumont (1970) and numerous scholars after him and maintained largely if not exclusively by the Brahminical point of view (see Burghart 1983), is that the renouncer is typically and fundamentally an individual who has severed ties with family life and responsibilities in order to pursue spiritual liberation or *moksha*. Most Hindus expect the renouncer life to be characterized by asceticism, celibacy, and itinerancy, though there are plenty of variations on ascetic practices and modes of living. Although men, who by virtue of their gender are granted more freedom, are more likely to become renouncers, some women also do take renunciation, as seen in Denton 1991; Hausner 2007; Khandelwal 2004, 1996, 1997; Ojha 1981, 1988; and in Khandelwal et al. 2006. The predominance of male renouncers holds true in Bengal as well as elsewhere in India, and early conceptions of Bauls, as discussed previously, of a lone man wandering the countryside dressed in the ocher of *sannyās* and carrying an *ektārā* in his hand, confirm this perception.

*Sādhu*s, including Bauls, in Bengal are ambiguously situated within a landscape of the pan-Indian *sādhu samāj* or community of renouncers. Speaking of *sannyāsinī*s in north India, Meena Khandelwal (2004) has argued that because this *sādhu samāj* has no centralized authoritative hierarchy, there are many cracks that allow for the participation of independent renouncers, including women and low castes, as well as different interpretations of *sannyās*. This is all the more true of Bengal, where *sādhu*s live on the periphery of the *sādhu samāj*. Nonetheless, Baul women's reinterpretations of *sannyās* are best understood if examined first in relation to the *sādhu samāj*.

Throughout most of India, an individual typically takes initiation into one of the several different *sādhu* organizations when she or he decides to become a renouncer. Some of the orders considered most prestigious and orthodox are those established by Sankara in the ninth century. Sankara founded ten Dasanami orders and four monastic centers to oversee broader regions in India. Overseeing the eastern and northeastern region, including the area of Bengal, is the monastic center of Puri, called Govardhan Matha. Puri is a pilgrimage site for many Bengalis, and some renouncers in Bengal claim affiliation with the Sankara orders in Puri. Followers of the Dasanami orders are considered Shaivas and are called *sannyāsī*s, though that term is not restricted to Dasanamis and certainly not in Bengal.

Rivaling Sankara's Dasanami orders, the *bhakti* (devotional) movement spawned four traditional Vaishnava communities, or *sampradāy*s (*chatuḥ sampradāya*): Sri-Vaishnavas, Nimbarkas, Vishnuswamis, and the Madhvas. All of these *sampradāy*s originated in southern India except for the Nimbarkas, whose founder came from south India and settled in Brindaban in north India (Uttar Pradesh). However, three additional northern Vaishnava sects—the Ramanandis, Pustimargis, and the Gauriya (Bengali) Vaishnavas—emerged later and claim that their lineages have links to the older and more prestigious southern lineages—Sri-Vaishnava, Vishnuswami and Madhva, respectively.[4] There appears to be little evidence that direct links actually exist between these northern lineages and the more prestigious southern ones, and it is likely that the attempt to make such a connection reflects strategic maneuvering more than historical reality.[5]

Although the Sankara orders carry some weight in Bengal, it is *bhakti* that became the prominent mode of religiosity in Bengal, particularly with the revivalist work of the famous Bengali Vaishnava Caitanya (1486–1533). However, these four traditional Vaishnava *sampradāy*, like the Dasanami orders, have at most only minimal presence in Bengal. It is probably partly because none of the traditional four Vaishnava *sampradāy*s has a significant presence in Bengal that in other parts of India the Bengali Vaishnavas (*gauṛiya baishṇab*) have a reputation, as I discuss further below, of being loose with rules, such as celibacy, vegetarianism, and maintaining strict lineages.

Under the enthusiasm and leadership of Caitanya, the *bhakti* movement spread rapidly throughout Bengal, where it also took its own distinctive form. Caitanya, understood by followers to be Radha and Krishna in one human form, established loving devotion as a new model of *dharma* "that supersedes in excellence and relativizes (though it may not invalidate altogether) other forms of *dharma*, including certain kinds of Vedic and other Brahmanic *dharma*" (O'Connell 1996–1997:199). In the community of Caitanya Vaishnavas, everyone, regardless of caste, gender, or class, was worthy of experiencing *bhakti* and being supported in that endeavor.[6] Since *bhakti* emphasizes a more direct and personal relationship with God, unmediated by Brahmin priests, it tended to clash with the hierarchical Sankara orders. Even so, Caitanya took initiation as a *sannyāsī* into a Sankara lineage, the Bharatis, in order, it appears, to be taken more seriously by those who still emphasized the Brahminical system and the related Dasanami (Sankara) orders.[7] According to the *Caitanya Caritamrita*, the definitive history and biography of Caitanya, he decided to take renunciation after an incident in which several angry students criticized him for his practices (Kaviraja 1999:327). "Thus I must certainly take *saṃnyāsa*; they will bow to me as a *saṃnyāsin* who is to be honored. They will have to bow, and in this their transgressions will be wiped away; I shall cause *bhakti* to arise in their stainless hearts. Then all these disbelievers will be saved" (328). This type of tension between *bhakti* and the more hierarchical *sannyāsī* orders continues today,[8] including, at times, among Bauls. Bauls and other groups influenced by *bhakti* are often criticized because of their unorthodox practices and beliefs that challenge the Brahminical system, and sometimes individuals in these groups feel the need, like Caitanya, to gain legitimacy and respect through strict observances of rules and proper maintenance of *sannyāsī* lineages.[9]

Those groups in Bengal who have direct links to established *sādhu samāj* centers elsewhere, such as between the Gauriya Vaishnavas in Nabadwip (West Bengal) and Brindaban (Uttar Pradesh), tend to share their ideologies and to search for legitimacy via lineages and observances of such traditional rules as celibacy and vegetarianism. For this reason, when the Gauriya Vaishnavas tried to establish themselves in the northern pilgrimage site of Brindaban where the local Vaishnava community recognized only the legitimacy of the four Vaishnava *sampradāy* mentioned earlier, they created a link with the lineage of the prestigious Madhva *sampradāy* of the south[10] and continue to demonstrate, to varying degrees, their strict adherence to Vaishnava asceticism. However, the Gauriya Vaishnavas in the Bengal center of Nabadwip are considered less strict than their Brindaban counterparts.

Despite their efforts, the reputation of Gauriya Vaishnavas as fish-eating *bostam*s[11] who live in ashrams with their wives or other women persists and is not altogether unfounded. This reputation is due not only to the limited presence of the more traditional and orthodox sects of the *sādhu samāj* but also to the strong presence of Tantra and its influences on many groups, including some Vaishnavas, in Bengal. In fact, in literature and popular imagination throughout India and even in Pakistan, Bengal has the reputation of being home to Tantric magic, dangerous women, and unorthodox *sādhu*s. Gauriya Vaishnavas and others in Bengal who have tried to maintain some semblance of orthodoxy have therefore faced an up-hill battle. Further complicating matters, Gauriya Vaishnavas have had an unwilling connection with the Tantric-influenced Vaishnava Sahajiyas, who, during medieval Bengal, adopted the appearances and outward behavior of orthodox Gauriya Vaishnavas but engaged in unorthodox ritual practices, including sexual intercourse intended to unite the cosmic principles of male (Krishna) and female (Radha). Vaishnava Sahajiyas also appropriated important texts, gurus, and lineages from Gauriya Vaishnavas, incurring the wrath of the latter.[12] *Jāt baishṇab*s, who may be an offshoot of Gauriya Vaishnavas, also have a reputation for licentiousness behavior. Let us also not forget that some Bauls consider themselves Vaishnavas or *jāt baishṇab*s and similarly draw on Radha–Krishna imagery for their practices and theology. Gauriya Vaishnavas have vehemently condemned these groups, but some damage has already been done to the reputation of the orthodox group, particularly in the eyes of other orthodox communities beyond Bengal. It should be kept in mind that the boundaries around these groups are very fluid, but for our purposes here, the existence of these groups in Bengal has not only helped diminish the influence of the more orthodox visions of renunciation; it has also widened the pool of possibilities from which individuals, including women, may draw.

Aside from—and despite—such organizations as the Gauriya Vaishnavas in Nabadwip, which cultivate ties with other orthodox communities, the majority of other *sādhu*s in Bengal follow and participate in loosely organized communities and remain predominantly outside the larger *sādhu samāj*. As Jeanne Openshaw states, "Just as, in the case of householder society in Bengal, the theory of the four 'classes' (varnas) is reflected in an incomplete way on the level of social structure, so too the hierarchical structures of the society of renouncers are present in embryonic or fragmented form, and are elaborated if anything on the terminological rather than the organisational level" (2002:128). As a result, there is much more room in Bengal for a variety of views on renunciation, reasons to take it, and ways to do so. Thus Baul renunciation, though certainly controversial among many in Bengal, has emerged within a larger pool of similarly loosely structured *sādhu* groups and goes largely untouched by more strict lineages.

Although Baul renunciation bears only minimal similarities to classical renunciation, it is not alone in complicating and obscuring the householder–renouncer divide among Hindus in India. As Richard Burghart (1983) demonstrates, there are many different kinds of renouncers, including those who do not abandon householder status. Furthermore, there are several castes that have their identity rooted in renunciation, despite the fact that they live and propagate in householder roles. Nath yogis, for instance, embrace both a renunciant path and a *jāti* group identity. As Ann Grodzins Gold shows, Nath renouncers and householders are often critical of each other, such that renouncers argue that householder Naths are fallen ascetics who could not resist the temptation of women (1992:47–48) while householders claim "that living in the world offers no impediment to spiritual achievement" (49). Despite these criticisms, Gold demonstrates the ways in which both Nath paths frequently merge and blend and that to separate the two groups is overly simplistic. Peter van der Veer (1988:72) mentions that some Ramanandi castes in western India are constituted by ex-*sādhu*s who had chosen to revert to householder status but were not accepted by members of their original high caste *jāti*s. Similarly, in Bengal, *jāt baishṇab*s have their *jāt* identity also rooted in renunciation, though they usually live as householders. Like the Naths, householder *jāt baishṇab*s are often considered fallen ascetics who have come to occupy an ambiguous place in the caste system. According to Joseph O'Connell (1982), *jāt baishṇab*s can be considered an endogamous *jāti* without affiliation to the traditional four varnas and can be joined by those of any caste. Being thus outside the varnas, *jāt baishṇab*s argue for a position at least equal to Brahmins if not higher.[13] Some *jāt baishṇab*s, including a few Bauls I met who counted themselves also as *jāt baishṇab*s, wear a sacred thread and/or claimed to be Brahmins, obscuring yet again the lines between householder and renouncer.

While the examples above certainly cloud the householder–renouncer distinction as well as the renunciation ideal of celibacy, many individual renouncers–both men and women–complicate other ideals.[14] Burghart suggests that this diversity among those who take renunciation can be understood when one realizes that it is not necessarily the social world that is being renounced but, rather, the "transient" world. The "release from the transient world (*saṃsara*) is both the purpose of the individual act of renunciation as well as the promise of the preceptors of the various ascetic sects. The transient world, however, is not coterminous with the social world, and various sects have understood or differently emphasised the way in which the transient world is sustained and hence the way in which the individual's relationship with it can be severed" (1983:642–643). Bauls, as will become clear, do not necessarily renounce the social world when they take renunciation, and in this and other ways they can be seen as further obscuring the householder–renouncer divide.

Expecting Renunciation: Understandings of Baul Renunciation and the Importance of *madhukarī*

Bauls may live on the periphery of the *sādhu samāj*, but the allure of *sannyās* captures the imagination nonetheless. This is particularly true for the *bhadralok*, who attempt to sort out evidence of authenticity among Bauls. But it is also true for Bauls who draw on *sannyās* as a strategy for creating and articulating their lives as suitably unencumbered.[15]

As I listened to Bengalis expound on the question of Baul authenticity, I noted that renunciation often loomed large in people's minds, and not surprisingly, people also had different ideas about the significance and meaning of Baul renunciation. Living in Santiniketan, I heard many elite Bengalis and Bauls claim that *madhukarī*,[16] or begging for alms, was a clear sign of a real Baul because they associated the practice with renouncer or *sādhu* traditions. This is partly due to the idealistic stature attained by Bauls in this area, such that many Bengalis prefer to connect Bauls with the more prestigious *sannyāsī* traditions. Furthermore, many Bengali Hindus maintain that giving alms to those who have fully devoted themselves to a religious path is a duty of householders and will bring merit to the donors. For some Bengalis, this emphasis on *madhukarī* is an attempt to separate so-called real Bauls from artists (*śilpī* or *gāyak*) who rely on contributions and payment at programs. The underlying assumption here is that only those who have taken renunciation are entitled to live from the alms of *madhukarī*, and those Bauls who have taken renunciation are seen as having taken the necessary departure from worldly concerns and greed. In contrast, however, those Bauls who do not do *madhukarī* are considered to be Bauls only for the gain of wealth and fame.

In the environment of Santiniketan where Bauls are as common a sight as foreigners, however, those who want to live from *madhukarī* do not necessarily need to prove their lineage or status, particularly to the transient *bhadralok*, foreigners, and train passengers, all of whom serve as likely patrons. If gaining support from transient patrons is the goal, all Bauls need to do is dress the part and perform the role.

In fact, there is an implicit ambiguity both in one of the Bengali terms most used for Baul renunciation and in the external markers of a renouncer. Baul renunciation is typically called *bhek* (and has Vaishnava associations) or *khilāphat* (the term used mostly among Sufis, though Muslim Bauls use *bhek* as well). Other terms also used are *sannyās*, which has its association within the larger *sādhu samāj*, and *tyāg*, which means giving up or relinquishing, and the Baul renouncer may variously be referred to as *bhek-dhārī*, *bairāgī*, *sannyāsī*, or *tyāgī*. The term *bhek*, which was most often used among Bauls I knew, also refers to the attire of an ascetic, particularly a Vaishnava ascetic, and the putting on of that attire. In the eyes of the uninitiated public, these understandings are typically conflated so that the appropriate clothes indicate both a Baul and a renouncer. Bauls frequently told me that they wear ocher-colored clothes, regardless of whether or not they are renouncers, because it is expected of them in society (particularly when performing). Even those Muslim Bauls and Vaishnava Bauls who tend to wear white instead of ocher sometimes wear ocher when performing in public because much of society (including in predominantly Muslim Bangladesh) connects that color with renunciation and believes that renouncers are entitled to request alms, as Bauls are sometimes perceived as doing when they perform. Thus the definition of *bhek* suggested above holds some currency for Bauls: that is, wearing the appropriate clothing of a renouncer is to some extent equated with being a renouncer—especially to transient sponsors. This is not so much the case in other areas, however, particularly for Bauls living in villages where acquaintances are aware of their status, reputation, and whether or not they have actually formally taken *bhek*. Openshaw (2002:135), however, states that some Bauls who have not taken formal *sannyās* may still be able to receive alms from people who know their actual status if these Bauls have demonstrated their accomplishments in other ways, such as with their *sādhanā*.

While wearing ocher-colored clothes or performing *madhukarī* may satisfy patrons' feelings about their own religious duties, expectations that Bauls take *bhek* and live off *madhukarī* are not uniformly reflected in Baul practices.[17] One of the reasons Bauls have conflicting and ambiguous views on renunciation stems from the socioreligious contexts in which particular Bauls find themselves. Because Muslims in general applaud householder life and responsibilities over renunciation, Muslim Bauls tend to take renunciation less frequently than Hindu Bauls. Vaishnava Bauls in the Santiniketan–Bolpur area, conversely, are more likely to talk of the value of *bhek* (though many may never take it) in part because of the Hinduization of Bauls reflected in the view that many use *sannyās* as a measure of authenticity.

Although the socioreligious environment may color the way Bauls view renunciation, there is no consistent perspective on the matter among Hindu and Muslim Bauls. Since each guru is an authority on the best way to progress, there is no uniform Baul path. Furthermore, a majority of Bauls are householders regardless of the level of their practices and expertise. Thus renunciation, though it may be viewed by some as an ideal way to relinquish societal obligations and devote oneself more fully to *sādhanā*, is not particularly seen as a culmination of one's spiritual endeavors. Furthermore, as pointed out by Openshaw (2002:140-51) and also corroborated by my fieldwork, the guru who bestows *bhek* is not necessarily seen as the most important guru to Bauls. Among the Hindu Bauls I interviewed, most claimed to have two or three gurus, distinguishing between *dīkshā* guru, *śikshā* guru, and *bhek* guru. Sometimes there would be two (or more) *śikshā* gurus,[18] at least one of whom taught Baul songs. It is quite common for Vaishnavas and Bauls to have at least a *dīkshā* guru, one who bestows a *tulsī* bead necklace and a mantra though offers little or no instruction. The *śikshā* guru, on the other hand, is credited with being the most important, for it is from this guru that one learns the practices and teachings of Bauls as well as the meanings of Baul songs. Openshaw (2002:140–143) argues that because a Baul may have multiple gurus and value the *śikshā* guru over the other gurus, the role of the *bhek* guru as well as the status of *bhek* is effectively devalued.

Bauls appear equally conflicted about the role of *madhukarī*. In my fieldwork, Bauls who claimed that *madhukarī* is essential to the Baul path explained that begging serves to make them humble (*lajjā*)—in this context a very Vaishnava sentiment—and that it allows them to connect with people. Networking is considered important on several levels, including spreading their ideological message through

their songs and gaining potential sponsors for future performances. Although
Phulmala, for instance, complains of the hardship of singing on the train, she
appears to really enjoy interacting with people and claims this is how she has
received invitations to some of her main performances, leading also to tours abroad.
Furthermore, many claim that even Bauls who have plenty of disciples and have no
need to beg for money or food should participate in *madhukarī*. Sanatan Das Baul
from Bankura is well known for his repertoire of songs as well as knowledge of the
Baul life, *kīrtan,* and *deha-tattva* and has disciples from all over the world who
support him, yet he regularly goes out and begs from those in nearby villages.

Other Bauls downplay the importance of *madhukarī*. In fact, the tendencies
among Muslim Baul renouncers particularly challenge the idea that *madhukarī* is a
defining characteristic of renouncer Bauls. Following the Islamic emphasis on
family and work, Muslim Bauls tend to believe they should have occupations, and
indeed many also tend to downplay the importance of taking *khilāphat* or *bhek*.
One Baul couple I met in Jhenaidah claimed to have taken *khilāphat* after having
their children, and for some time the man continued his job as a gardener in the
nearby police station in order to support his family. At the time I met them, his now
grown son had taken over that job while he himself was bringing in income from the
donations of disciples. Lalan Shah, whose songs constitute much of the *bāul-gān*
repertoire today, purportedly made his living selling betel nut. Sources say that in
his later life he had enough disciples to support him and thus no longer worked, but
begging was not portrayed as an esteemed option. Ābul Āhsan Caudhurī, claiming
that Lalan was a strong believer in work and did not care for begging, attributes the
following saying to him: "Excellent crops, independent business, service job, and at
the end alms; begging is the filthy work of lazy people" (1997:132). He goes on to
state that Bangladeshi Bauls tend to be cultivators and craftspeople, especially
weavers, though many of them have left their hereditary occupations in order to
become shopkeepers, businessmen, and laborers or to take low-level service jobs
and that very few rely on begging. Openshaw mentions that in Krishnapur P.S.
Bauls include "farmers, landless labourers, petty traders, barbers, blacksmiths,
conch-makers, shop-keepers, deed-writers, schoolmasters, technicians, and
renouncers" but that renouncers "are supported by their disciples, from ashram
land or from alms-taking without reference to singing" (2002:98).

Other Bauls prefer to earn their living not through *madhukarī* but through performances,[19] particularly in the Santiniketan–Bolpur area. Many of them claim that
madhukarī would decrease their chances of getting invited to performances. Jaya
told me that if she and her family were really in need, they would go out and do
madhukarī but that it would look bad in the eyes of the villagers. Villagers would
tell her that she, being young and healthy, should get a job; potential patrons would
think that she had lost her talent and would not invite her to programs. When I
mentioned to Jaya that many Bauls, like Phulmala, did *madhukarī* on trains, she
countered that that proved her point: Phulmala no longer gets invitations to programs. Although in my observation that is not completely true, I did find many who

concurred with Jaya that *madhukarī* had negative implications, limiting one's opportunities to earn income in the more prestigious occupations of performer or as a guru of songs and/or *sādhanā*. Rina, for instance, felt that some day she might take *bhek* with her husband but that doing so would likely coincide with a natural decrease in her desire to perform songs for others. Although she might consider *madhukarī* when she is much older, especially if she does not have a community of disciples or family members willing to support her, she now also believes that *madhukarī* would detract from the weight of the messages she is committed to communicating. Similarly, other Bauls claimed that having disciples provided them with enough income so that there was no need to beg, an activity they dismissed. For a Baul, having disciples is like having children who will provide support to the guru, especially as he or she ages. The preference some Bauls give to *madhukarī* as a way of life should not be overlooked, as it clearly signifies the prestige associated with *sannyās* and a sense of humility some value. But given the diverse ways in which Bauls actually make a living and that argue in favor of certain occupations over others, using *madhukarī* as a way to measure Bauls and Baul renouncers has more to do with other peoples' expectations (e.g., *bhadralok*, Brahmins, *sādhu samāj*, and scholars who unquestionably accept such perspectives) than it does with Bauls.

There is thus an obvious disjuncture between the expectation, held by many non-Bauls, that Bauls *should* take renunciation and the views held by Bauls themselves. Openshaw argues that renunciation among Bauls is more of a "received" category than a "native" one (2002:125–139), yet because renunciation is an aspect of Baul life, many scholars and laypeople have attempted, unsuccessfully, to pin it down. My research findings support this view. Furthermore, because some Bauls are aware that potential sponsors place a particular value on renunciation, Bauls also frequently cite those very aspects that are valued as reasons for why they have taken renunciation (for example, being able to do *madhukarī*, the valued humility that comes with begging, earning the respect of householders, etc.). Thus the question remains as to whether they have taken renunciation because of the fringe benefits gained by meeting expectations of potential sponsors or for other reasons more intrinsic to the nature of renunciation.

I believe that renunciation (as well as *madhukarī*) is a strategy used only by *some* Bauls and is neither a central defining characteristic nor a pervasive goal and status marker among Bauls. This is not to say that Bauls cynically don the attire and enact the part for the benefits they may gain. Rather, renunciation and *madhukarī* are symbols with myriad meanings from which Bauls can draw—selectively or simultaneously. Certainly the motivations for taking Baul renunciation appear to differ from the view that *sannyās* is an important step intended to cause the realization of illusion, or *māyā*, on the path toward *mokṣa*. Renunciation for Bauls has a distinct flavor that sets itself apart from mainstream paradigms of renouncers whose lives are characterized by celibacy, asceticism, and uninvolvement in worldly concerns. Yet the lives of Baul renouncers are also informed by those ideals, even if they oppose them. For instance, drawing on *sannyās* ideals and patterns of living, Bauls similarly emphasize the expectation of detachment. However, detachment may manifest itself in several different ways: in the view that *yugal-sādhanā* is done to cultivate love and an experience of the Divine as opposed to earthy, carnal lust; in the practice of *madhukarī*; or both. Detachment may also be expressed through the binding commitment among Baul renouncers to no longer have children, an idea that seems fitting with normative views of *sannyās*. Yet the method for accomplishing this goal is *yugal-sādhanā* rather than celibacy. Furthermore, most Bauls would agree that renunciation is ideally taken as a couple with the purpose of pursuing their *sādhanā*. In fact, many severely criticize the practice of taking renunciation as an individual and would consider any individual alone as not a genuine Baul because of the centrality of *sādhanā*. Followers of Lalan (*lālan panthīs*) in Kusthia are adamant that an individual cannot take *bhek* alone. Nonetheless, despite the strong stance taken by many Bauls on this issue, there are individuals who take renunciation alone and who nonetheless consider themselves Bauls.[20] (I will return to the discussion of single Bauls and couples below.)

Regardless of whether it is a couple who have or an individual who has taken renunciation, their lives are not necessarily characterized as being uninvolved in the world. Madhabi's parents, who took renunciation when they were pregnant with their one child, maintain close contact with Madhabi and their grandchild. Madhabi did not take *bhek* until her own daughter was married and her future thereby taken care of because she considered that marriage to be her last major responsibility as a parent. This sentiment would be shared by most other renouncers as well: do not abandon familial responsibilities until they have all been met. Although Madhabi's child is now successfully married, Madhabi has by no means completely cut ties with her, or with her own parents for that matter. When I went with Madhabi to visit her parents, I saw a family who expressed great affection and care for one another. Madhabi and her parents are not unique in this regard; of the Baul renouncers I met in West Bengal and Bangladesh, most of them maintained at least some contact with family.

So why take *bhek* if it is not essential to the Baul path and does not indicate a radical departure from householder life? Bauls frequently explained that the reason one would take *bhek* is to loosen society's hold on them.[21] For some this was so that they could have more time for *sādhanā*; for others, it was to remarry (such as a woman to marry a second time) or to marry a person who others considered to be unsuitable. Similarly, Bauls also take *bhek* in order to gain the more respectable status of renouncer and the concomitant entitlement to seeking alms. Because it is usually couples who take renunciation, there is no shortage of women renouncers. Many women become Bauls and take *bhek* along with their husband, pursuing a spirituality that has its base in a variety of practices concerning the body, including sexo-yogic rituals. Other women, however, take *bhek* alone and sometimes despite their husband, providing themselves with sanction to move around unaccompanied and/or to collect alms. I would say that among Bauls *bhek* is *in part* a strategy of negotiating with societal expectations, and it is on this aspect of renunciation that I focus for the remainder of this chapter.

So much for the messiness of ideals. I now return to the lived experiences of Bauls I met.

Baul Women Renouncers and Their Position and Identity in Society

There are two circumstances in which a Baul woman might take renunciation: alone as a single woman (either separated, widowed, or unmarried) or with her husband. I did not run into any women who had taken renunciation while still living with their nonrenouncer husbands, and given the couple-oriented nature of Baul practice, it really would not make much sense for them to take *bhek* without their husbands. The stories of those women who had taken renunciation alone were much easier to collect in part because their circumstances as single women were unusual, and, as a result, these women often felt they had a story to tell. It is also with these single women that questions of renunciation were more likely to arise on my part, primarily because Baul couples who had taken renunciation often resembled non-renouncer Bauls, and thus I tended not to explore this aspect of their lives, whereas with single women I was searching for ways in which they manage their obviously challenging lives, and renunciation emerged as a strategy. It is because of my admittedly biased attention to single Baul women renouncers that I give them considerably more space below, though given the general lack of attention to such women I hope that my initially unchecked focus proves fruitful. It is therefore also not clear to me if renunciation is a more important transition for these single women than it is for women living with their husbands or if renunciation came up more in our conversations because I asked about it. Renunciation has significantly different meanings for married women and single women. However, in both cases, as will be shown below, renunciation can either enable a normal life or permit nonconformist behavior.

RE-CREATING RESPECTABILITY AS HUSBAND–WIFE BAUL RENOUNCERS

Although couple-oriented Baul renunciation challenges many orthodox expectations of renunciation and spiritual practice, Bauls nonetheless draw on ideals in order to create a meaningful life and garner respect in the communities in which they live. This is not to say that Bauls attain the same stature as bonafide *sannyāsīs*. If asked, most Hindus would likely agree that celibacy is a higher road to spiritual knowledge. However, Baul couples offer other things to their communities, such as music, advice, and, for those who are interested, knowledge of methods to prevent pregnancies even within healthy householder life (i.e., without practicing celibacy). In this section I discuss the ways in which Baul couples use renunciation to gain freedom and/or respect and how they attempt to maintain their good standing. What this section does not address—and this awaits another research project—is how the community of non-Bauls views and interprets the nonconformist householder/*sannyāsī* lives of Baul couples. That is, this section highlights Baul perspectives and actions, not the perspectives of their neighbors.

Many Baul renouncer couples, like Madhabi's parents, have followed traditional South Asian marriage patterns with arrangements made by parents. For them, renunciation occurs later as a choice made by the couple. For others, renunciation takes place at the time of marriage, sometimes between people whose marriage would not be sanctioned by their community and family. While Baul renunciation does not necessitate severing ties with one's past and family, Bauls sometimes use renunciation as a way to break with the past and begin anew. In fact, one reason renunciation appeals to some people is that it provides a way for a so-called unsuitable couple to break away from their community and family to live together.

This was the case between Jamal and Pushpa, whom my husband Ed and I met in Jhenaidah, a small town in the western part of Bangladesh, during the summer of 2000. Most of the story of their meeting was told by Jamal, though Pushpa wandered in frequently during breaks from cooking and cleaning to interject a few details. The story began when I asked Jamal when and how he became a Baul.

> JAMAL: In 1971. The time of the war. Then. And the woman, my *saṅginī*
>   [partner], she's a Hindu.
> ED: Oh. And you're a Muslim.
> J: I'm a Muslim man.
> LISA: How did the marriage happen?
> J: When we saw each other, there was love [*prem*].

As I mentioned in chapter 3, Jamal claims that Pushpa is his *saṅginī* and not his *strī*. He explained that *strī*, or wife, is a social category, existing in the mundane world, whereas he and his partner, being renouncers, reject (aspects of) this social world. Similarly, he asserts that Bauls do not have marriages, that too being a societal (*samājik*) matter.

During the Bangladesh Liberation War of 1971, the Pakistani army systematically tried to destroy opposition to their rule. Their primary targets were those perceived as constituting a threat to Islam, including the educated elite, Hindus, and marginal people, such as Bauls. Jamal's father, a conservative Muslim, was already angered by his son's interest in Bauls. When the war began, Jamal left home and hid out with the street sweepers who, though they were Hindus, provided too valuable a service to the Pakistanis to be under any significant threat. Furthermore, the sweepers were mostly outsiders, coming largely from Bihar and speaking mostly Hindi, so generally they were not considered as being involved in the war. Jamal stayed among the sweepers, learned Hindi, and pretended to be one of them in hopes of being overlooked by the army and its supporters (*rajakar*). This in itself was certainly an affront to his father, but after Jamal met and fell in love with Pushpa, a young Hindu woman from the sweeper caste, his father became furious.

JAMAL: There was no compatibility between my father and me! He used to really beat me.

LISA: But if she's a Hindu, then she could become a Muslim. But that didn't happen?

J: Yes. She became a Muslim.

ED: And still your father was angry?

J: Very.

L: So you got married without any support from your father?

E: Is that why you left home to marry?

J: Yes. It was a long time ago. I don't go near my father [anymore].

On another day, Jamal described the fights between him and his father, pulling off his shirt to reveal a four-inch scar from a knife wound. His father beat him several times, nearly killed him at least once, and Jamal also ended up spending time in jail (the exact reason for this was unclear) where he was further beaten. Becoming a Baul for Jamal was colored by personal and national struggles. Jamal said that after marriage "my father didn't give me any place in the family. I used to travel around and play *bāul-gān*. In 1983 when I had two kids, I had to get a job. I used to run around and sing songs. Now I don't do that any more. I sing for myself; I make up songs. When you travel around, make songs, make money, then it's your occupation" (*peśā*).

Since Jamal, raised in a middle-class Muslim home, and Pushpa, a poor Hindu sweeper, were not allowed by either family to marry, renunciation became a way for them to re-create their identities and live together. However, renunciation was by no means central to their beliefs and lifestyle; they currently live a sedentary life in a home with their sons. Although Jamal took a job tending the garden at a nearby jailhouse when they had children, one of his now grown sons has taken over that job. Jamal explained that having children was a deterrent to his spiritual pursuits and Baul lifestyle, as he and his partner were no longer free to move around but had to maintain a family. Since he stopped working, Jamal's personal income comes primarily from his disciples, and he spends most of his time in a small room built a few yards away from the main compound, where disciples and neighbors regularly visit. Now that their sons are grown, Jamal and Pushpa remain sedentary, even though their family obligations have been met.

Pushpa was reluctant to talk about her early life, but she was very clear that what she liked about being a Baul renouncer was the idea that everyone was equal: Hindu, Muslim, and Christian; husband and wife; high caste and low caste. These ideals are understood as all the more valuable given the circumstances in which Pushpa and Jamal met and married. However, even though Pushpa stated that it was equality among humans that she liked best about Baul philosophy and life, in my few days with the couple, I observed what appeared to be an unequal distribution of labor in the home. Pushpa cooked and cleaned from morning until dusk when we left, while Jamal sat either in the small room or under a cluster of nearby trees with his disciples and us asking questions. Even when I remained with Pushpa, sitting near her to ask questions, she never paused in her work. I did not stay with the couple long enough to make any definitive conclusions about this observation, but this distribution of labor is typical among Bauls, even those proclaiming the high status of women among them. Nonetheless, it should be kept in mind that a division of labor does not automatically imply inequality or women's subservience.[22]

Although the current lives of many Baul renouncer couples I met do not appear to differ significantly from other couples who also live sedentary lives and hold occupations, it is clear that renunciation for some couples is motivated by real concerns about their positions and options in society. Bauls who have gained a reputation in their village communities as renouncers are often afforded more freedom and respect, and this is particularly valuable considering that Bauls depend on those communities for their living and peaceful existence. Thus Jamal and Pushpa, after severing ties acrimoniously with their natal families, are able to live together and raise their family.

The reputation Baul renouncer couples may establish in their community evolves also from mutual exchanges. Bauls who have gained a positive reputation often have disciples who come to them for advice on matters of spiritual discipline and everyday life. Whenever Ed and I showed up at Jamal and Pushpa's home, they were flocked by disciples, and others from the community also visited Jamal for advice. Jamal and Pushpa are supported by their sons and by their disciples, but they gain those disciples because they have knowledge that is valued. Madhabi's parents, living quietly in their ashram, depend throughout the year on the alms they receive from their neighboring and nearby villagers. In return, her parents organize and offer an *utsab* (festival) once a year, feeding the entire village and performing *pūjā*. I attended a similar *utsab* at the ashram of Sanatan Das Baul in 1999. The amount of effort and expense involved was significant as a few hundred people showed up for the meal and the all-night Baul and *kīrtan* performance. If the turnout of such an event is any indication, I would say that these Bauls had gained the respect of the people of the village in which they live.

Respect is always dependent on behavior and needs to be maintained. If couples do not behave in ways that are perceived as right, then the respect and prestige of being a renouncer is lost. Although many factors come into play here, I am focusing primarily on the subject of Baul nonprocreative *sādhanā*—which is both linked and in opposition to *sannyāsī* ideas of asceticism and detachment. If one thing can be said to differentiate renouncers from nonrenouncers, it is the injunction for renouncer couples to abstain from having (any more) children. Being successful in *sādhanā*, with the necessary proof of not getting pregnant, not only gives one prestige in the community; it also is required in order to maintain one's place in the Baul community. When Madhabi's parents stated they took *bhek* after conceiving Madhabi, they spoke specifically of their need to demonstrate their seriousness in order to maintain their good standing within the Baul community. However, what initially surprised me is that despite efforts to keep rituals secret, it is well known that Bauls have methods for preventing pregnancy. The first time I became aware of this was when a Muslim rickshaw driver and I left the home of a young Baul couple. The rickshaw driver had been helping me locate Bauls early on in my research, and we often exchanged impressions after meeting with Bauls. This time he told me that he did not think the couple he had taken me to meet was really Baul. When I asked him for an explanation, he said that the young couple had a child, and Bauls are not supposed to have children. He and other non-Bauls I met also expressed an interest in learning from Bauls in order to stop having children. Since this rickshaw driver was the father of several children and was currently struggling to raise money for his daughter's dowry, avoiding further pregnancy was undoubtedly on the forefront of his mind. On the other hand, many Bauls, such as Madhabi's parents, expressed certainty that neighboring (non-Baul) villagers had no idea about the actual nature of their rituals.

Nonetheless, the majority of Baul renouncers I met, like Jamal and Pushpa, had children, and they all claimed, perhaps conveniently, that they took renunciation *after* having children. When such claims were made, others, however, sometimes contradicted them. This was common, but the most extreme case of this was between Jamal and Pushpa and another couple, Nur Ali and Rabeya, whom we visited on alternate days during our stay in Jhenaidah. Both couples dismissed the other as fakes, stating as proof the others' failure at *sādhanā* and resultant pregnancies. None of these supposed pregnancies came to term (except for the children Jamal and Pushpa claim they had before taking renunciation), but Nur Ali went as far as to say that Jamal has killed many thousands of seeds through inappropriate practice, for example, withdrawal and spilling of semen.[23] I cannot verify these claims about either couple, but what is evident here is the injunction against pregnancy while practicing *sādhanā* and the use of such "mistakes" to criticize Bauls.

Thus Baul couples must cultivate and maintain their reputation as Bauls, as renouncers, or as common villagers in order to be accepted in the community in which they live. While this may involve a careful balancing act on the part of the couple, it is doubly challenging for a single woman whose single status already suggests aberrant behavior.

STEPPING OUT ALONE

Taking renunciation in many South Asian traditions involves an individualized act of removing oneself from normative householder roles. A woman who takes this step typically goes against society's expectations of her by leaving behind traditional gender roles, particularly those of wife and mother. Women who take renunciation without a husband in an otherwise couple-oriented Baul tradition, however, are further challenged by the fact that they do not follow Baul expectations of ritual practice. The single Baul women renouncers with whom I spoke were very aware of these tensions, of the problem that the cloak of renunciation under which many of them were seeking protection did not provide them with the solace of spiritual development that comes from *yugal sādhanā*. Equally conscious of those tensions were women who blatantly rejected *yugal sādhanā* in favor of an independent life without a husband. This ambivalence about taking renunciation, which is shared by many Baul women and is reflected in their statements, concerns, and stories, is grounded in their gendered positionality: their positions both as Bengali women and as Baul women set them up as needing a husband. Even women who consider taking renunciation with their husbands may fear the repercussions of severing ties with their social roles as Bengali mothers and wives, and this is largely due to the potential of ending up alone, that is, without a husband and ritual partner. As one Baul woman, Nirmala, explained: "For an 'Indian' woman, the husband is everything." By extension, I suggest, so too is her position as a wife. Whether Baul women who take renunciation without a husband do so defiantly or ambivalently, the husband and her status as a wife factor in as major concerns.

In the sections that follow, I focus on several different women, starting with Kangalini Sufia, Rajani, and Madhabi, all of whom took renunciation after leaving their husbands. By drawing out the similarities and differences among these women, their concerns, and how they represent their lives, a portrait of Baul women who argue both for and against (sometimes simultaneously) renunciation emerges. Almost all of the women I discuss are ambivalent about taking renunciation without a husband. In this regard, Rajani is an exception, yet this is not a surprise given that she positions herself only marginally within the Baul world—and not at all in the couple-oriented tradition. I argue that women's decisions to take Baul renunciation are not so much a reflection of expectations from within the Baul community as they are considerations about these women's situation vis-à-vis the larger non-Baul society in which they live. Even with all the ways in which Baul renunciation is unconventional, renunciation for Baul women is still one of the most radical expressions of unencumbering.

(NOT) GRABBING HER HUSBAND'S FEET TO STAY

Single Baul women renouncers draw selectively on characteristics of both Baul renunciation and more conventional *sannyās*. They demonstrate the fluidity of these traditions as well as their own resourcefulness in drawing on traditions to craft a meaningful life. Madhabi, Kangalini, and Rajani all took *bhek* after their marriages were over and, in so doing, gained a certain degree of freedom, respect, entitlement to alms, and reason to be women alone. As Baul singers, they also gained an extra amount of economic independence. But their reasons for being alone are quite different, and as a result they position themselves differently within the Baul-householder-*sannyāsī* matrix.

Kangalini Sufia's story about taking renunciation is particularly interesting because of how she has navigated through many different situations and roles. She has, in a sense, tried it all: daughter, wife/daughter-in-law, single mother, and renouncer (with infant); single Baul and married Baul; Hindu and Muslim. Since her story has been told earlier, I will summarize only a few points here. Kangalini was born Hindu in Bangladesh. Her marriage was arranged when she was around age seven, and she had a daughter by that marriage. Her husband used to beat her and treat her poorly, so after much difficulty, she returned to her parents' home. After her father and brother were killed during the Bangladesh Liberation War of 1971 (because they were Hindus), her mother brought Kangalini and her infant to a Vaishnava *sannyāsī* who promised to take her in and give her instruction. In the care of this guru, Kangalini took *bhek*, probably around the age of 15. Later, she took a guru who instructed her in Tantric practices as well as songs. It is from him she says that she began learning Baul songs, and after leaving his care she took the path of a Baul. At some later point she became a Muslim and married a Baul.[24]

Although she is now one of the best-known Baul singers and songwriters in Bangladesh, clearly her decisions were strategies for dealing with being a young woman alone. As Kangalini claims, it is precisely because she is a woman that she became a Baul: "If I was a man, I would have stayed in their world. Whatever my family occupation [*jāti byabasā*], I would just have done that." Like with Madhabi, who also had to deal with being a young husbandless mother, taking *bhek* gave Kangalini's single status some legitimacy and entitled her to live from alms. But Kangalini was quick to explain that this was not enough: being a Hindu in Bangladesh was a source of difficulty, and hence she eventually became a Muslim, repositioning herself in what has increasingly become the normative religion of that nation.

Since Baul renunciation is couple-oriented, as is most of normative society in South Asia, single Baul women frequently bemoan the lack of a husband. This was certainly true of both Kangalini and Madhabi. As a young woman raised within the Baul path, Madhabi directed most of our conversations back to the absence of her husband, feeling that loss on several levels. Her parents expressed a particular concern about her lack of a partner for *sādhanā*, and as Bauls they all viewed taking *bhek* alone as problematic. Although I do not want to undermine Madhabi's commitment to the Baul path, it seemed she was equally concerned with how being single impacted her situation vis-à-vis the larger society. Drawing on the image of an individual *sannyāsī* through her clothing and behavior, she claimed that identity publicly in order to legitimize her status of being alone. But *bhek* did not enable her spiritual practice, and for that reason Madhabi feels doubly agitated by her current situation. Kangalini, however, took *bhek* as a way to further negate her already failed status as wife. That is, *bhek* was originally a solitary pursuit for Kangalini, with no ideological assumption that a partner was needed for spiritual reasons (though she never forgets that a partner is needed for societal reasons). Since she became a Baul some time after her marriage ended, and after having taken *bhek*, only later did Kangalini position herself within the couple-oriented tradition. That said, she now views herself as situated squarely in the Baul path, and her Baul identity is integral to who she is. In fact, her current identity as a married Baul supersedes that of renouncer, further emphasizing the importance of marriage to her.

In stark contrast to both Madhabi and Kangalini is Rajani, who embraces the role of a solitary *sannyāsinī* (or, to be more specific, *bairāgī*). An older woman living near Bolpur–Santiniketan, Rajani defiantly left her husband soon after marriage in order to devote herself to her religious pursuits, singing Vaishnava songs and reciting the name of Krishna. Reflecting the blurriness of boundaries among religious paths, Rajani casually positions herself within the Baul tradition through some songs and friendships. "Baul, Vaishnava, they're the same thing," she told me when I asked how she identified herself. Calling herself a Baul today is a reflection of both the ambiguity and the versatility of the term as well as her awareness that for some people in the Santiniketan area (including foreigners), being a Baul is more attractive than being a Vaishnava. I include her here not to argue that she should be included in discussions about Bauls, but because she—and her advice to another Baul woman—provides an interesting contrast to Kangalini and others. Her association with Bauls has occurred later in life (the ashram in which she currently lives with other single women is located near some Bauls she regularly visits), and she does not share the Baul reason for taking renunciation in order to focus on *yugal-sādhanā*, though clearly other single women also are not practicing *yugal-sādhanā*. Rajani's *sādhanā* is defiantly independent of her husband, and though she is aware of the injustices faced by women, she never in my presence claimed she needed a man for any purpose, ritual or otherwise.

Rajani and Kangalini took *bhek* after leaving their husbands, but their memories of why they left marriage are articulated quite differently: whereas Rajani deliberately left her husband in order to pursue her spiritual path, Kangalini left because her husband was abusive. It is likely because of these different reasons as well as the divergent directions their lives have taken—one living in an ashram and singing for alms, the other performing on big stages both in Bangladesh and abroad—that the stories they tell of their previous marriages demonstrate radically different ideas about appropriate wifely behavior and responsibility to one's husband. Rajani claims that she wanted an independent life all along and that she was frustrated that her husband prevented her from doing what she wanted to do. When she reflects on her married life, she talks about the longing she felt when she heard the songs of wandering mendicants and traveling performance troupes—especially those that sang *kirtān*. Since she had no children from her marriage, she was able to break ties with her husband, encourage her in-laws to find another wife for him, and then leave that life behind. In fact, she describes leaving her husband with some pride, demonstrating her defiance against the traditional wifely role given to her by exclaiming, with a gleam in her eye, that it was *she* who had left *him*.

In contrast, Kangalini is conflicted about what she should have done in her previous marriage. "Maybe I was at fault," she suggests; "Maybe I did something wrong. Now my husband is very reddish—like you. His skin was light skin. I was black. Maybe that was my fault. I was black."[25] In most versions of her life story, she claims that her husband died and that it was as a widow that she began her life as a Baul. This is the version she first told me as well, but during a much later interview she changed the story and said he is still alive and that she left him because he was extremely abusive. There is no defiance in her voice when she talks about how she left. She says she tried to stay, to do everything right as a wife, but that he continued to abuse her. In one interview, she claimed that if she had known then what she knows now, "I would've grabbed my husband's feet and stayed. Even getting beaten, I wouldn't have left his house. But then I didn't understand this! I didn't know." Kangalini, then, does not readily articulate defiance against the dependence of women on men and, indeed, at times states it is a woman's duty to fulfill such roles:

> In the Qur'an Sharif, there's a light. It is known that by serving the husband, [one] can get close to Allah and go to heaven. You have to take care of the husband: wash his feet; dress his hair; wipe his feet. Only loving him privately is not enough; you have to show how you love him. You have to give him all kinds of things. You have to give him whatever a woman has. Even if a husband beats her, you can't counter him. Wherever a husband puts his hand on a woman, that place is heaven. All this we [women in general] didn't understand before. If we understood this, I think that a lot of women would stick with their husbands no matter how they were abused.

Unlike Rajani, who rejected societal roles and expectations to find solitude and refuge in ascetic devotion, Kangalini is a public woman who has reason to be concerned about how others view her. Her life as she describes it is marked by struggles, and in her story she articulates numerous attempts to create a more positive identity and position in society. These attempts at negotiation did not only occur in the past, however; they continually occur as she tells and retells her story, sometimes refashioning her life to meet local ideals of virtuousness. For instance, she tells most people that she is a widow, even as problematic as that status is, instead of revealing that her husband was abusive and is still alive. Many Bangladeshis would agree with her view that a wife should remain with her husband no matter what. While it is very probable that such contradictions can coexist in the life of a woman whose path diverges from mainstream norms, Kangalini also modifies her views depending on her audience. The above statement concerning a woman's duty to her husband was made during my seventh visit with Kangalini, but it was the first time I appeared with a young Bangladeshi woman to assist me. Although previous conversations had also been scattered with statements in which it seemed that Kangalini supported traditionally accepted roles for women, in the presence of a foreign ethnographer she mainly highlighted her own ability to overcome obstacles. In this particular interview, Kangalini clearly echoed a common Hindu and Muslim belief that serving one's husband is the essential path to reach God. It seems unlikely that Kangalini actually agrees with this view, since so many of her own actions and circumstances demonstrate otherwise. Most obviously, though she says a woman should remain with even an abusive husband, she herself left her first marriage and has in fact left at least two other marriages. It is possible, however, that since she has become a Muslim and learned the rules of the Muslim society in which she lives, she is able to articulate those rules and expectations when she feels it may enhance her position or be appropriate. My assistant that day was unknown to her, but she was a young Muslim Bangladeshi woman, and it is likely that Kangalini was inclined to support traditional roles for the benefit of my assistant.

I have suggested that Kangalini verbally upholds normative roles even while subverting them in practice partly because she sometimes desires to put herself in a virtuous light. In her study of *sannyāsinī*s, Khandelwal suggests an additional reason why Kangalini may evoke normative roles. Khandelwal (1996:117) notes that female *sādhu*s usually discourage other women from renunciation in part because "it is contrary to the ideals of sannyasa to recruit followers" and also because *sannyāsinī*s tend to believe that people should experience family life before choosing renunciation. Khandelwal goes on to demonstrate that this is particularly true of *sannyāsinī*s for whom renunciation has involved many challenges. Although my unmarried assistant expressed no particular personal interest in the Baul path, it is likely that Kangalini feels it her duty to encourage women to follow a path that she herself did not. I believe that Kangalini's purported support of mainstream roles for women is in part due to her experience that taking the path of a Baul as a woman is extremely difficult. This is indeed evident in the sentiment expressed at the very beginning of our first interview: "My Baul life is a life of pain," as well as many other descriptions she gave of her life as a Baul. Although she has been very successful as a Baul singer, her statements suggest that she believes others may find it easier to remain traditional wives, even if married to a man who is abusive.

Regardless of what she says, it is clear that Kangalini did not grab onto her husband's feet and remain with him. Instead, she re-created herself several times, demonstrating her own capabilities and resourcefulness. Rajani, on the other hand, deliberately let go of her husband's feet (indeed it is hard to imagine she ever held on to them) in order to strike out on her solitary spiritual path. Both are capable and independent women; both are singing their hearts out. But while Kangalini seems reluctant to openly acknowledge that she, as a Baul woman, has actually managed fairly well without her first husband, Rajani expresses a very different view about marriage, as the following section demonstrates.

"WHAT WILL COME OF STAYING IN THIS HOUSE?" THE PULLS OF *MĀYĀ*

On one of the days that I went to see Rajani I arrived with a young Bengali Hindu woman, who assisted me with interviewing. There were two ashram residents (at the time I was there, only women were living in the ashram, except for the young son of one woman) who stood around talking with us, and during our conversation, Nirmala, a neighboring Baul woman, arrived and joined in. When Nirmala learned that my assistant, in her midtwenties, was still unmarried, Nirmala praised my assistant for not having met the difficult fate of marriage. Rajani and Nirmala agreed that "marriage is a hard life" and that once you have children, it is very difficult to become independent.

As the women debated whether or not it is possible for women to become independent, Rajani told my assistant: "It's possible to be free. If you pray to Him, if you like to be with Him, He will make you free." My assistant then asked, "That means you should not be involved in *māyā*?" To which Rajani responded: "You should not be involved in *māyā*." *Māyā* is generally used to denote the ties of family and friends, or the "web of attachments, affections, jealousies, and love that in Bengalis' eyes make up social relations" (Lamb 2000:28). Although Bengalis often refer to this web of *māyā* as the affection that develops between people, it is also seen as the cause of much suffering.[26] When Rajani tells my assistant to avoid *māyā*, she is advising her not to marry and have children. Although Rajani does not articulate that she should become a renouncer like herself, she does hint at the possibility through her suggestion that devotion to God would enable her to be free. In this way Rajani differs from both Kangalini and the *sannyāsinī*s discussed by Khandelwal. For Rajani, householder life is clearly the more difficult. When talking to someone who has a problematic marriage (Nirmala) or who expresses hesitation about embracing the institution (my assistant), Rajani sees little reason to discourage them from abandoning married life altogether. For Rajani, the solitary path is clearly the better one.

Rajani is following the footsteps not only of *sannyāsinī*s but also of some women *bhakta*s. While women can have *bhakti* to God while still married to a human husband, there are plenty of examples in which women's *bhakti* and marriage conflict. Mira Bai and Radha are two well-known examples. Mira Bai's story is of a woman whose *bhakti* to Krishna was so strong that it threatened her marriage and prevented her from fulfilling her duties in the house of her in-laws. For many, Mira Bai is an ideal model of the *bhakti* saint because her gender made her devotion all the more sincere and her effort to be with Krishna all the more dramatic. Nonetheless, as Lindsey Harlan (1995) shows in her work on Rajasthani Rajput women, while some women claim to admire Mira Bai for her religious devotion, they also criticize her for not following her duties as a wife and for "transgressing *pardā*" (purdah), demonstrating that this tension between marriage and devotion is never fully resolvable. Similarly, Radha's *bhakti* to Krishna causes her and the other *gopī*s to leave their home and husbands secretly in order to meet with their divine object of devotion. Radha and the *gopī*s remain married (Krishna left town, never to return), but it is clear that their hearts are with Krishna and not the household into which they had been married. Vaishnava Bauls often claim that the love Radha has for Krishna is the most ideal form of love and aspire to attaining this in their own couple-oriented *sādhanā*. Rajani, however, prefers to skip over *yugal sādhanā* in order to focus exclusively on her love for Krishna, following a solitary path of devotion.

Clearly Rajani's religious needs were not met inside the family household. For that reason, she emphasizes the binding nature of marriage and how rare it is to get a husband who allows one the freedom that she, my assistant, and Nirmala appear to desire. Furthermore, Rajani believes that having children further binds one to the net of *māyā*. Rajani was able to sever those ties because she did not have children and because she was able to satisfy her husband's need for a wife by encouraging him to be married again. These points come through in the following passage of conversation, starting with Nirmala's complaints about her marriage:

> NIRMALA: [The pain of a bad marriage] penetrates deep into the mind. Suppose you have lost your hand, will it grow again? A doctor could set it again, could put a plastic hand there, but can I use it like my own hand? No, I cannot. It's very difficult to wipe away a mark. No, it's impossible, impossible. My grandfather was a very learned man, very good man. In our childhood, we have heard Bhagabat, Ramayan, Mahabharata, Caitanya Caritamrita—everything! I studied a little. I understand all these things. Still I didn't find *ānanda* [happiness or bliss, in this case probably both spiritual bliss and marital happiness].
>
> RAJANI [to my assistant]: This net is very strong, daughter. One has to give Him [God] this soul. If someone else [husband, or a bad marriage] takes the soul away with him, there is nothing that can hold it back. For this reason I am running away [from worldly concerns]: one pulls me in this way, another pulls me in another way.
>
> N [INTERJECTING]: You cut all ties and left everything. I cannot go away like that. I do not have the courage. [Nirmala is married with four children.]
>
> R [indicating that this is in part what has held her back]: If I had a child, then I couldn't do it. He [husband] is someone's son. He came again and again to take me back, and again and again I sent him back [alone]. I told my mother-in-law to marry him off again. That would be good. Then he wouldn't come again, and I could say "*haribol*" [chant the name of Krishna (Hari)]. Yes, I am telling the truth. Everybody went to choose a wife for him. I [then] went to Brindaban;[27] from Brindaban I came here.

Rajani, who at our request had earlier sung a few songs, sang another one to illustrate her own *bhakti* and her decision to leave home. She accompanied herself with *kartāl*s (small cymbals) and sang with a voice slightly shaky with age, but her eyes emitted the strength behind many years of determination.

> I won't stay in my house, oh sweetheart.
> I'll leave saying Gauranga [Caitanya] and crying.
> Oh I won't stay at home anymore.
> Oh that eternal form of Gauranga is very beautiful.
> One can't keep it in one's vision.
> I won't stay at home anymore, sweetheart.
> Oh those smart clothes and young age.
> My heart's delight is Gaur.
> Young girls don't keep [unclear]
> Oh, I'll shout Gauranga and lift up my arms [in dance].
> And I won't stay at home anymore, oh sweetheart.

With a nod of her head as if to emphasize the instructional truth in the song, she concludes, "What will come of staying in this house? Day and night, this person says one thing and that person says another [i.e., they pull you in different directions]. I'll sit somewhere alone and chant Govinda's [Krishna's] name."

Nirmala, who had expressed a longing for the presumed freedom shared by my assistant and Rajani, both of whom live without husbands, on many occasions told me how fed up she was with her current situation. Her frequent complaints of ill health, unhappiness, and the status of Indian women merge with her complaints of living with a husband and sons who do not look after her. She claimed she wanted to leave home and be independent. She often said she was looking for a job, doing anything, she said, "Cooking, cleaning.... I can do everything," and she even offered her services to me. One day when Nirmala and I were taking a rickshaw to visit a nearby temple, she confided that if she could sing, she would surely leave. Then she would have a way to support herself and would not have to remain in misery at her home. But, she said, she cannot sing.

Despite her apparent desire to leave her unhappy situation, in actuality I saw little evidence that she ever seriously intended to leave. Several times she suggested taking me somewhere, offering her assistance and/or company. On some occasions I attempted to pursue her offers, and I even offered her some work as an assistant, which would involve short, or long, excursions. But despite her apparent eagerness to take these trips, she was able to follow through with only one of them; the other times, she begged off. As Rajani pointed out in the above conversation, "This net [of *māyā*] is very strong." Despite Nirmala's proclaimed interest in breaking ties and gaining independence (e.g., financial independence), what she really wanted was for her situation at home to improve: she wanted her sons and husband to look after her, to treat her with respect, to pay attention to her. Furthermore, I suspect that Nirmala really did not want to sacrifice the comforts to which she is accustomed or the proximity of even neglectful sons.

Evident in Nirmala's statement that she wished she could sing is the fact that singing is sometimes a ticket for women to gain some independence, and Madhabi, Rajani, and Kangalini are women who are able to survive financially on their own because of their ability to sing. Having the ability to draw an income is certainly a major step in achieving independence. But despite Nirmala's claims that she could possibly manage with other work, she instead hesitates repeatedly in achieving her proclaimed goal. Choosing to remain in her unhappy home, Nirmala demonstrates the binding nature of *māyā* about which Rajani cautions my assistant and which Rajani sees herself as successfully severing.

Clearly there are many reasons why a Baul woman might not want to take renunciation. Not only is the Baul path difficult, particularly when pursued by a single woman, but the ties of *māyā* bind one to a life cushioned by some degree of certainty about one's roles and expectations. Even if one is unhappy in one's domesticity, "staying in this house" constitutes a familiar world, and for that reason it may be hard to abandon.

In actuality, I only occasionally heard Bauls describe *māyā* as something that prevented them from taking renunciation. As the previous section demonstrated, Baul couples who renounce typically remain householders and maintain connections with family. Therefore, leaving family life in order to dispel the *māyā* associated with familial ties makes no sense to most Bauls, even if some complain that family life distracts them from their spiritual practices. Even single women Baul renouncers, like Madhabi, maintain close contact with children and parents. Thus *māyā*—if we understand this as the attachments that keep one involved in the world—itself is not really challenged by Baul renunciation. In Nirmala's case, however, the only reason for her to take renunciation would be to break away from her husband and family, and for this reason she feels the pulls of *māyā* keeping her in a familiar, though unhappy, home. As a Baul, she has little religious reason to leave. Perhaps that is also why she does not experience the intense pull felt by a small minority in society to take a solitary journey toward *moksha*. Her own complicated religious practices (*sādhanā* in which she no longer engages, possession by the goddess, and other domestic Hindu rituals) have long existed within her home. She does not need to leave the home like Rajani does in order to focus on her religious pursuits, and indeed she never claims that it is for religious reasons that she would consider leaving that home.

Given that Baul renunciation does not necessitate breaking ties with family and community, as it does in most other South Asian traditions, what then does it mean for a woman to take renunciation? I have suggested so far that Baul renunciation functions to unencumber single women in some positive ways, particularly by relinquishing—at least to some degree—the public need for a husband. In the process, women gain a reason to be alone, to travel outside the household, and to receive alms. For those with a good singing voice, they also gain extra income and opportunities to wander. Rajani, Kangalini, and Madhabi all share these benefits from their renunciation. But Rajani differs from the other women in one crucial regard: for her, a husband is an impediment to spiritual practice. Given that Baul renunciation is ideally couple-oriented, the feelings most Baul women have about taking *bhek* alone are clearly mixed, as we have seen. In the following section, I turn to Madhabi and Jaya, who also have mixed feelings about Baul renunciation, suggesting that their apprehensions help us understand other aspects of what it means for a woman to be a Baul renouncer—even for those who are married.

THE VALUE OF LIVING IN SOCIETY AND BEING A WIFE

The more time I spent with these women, the more evident it became that there is a significant tension between having—or wanting to have—a husband around and not. Baul renunciation poses particular challenges for women because a husband is needed both for religious as well as societal reasons. It is largely because of these challenges that Madhabi does not want her now married daughter to become a Baul and why Jaya, who introduced me to Madhabi, states she does not want to take *bhek*.

As mothers of daughters, Jaya and Madhabi feel their situation is especially precarious. When Jaya first suggested I talk to Madhabi, she described her as a *bairāgī* Baul who was having a very difficult time because her husband had abandoned her. As Madhabi's own story unfolded, she too articulated her husband as the source of her problems, and she was left with the responsibility of arranging for their daughter's marriage and dowry.

On the day that Madhabi took me to her parents' ashram, where I also met her daughter and son-in-law, we sat on a hill overlooking a pond. Her daughter was around 15 years old with long thick hair loosely draping down her shoulders and big doe-like eyes. Her responses to my questions were usually monosyllabic and uttered quietly, but Madhabi, who had wanted me to interview her daughter, would frequently instruct her in what to say or jump in with her own comments and clarifications. I learned very little about her daughter that day, but I learned quite a lot more about Madhabi. When I asked the daughter if she had learned Baul songs, her quiet "no" was followed by Madhabi's interjection that being a Baul is not such a good thing, suggesting that she had not wanted her daughter to be a Baul. Up to that point, Madhabi had in our interviews kept two discursive threads somewhat separate: she was miserable because she had a husband who was abusive, irresponsible, and selfish, and she found peace singing Baul songs. If there was any connection between the two, it seemed to me, it was that being a Baul and singing Baul songs had been a way for Madhabi to deal with her circumstances: singing both provided a small income and offered her some peace of mind. But usually she articulated a contrast between the peace (*śānti*) and happiness (*ānanda*) she gains from singing Baul songs, traveling around, and mixing with people and the *lack* of peace in her marriage: "This marriage has been really unpeaceful" (*aśānti*).

When I asked her daughter if she learned Baul songs, Madhabi revealed a causal relationship between these two threads: her own misery was in part due to being a Baul. That is, rather than emphasizing the peace that can come from the Baul path, she revealed that being a Baul can actually bring one misery because a Baul woman's husband may leave. Because of the precariousness of Baul marriages, Madhabi wanted to make sure her daughter would not become a Baul, and she tried to do this in at least three ways: First, she did not teach her daughter Baul songs but instead had her attend school. Although Madhabi's daughter was only in school up to grade five (at which point her marriage was arranged), she got the message that schooling and being a wife were more important than singing. This contrasts with Madhabi's own childhood, during which, in addition to receiving some schooling (also up to grade five), she enjoyed and participated in singing with her parents at home.

Second, Madhabi made sure that her daughter married a good man, and this was accomplished in part by providing a dowry and wedding ceremony. Madhabi's many articulated worries about getting her daughter properly married demonstrate her determination to make sure that her daughter does not have the kind of life she has had to lead. Thus Madhabi explained that her family sold part of the ashram land to pay for the dowry: "I gave 24,000 rupees. . . . I counted it and gave it to my daughter. On my daughter's ears, throat, wrists [ornaments]. . . . [And] I gave a wedding." As she describes it, her daughter's wedding included the services of a Brahmin priest and displayed an appropriate amount of fanfare, both being needed to demonstrate her family's commitment to their daughter and to provide some degree of insurance that the bride will be respected in her in-laws' home. Furthermore, bringing me, a foreigner with seemingly great prestige and power, to her parents' ashram and arranging for me to meet her daughter and son-in-law (and then asking me to interview her daughter) further enhanced her daughter's position. Although I had often felt like I had been "shown off" by my interviewees, I later realized that my presence was at least partly a substitute for her family's lack of other resources for providing gifts for the daughter. During the day I was there, Madhabi complained many times that she had nothing to give her daughter and that her daughter's father never gives anything—money, food, or gifts. Then, toward the end of our visit, Madhabi pulled me aside and asked if I could give her daughter some money for a sari. I had not gotten the hint embedded in her complaints about her own lack of financial resources.

The third way in which Madhabi has attempted to ensure that her daughter will not become a Baul is by not remarrying. Although she could draw on her freedom as a Baul to remarry, Madhabi instead emphasizes her position in the Hindu Bengali society and states that remarriage would look bad in the eyes of that society, negatively affecting her daughter and in-laws. So she claims: "I won't marry again. . . . I have a daughter, a son-in-law. It's a 'prestige' thing. In our society, two marriages are a matter of 'prestige.' *Badmāś*; they do that." When I mention to Madhabi in another interview that Bauls frequently do remarry, she agrees and tells me that those who do are *badmāś*. Madhabi cannot deny being in the Baul or Vaishnava path herself, and the marginality implicit in being in this path is further heightened because her husband has left her, leaving her alone and without the protection of a husband. But despite these factors, she still tries to demonstrate the many ways in which she has done the right thing as a Bengali woman. In addition to providing for her daughter's marriage, this means not remarrying. But it also includes taking *bhek*.

Madhabi took *bhek* in part because it served to legitimize her position of being alone, a decision motivated by her options within the larger Bengali society more than her options among Bauls. Baul remarriages are fairly common, and Madhabi would have had the support of her parents to have married again. Madhabi's parents emphasized their disappointment that their daughter lacked a partner for *sādhanā*, and, although they did not express it during our interview, I feel certain that they are concerned about her not having the protection of a husband. Furthermore, because her parents have some ashram property, they would probably rather Madhabi get a supportive and trustworthy spouse so that they could leave the property to both of them and not have to worry that her previous or a future husband might again abandon Madhabi and sell the property. Madhabi says she will get the property herself if she remains alone, but she doubts there will be anything left by the time her parents die. Since there are no young males contributing to the household, any difficulties her parents face, such as illness, will most likely have to be met by selling off remaining portions of the land. If Madhabi had a husband who was willing to help maintain the household, the two of them would probably be able to keep the ashram after her parents' deaths.

Thus there are many reasons why Madhabi could, as a Baul woman, remarry. I suggest then that Madhabi's decision to become a renouncer reflects her effort to create a meaningful life and future in light of the somewhat restricted pool of options available to her. As a young single Hindu woman abandoned by her husband who has since remarried, her identity is problematic.[28] A husband's abandonment or death is equally problematic, and Madhabi revealed a common perception, often attributed to Hindu widows, that her misery was likely her fault: "In a past life I did something," she says. After her husband left, her social identity as a wife was shattered, and she turned to her responsibilities as a mother to look after her daughter's well-being and marriage.

Rather than seeing *bhek* as a negation of her past identity, Madhabi uses that symbol for its agentive power to re-create herself and rebuild her status. Taking *bhek* not only legitimizes her single status in Hindu society, it also conveys the message to her son-in-law's family that she believes marriages to be final. What Madhabi will do when her daughter successfully bears a child—especially if it is a male child—remains to be seen. I speculate that once a child is born, Madhabi will feel her daughter's security is more assured, thereby freeing up Madhabi to make a different choice—possibly remarrying.

In introducing me to Madhabi, Jaya was trying to demonstrate that Baul women are vulnerable in ways that Baul men are not. Jaya knows that her husband could also leave her, and she is torn about the question of taking *bhek*. On the one hand, she says that she would like to take renunciation because she really wants to move to another level and learn more from her guru. She would also like to be able to sit among her guru and other *sannyāsī*s, sharing meals and conversation with them. Thus Jaya feels *bhek* is the logical next step on her path. But Jaya is also very concerned about her and her daughter's future. Having seen so many Baul men leave their wives and family, and knowing that her husband could easily do the same, Jaya has decided, for now, to remain in society with the hope that that will give her the protection she needs. So when I ask her if she wants to take renunciation, she explains: "I live here. I won't leave from here [community]. So I have to follow the community. I said one time that if [my husband] ever leaves me, then the community will look after me. My community will keep me safe/fine. But if I leave society now, if I go against society, then later it will be very difficult for me. Community is another level of existence. Whether we agree with it or not, I have to live in that society."

Jaya thus expresses a tension between being in society (*samāj*) and stepping out of society's realm of protection through renunciation. Her statements suggest that even as a Baul woman, she can maintain an image of living in society, cultivating the ties of *māyā* with her non-Baul neighbors. In fact, she and Madhabi both say that so long as they behave correctly, they will be viewed positively and receive protection. But Jaya also suggests that even the more ideal couple-oriented Baul renunciation may pose a risk to some women. While renunciation can help couples become more unencumbered in order to re-create their status and focus on *sādhanā*, being unencumbered might also remove women from the kinds of protection that neighbors are willing to give women who adhere to normative marriage life. On the other hand, for a woman abandoned by her husband, like Madhabi, renunciation provides a semblance of normalcy to her obviously aberrant position as a young single mother in rural Bengal. Given that the wandering and singing Jaya and Madhabi do not represent normative roles for women, it is notable that in their daily lives they position themselves within the comparatively more conventional roles of respectable wife or ascetic *sannyāsinī*. In so doing, they draw on their capacity to act while trying to ensure that society will protect them even as they create a different path for themselves.

"BACK THEN I HAD NO SENSE": SEVERING TIES AS A *PĀGAL*

Unlike Jaya, who views renunciation as potentially threatening to her role as wife and mother, other women, such as Rajani (discussed above) and Nur Jahan (discussed here), are eager to sever ties with the mundane world and would happily abandon conjugal life.[29] In their efforts to live a religious life, they show that for some women, marriage and religiosity are not compatible. But while Rajani is able to turn to the *sannyāsī* tradition as a way out of her socially prescribed role of wife, Nur Jahan draws, ultimately with less success, on other options for evading the mundane world of marriage.

Nur Jahan is a Muslim Baul woman I met in Sylhet in 1999. Although she did not take formal renunciation, her story is relevant here because she did leave society in a similar way. As a Muslim woman, the institution of renunciation, more readily associated with Hindu traditions, is not really an option for her. Some Muslim Bauls do take *khilāphat*, particularly in western Bangladesh (as we saw with Jamal and Pushpa), but Nur Jahan's association with those Bauls appears to be negligible. Although Rajani met familial resistance when she left conjugal life, there was an established institution of renunciation that she could join and that, as a Vaishnava, she would have been familiar with. Nur Jahan, however, probably did not consider taking some formal renunciation largely because her day-to-day experiences would not have presented her with the option: the Bauls in Bangladesh who take *khilāphat* are not in her circle of contacts. Sufis, with whom she had contact, do take renunciation, but due to the Muslim emphasis on marriage and family life, this renunciation rarely includes abandoning conjugal life. I have often heard it said that when a Muslim saint, *pīr*, or mystic remains unmarried long past the typical marriage age that he has merely not yet found the right partner. Munibor, the unmarried Baul singer and hafiz who introduced me to Nur Jahan, explained that Shah Jalal,[30] the Muslim saint for whom the main *māzār* of Sylhet town is dedicated, had intended to marry but died unmarried at an old age because he had not found the right woman. I heard the same explanation given for Munibor, who was in his mid-40s when I met him.

Although I do not have comparable examples of single women in Bangladesh being excused from marriage because "they have not found the right partner yet," Nur Jahan provides an example of someone who tried to remain single. Her attempts, in this case largely unsuccessful, are not without precedence in the Sufi world. Indeed, one of the major early influences of Sufism, Rabi'a of Basra (d. 801), refused to be married. Margaret Smith explains that "like her Christian sisters in the life of sanctity, Rabi'a espoused a heavenly Bridegroom and turned her back on earthly marriage even with one of her own intimates and companions on the Way" (1984[1928]:13). Rabi'a is said to have rebuked several marriage proposals, claiming in response to one of them that "renunciation of this world means peace, while desire for it brings sorrow.... God can give me all you offer and even double it. It does not please me to be distracted from Him for a single moment" (11, quoting Munawi).

Nur Jahan's desire to remain single did not have the effect that it did for Rabi'a, whose historical renderings describe her as spiritually advanced, very influential, and worthy of great respect. It is likely that life circumstances and social pressure did not give Nur Jahan the option of merely refusing marriage in favor of a life devoted to God. I argue that instead of taking renunciation or *khilāphat*, Nur Jahan draws on the Islamic notion of *majzub* or the Bengali *pāgal*. As her stories below demonstrate, she clearly sees herself as wanting to abandon her societal roles and responsibilities, particularly those related to being a woman, in order to pursue spiritual goals, and these desires are similar to many of the stated desires of people who do take renunciation.

Nur Jahan's life story, as she told it one afternoon, is full of tensions between different ideals and expectations. On the one hand, she claims to want only to sing her devotion to Allah; on the other hand, she feels pulled to live in the mundane world, to act in ways appropriate to a Muslim woman. She refuses to get married; and then she does get married, reportedly under duress. She wants to be close to Allah, feeling no gender distinction in her role as devotee, yet she also wants to be a good woman and recognizes that this desire pulls her away from her chosen expression of devotion. In her life story, Nur Jahan never seems to find a balance between the different pulls she experiences but, rather, goes from one extreme to another, trying in turn to fulfill her own longing and the expectations she thinks others have of her.

It is telling that the story she told me was focused on her youth, the years between age nine and her midtwenties, when she was most consumed by her devotion to Allah—30 to 40 years ago. Yet, though she focused mostly on those early years, she claimed not to remember them or at least not sections of them. It seems as though her claims of not remembering somehow distance her from assuming responsibility for those actions. As she says, she was *pāgal* at that time.[31] After stating her place of birth (near Dhaka) and father's name, she begins:

> People say when I was 9 or 10 years old, I was of a different kind. I did not learn my lessons. I used to live an abnormal life. For instance, I went down into the water even in the winter. While I was staying in that cold water, my parents sat beside the pond for the whole night. How much difficulties they endured for me! Then they decided to keep me in chains. Many years passed like this.

Nur Jahan explained that her condition became a special matter of honor for her parents when it was time for her two younger sisters to be married. Although she was supposed to get married before her younger sisters, she had no interest in "living in this world." She added, "The village council [*pañcāyet*] talked to my father seven times: 'Our village's reputation is ruined by your daughter. She visits *māzār*s improperly,' they said....Many religious healers came for my treatment. I beat them, and they went away. They went away with dishonor." For several years in her youth, Nur Jahan stayed in *māzār*s, dressing and behaving as a *pāgal* and singing what she calls Baul songs.

> I stayed in the shrine of Shah Ali Baghdadi for about three-and-a-half years. This is in Mirpur. There was a flower tree, but it wasn't alive. In the daytime I stayed under the tree and in the nights in water. Those who saw me [at that time] now say that I used to beg from them. That is, when I was hungry, I asked for food. I was not the least interested in worldly affairs. I visited three hundred and sixty shrines in Bangladesh. I also visited the *māzār*s of one hundred and twenty thousands of saints, situated in Sonargoan. Seventeen other *pāgal* people [traveled] with me also. The shrine of one of them is now situated in Ghorashal. He was called "Lengta Pagal" [naked madman]. If he kicked a dead cow, it would stand up. We threatened him: "If you do these things again, we will not take you with us." A machete was always with me. I used to cover my body with a black cloth except for the face. I did not wear any ornament on my nose.
>
> Persons who went with me were all educated. They studied up to the master's level. Only I was uneducated. I had spiritual knowledge. When I was mad, I always sang. I like to sing very much.
>
> I had matted hair. This is now at the *māzār* in Azimpur. The *māzār* is situated near the second gate. It is called "Telsha Baba's Mazar." He was a madman. He was called by that name because oil always trickled down his head. One day he shouted to me: "You crazy woman! I want your matted hair!" Then my [fictive] mother told him "On my order, I have some prayers to do. After [my prayers] you will cut her matted hair off." Telsha Baba cut off my matted hair and shaved my head. He called other people and prayed for the salvation of the [departed] hair before the burial of that hair. They kept the hair with attar. I just saw what they did, but could not speak. They buried the hair at the *māzār*.

Although Nur Jahan suggested in the beginning that she did not remember much from the time she was *pāgal*, in actuality her story is rich with details about her travels, her companions, and her state of mind. What becomes evident in her descriptions is the common polarity of mundane and profane, of "worldly affairs" (*duniyadari*) and "worshipping/singing praises" (*bandigiri*). She was not interested in marriage or material well-being; instead, her "only practice" (*sādhanā*) was focused on "how to get God." Although there is the risk of overemphasizing the polarity of mundane and profane, often superimposed on cultural phenomenon without attention to variations and the significant ways in which worldly affairs and religiosity meld, what is noteworthy here is that Nur Jahan repeatedly stressed a conflict between these two paths and that she believes that one poses a challenge to the other. First of all, she originally rejected marriage in favor of a life committed to God. She was able to do this as long as she was perceived of as being *pāgal*; in that state, most men would not want her. Her appearance during that time, as she describes it, was certainly not inviting: she had matted hair, carried a machete, and wore dirty black clothes with no jewelry. Furthermore, she claims that she was able to forget about her own gender: "I lived a different life in my youth. I could not believe that I am a woman. When I stayed with men, I thought that I was a man too. Now I understand everything: good and bad, vice and virtue." These social distinctions were not as important in her previous *pāgal* state, living with other *pāgal*s. She was outside the rules, roles, and judgment of society. As is emphasized by many Sufis, in one's devotion to Allah, gender does not matter. However, Nur Jahan says that after she cleaned up (which she did with the help of a woman who used to visit her in the *māzār*s), she was forced to marry and that it became impossible to carry on as she had without a man. Participating in the world, she recognized the social constructions of good and bad, as she says, and realized her gendered role as a woman.

Having to turn her attention to worldly concerns, such as marriage, has caused her much unhappiness.

> I am a very unhappy person, you know. I got married, but not at my will. No, I had no desire [to get married]. People wanted to marry me. Then I had to surrender myself. It was a matter of honor. I was married at the age of twenty-five or thirty. People became crazy seeing me. So I was to be married. Can you get my point? My only desire was to get Allah through songs or music, reciting the name of Him, or through prayers, whatever. This was my only wish, to get Him.

She showed us the scars from being forced at knifepoint to "marry" a man who desired her. She bore him two sons but says she eventually left him because he refused to let her sing. Her current husband also tries to forbid her from singing, and she is ambivalent and worried about her ability to remain in this marriage and in this mundane world.

Now if I go back to that state of mind—pray/worship, only meditate on Allah and not think of anything else in this world—then I'll go back to being fully absorbed. Then I'll not be able to do anything [else]. That's why I am always keeping my mind on worldly affairs. If my mind goes back to that stage, I will not be normal.

Nur Jahan paused, and in a tone of resignation, concluded our interview:

I told you about my [fictive] mother.[32] She died and was buried in Azimpur [Dhaka]....She looked after me. She endured many difficulties for me. Sometimes she gave me food, but I refused to take [it]. I threw the food out. But she never beat me. She tried to make me understand. She did up my hair. She helped me in wearing saris also. She kept me inside the house. She did not let me out. Sometimes she told me to look at the mirror: "See how beautiful you are looking?" She wanted to arrange my marriage, but I replied: "I don't know what a marriage is. I don't want to know either." Now I am living a life similar to others. It came from Allah, so I don't blame others for this. Everything comes from Him. Nothing happens without His order. Isn't it?

As is particularly clear in the last few passages of our interview, Nur Jahan's story reveals multiple pulls between living a married life and worshipping God. Nur Jahan never fully reconciles these pulls. As she concluded our interview, Nur Jahan said that if she returned to her worship of Allah she would no longer be able to remain involved with worldly affairs. Her repeated emphasis on her longing to sing and to worship made me think that this was really a temptation, born at least partly out of her current dissatisfaction. However, she claimed that even this married life came from Allah. Though her life story reveals regret about her current situation, she emphasized that neither she nor the woman who helped her clean up to the point at which marriage became an option—or a necessity—were ultimately responsible for where she is today.

Nur Jahan clearly links her worship of God with losing her ability to stay engaged in the world, and reflecting back on the time in her youth when she was most immersed in worship, she calls herself *pāgal*. The Baul association with *pāgal* has been discussed before (see chapter 2), but a more nuanced elaboration is needed here in order to understand the myriad meanings and functions of *pāgal* in the case of Nur Jahan. Depending on the context and intention of the speaker, *pāgal* can be used both to dismiss and legitimize an individual. The few men who reluctantly introduced me to Nur Jahan told me she was a real Baul, and they appeared to have some respect for her. Munibor, whose fictive uncle's house my husband and I stayed in for three weeks, had agreed to help me find Baul women and eventually introduced me to Nur Jahan. We spent hours and days engaged in lively and interesting conversation with Munibor, during which time he occasionally discussed Baul women (and his views on women more generally), but he was extremely hesitant about actually introducing me to any. He and many other men I met in Sylhet were keenly worried about me spending time with Nur Jahan and other Baul women, whom they found problematic even if they considered them sincere in their spiritual endeavors.

When I finally had the chance to meet Nur Jahan, Munibor sent along Kasem, a neighboring friend who had been visiting regularly. Kasem sat with me and Ed while I interviewed Nur Jahan and a few times added questions for clarification. Looking back at the transcript of the taped interview, I found those few questions or statements to be very revealing of how he wanted us to understand Nur Jahan. The first interjection came soon after Nur Jahan began her story, describing, as quoted above, her behavior while living with her parents: staying for hours in the water, being chained to keep her in the house. Kasem then offered: "That is, you were *pāgal* then?" to which she responded "Yes, I was *pāgal*." Later in the interview, when Nur Jahan described how much she loved singing and how she received great happiness from it, Kasem interjected: "This means you love Baul songs very much," clarifying, presumably for our benefit, that the songs she had been singing were Baul songs. The third[33] time I heard him say something was to tell us that she has written several songs of her own. By identifying her as *pāgal*, her songs as Baul, and informing us that she had composed songs, Kasem was separating her from ordinary Muslim women, many of whom he and Munibor believed had questionable morals, and raising her status by emphasizing her spiritual and musical difference and competence.

I believe one way to understand the significance of her *pāgal* behavior and how her status might be raised through these identifications is by considering *majzub*, a concept widespread in the Sufi world, though generally not accepted or viewed positively by more orthodox Muslims. Although I do not recall[34] this term used in my presence to describe Bauls, Nur Jahan's description of her behavior most closely resembles that of a *majzub*, someone who has renounced society and worldly involvement by virtue of being an ecstatic. That is, a *majzub*, like Nur Jahan in her early days, does not know how to live in the world. Why a person so addressed is not merely considered mentally incompetent has to do with local interpretations of ecstatic devotion or divine possession (Frembgen 1998). Instead of seeing madness as a medical condition, it is understood as reflecting a close vicinity to God. "The *majzub* is one whose speech and actions appear to lack sense because his or her mind has been 'burned' by the closeness to God" (Ewing 1998:160). Furthermore, the *majzub* is "a 'wise fool' . . . considered exempted from following the religious law by God himself" (Frembgen 1998:144). She or he may be actively worshipping God as well, or it may be others who interpret a *majzub* as being spiritually gifted or acting religiously; often a person called *majzub* by one person is dismissed as mentally crazy by another person. The Bengali use of *pāgal* may also have this divine association, as seen when Bauls are described as being *pāgal* with love for the Divine, but it also can be used to degrade and dismiss someone, as seen in James Wilce's discussion (1998) of efforts by conservative Muslims to restrain an old man who preferred to sing aloud about his love for Allah.

In this case, I think that Kasem's use of the word *pāgal* in describing Nur Jahan reflects this localized interpretation of being "burned" by the closeness to God, as is perhaps more clearly recognized in the term *majzub*. That Kasem regards Nur Jahan's past *pāgal* behavior as suggesting closeness to God is supported by his earlier identification of her as a Baul, a term he used also for his close friend Munibor. Unlike most Bauls I met in Sylhet, Munibor is highly educated, intelligent, and charismatic. He is also the *ustād* or teacher of several students, and many come to listen to him tell moralistic and entertaining stories or to discuss the Qur'an and spiritual practices. In contrast, Nur Jahan is not educated, a point she repeated several times, indicating to me that it embarrasses her. Although Munibor and Kasem expressly stated they were ashamed and disgusted by the lack of education of many Bangladeshis, particularly Baul women, they appeared to make an exception in Nur Jahan's case. Furthermore, Nur Jahan is clearly a gifted singer. When I heard her sing, which she did when her husband was not around, I felt her deep and soulful voice filling the room with her intense sincerity, silencing those in its path. It seemed that Nur Jahan's ability to sing well and to compose her own songs as well as her *pāgal* behavior, if interpreted as reflecting closeness to God, served as grounds to grant her some respect by these scrutinizing men. Kasem and Munibor were not dismissing Nur Jahan by calling her *pāgal*; they were giving her a legitimate and, I believe, honorable excuse for her many years of living unmarried at *mazārs* and singing praises to Allah.

The concept of *majzub* also sheds light on Nur Jahan's attempt to renounce society. Unlike her Vaishnava Baul counterparts, Nur Jahan did not have an institution of renunciation to go to where she could delve unhindered into her spiritual world. She did, however, have the cultural constructions of *majzub*, shared by the Bengali *pāgal*, which offered her some insulation from worldly concerns. As Nur Jahan emphasized, "Yes, I am *pāgal*. But *pāgal* about singing. I am telling you the truth. I don't know what other singers do. My only practice was to worship God. I always tried [to figure out], how could I get Allah? I tried to do the things that would enable me to get Him."

Implicit in the concept of *majzub* and *pāgal* is the perspective that it is a condition not chosen by the individual as much as received spontaneously. While divine ecstasy reflects an embodied expression of all-consuming devotion that may arise from repeated acts of devotion, "*majzub* means a person being in a permanent state of ecstasy and divine emotion, in most cases enraptured since birth, but sometimes in response to dramatic visions or far-reaching experiences of the soul" (Frembgen 1998:145). Given that Nur Jahan claims she was a *pāgal* and does not remember much from her past, it may be difficult to conclude how much agency she had, especially if one is inclined to view her previous state as a medical condition. It might be tempting to see her madness as a desperate response to a constricting environment—one in which she, with her carefree and devotional spirit, did not fit. Nonetheless, even though Nur Jahan highlights those portions of her past life when she was wandering and singing, she presents her current state as one in which she consciously and actively engages in the maintenance of her feminine modesty and wifely propriety. Moreover, she interprets this current worldly life as being in accord with God's will, imbuing her daily acts with a different expression of surrender to God. Saba Mahmood makes a compelling argument that among the women in the mosque movement she studied in Egypt, ritualized behavior like veiling, praying, and crying during prayer were "understood to be disciplinary practices through which pious dispositions are formed, rather than symbolic acts that have no relationship to pragmatic or utilitarian activity" (2005:128). I would not go so far to suggest that Nur Jahan's displays of feminine modesty and wifely discipline are the same kinds of constructive and agentive projects performed by the mosque women. After all, she appears quite ambivalent about married and worldly life, even if she attributes it to God. Yet because she remains tempted by a *pāgal* life, she presents herself as having a choice to remain in her current situation. Thus, in contrast to the idea that a *majzub* is someone whose condition is involuntary, Nur Jahan claims she resists returning to a *pāgal* state. I suspect, then, that she does gain something from her current situation, perhaps the security of having a husband and some financial stability and perhaps also the recognition that she is conforming to what is locally considered to be Islamic feminine ideals.

Conclusion

Although many Bengalis connect Baul renunciation with *sannyāsī*s who relinquish ties with society in order to focus on *moksha*, I suggest that Baul renunciation actually has more to do with society than it does with goals on the Baul path. There is no essential reason intrinsic to the path of Bauls to take renunciation: it is not a requirement or an established step on the path, and as I discussed, renunciation does not necessarily indicate a dramatic transformation from householder status to ascetic, as is encouraged by many other renouncer traditions.

However, renunciation can be an important way to negotiate one's position in society, and I argue it is in this light that we need to understand these Baul women. Being a Baul woman is in itself a challenge to traditional roles for women, as I have shown. Renunciation further challenges their gendered role— not so much because their life circumstances change but because other people's perception of them does. But it is also this change in perception that entices some single women to take renunciation. As renouncers they are no longer viewed merely as unmarried women, widows, or wives abandoned by husbands but as women single-mindedly pursuing a religious path. Significantly, renunciation can serve as a way to provide these women with some semblance of normalcy (through the association with *sannyāsī* traditions) while at the same time enabling nonconformist behavior. This applies to Baul couples too, as they may also gain a cover of legitimacy that allows, for instance, an unsuitable couple to live together.

In reconfiguring their lives publicly and privately, Baul women draw selectively on aspects of both Baul renunciation and single-oriented *sannyās*. Here we see the differences between West Bengal and Bangladesh coming to the fore. In predominantly Hindu West Bengal, the various forms of *sannyās* color the imagination, pointing the way to different possibilities for pursuing an unencumbered life. But in Bangladesh, where Islam has increasingly become the norm, *sannyās* is marginalized if not nonexistent. For this reason, we see Kangalini's movement through different possibilities—from *sannyāsinī* to single Baul to married Baul—as a mirror reflecting the changing face of Bangladesh as it has moved from being tolerant of religious diversity to becoming a stricter Islamic nation. It is in the position of married Baul that Kangalini is finally happy (or perhaps as much as she can be, given the significant challenges that remain on her path). Kangalini is happy partly because her own preference for married life over celibacy is shared by Islam, and within that normative expectation, the couple-oriented Baul tradition has some small place. But this Islamic preference for marriage is also the root of Nur Jahan's troubles. One could imagine her preferring a life like Rajani—with no husband to keep her from singing about the Divine. But in the conservative region of Sylhet where Nur Jahan was living when I met her, such a path was available only to those playing the difficult role of the *pāgal*. This is not much of an option for someone who wants to keep at least one foot in society.

To return to the question of what these women are actually renouncing when they take this step alone or with a partner, I suggest that they are not renouncing society at all but, rather, society's expectations of them. As *bhek-dhārīs*, *sannyāsīs*, or *pāgals*, they have created for themselves a space in which they can choose how involved they will be with their family and community. For most of the women I interviewed, renunciation did not precipitate the severing of social ties but did provide an excuse for evading societal roles and expectations, and as single women alone they were then able to pursue their musical and/or spiritual path. Thus not only do they gain a certain amount of legitimacy for otherwise nonconformist behavior, but they also loosen society's claim on them, becoming more unencumbered in the process.

Concluding Thoughts

"Bauls Can Live Anywhere They Want!"

"How can I be a Baul when I have a roof over my head, a family...when I have all this?" It was Phulmala who said this to me when I met her in 2000. This sentiment was expressed by many women I met and reflects the encumbered nature of family life and the different pulls of responsibilities and of spiritual work. Although Phulmala may be saying that she has conformed to some aspects of society by raising a family and keeping a home, she is not in fact suggesting that being a Baul necessitates relinquishing societal roles and obligations to go live under a tree. Rather, she is emphasizing the challenges that living in the world pose to spiritual realizations. It is difficult to find time to focus on spiritual matters when there are children running through the house and when there is food to cook or money to earn. She is also alluding to the ineffability of being *bāul* and the difficulty of measuring progress on the path. To claim to have succeeded in becoming a Baul—or to being carefree—is to claim to have attained the spiritual realizations sought by those on the path. Most would not claim that success about themselves, no matter where they are on their journey.

In 2007, when I returned to Birbhum, Rina seemed to answer Phulmala's rhetorical question above. "Bauls can live anywhere they want!" she said. I had been summarizing some of my chapters to Rina, and she responded at length to the *bhadralok* claim that real Bauls live under trees (discussed in chapter 2). She immediately replied: "Do you think that if we live under trees we'll have time for *sādhanā*?! No, we'll be too busy trying to find our next meal." She tried to remember the lines of a song she had heard and paraphrased it as follows: "Live in a house, eat rice; live under a tree, eat fruit. But both must eat. Where's the difference?" She continued, "I've thought long and hard about this, and I think that there is no difference. We can do *sādhanā* in the house; we can do it under the tree. It can be done in a cave. Anywhere. But *sādhanā* can be done [regardless]. One can be a Baul while living in the household. One doesn't need to leave the house to be a Baul. Actually, I think it might be easier to do it in the house because under a tree there would be all sorts of interruptions!"

Although being unencumbered may help on the Baul path, Bauls I met are certainly not ascetics, and they never claimed that a life of denial will lead them to spiritual realizations. Having a family and house are not in themselves impediments to being a Baul. By 2007 Phulmala had left that house and family but not because she was trying to become more of a Baul. In fact, now that Phulmala has left her house and family, she appears even more preoccupied by the very worldly concerns of poor health and separation from her household. Phulmala sees herself as separating from the householder stage, but that separation is by no means complete, which is sometimes true of renouncers as well.[1] Like many of the Baul women in these pages, Rina also has had to juggle family, singing, and finding time for *sādhanā*. But how they juggle reflects not their failures in being Baul, but the diversity of the Baul path.

An underlying assumption of this book is that that there is no clear definition of *bāul*. The diverse women included in these pages should make that obvious. Although being a Baul may be characterized by adherence to the practices of singing and sexo-yogic rituals as well as the belief that all humans are to be respected, I believe that those are variables that different Bauls draw upon differently. The most common thread I found among the diverse Baul women I met was that being a Baul suggests nonconformity. Bauls position themselves in opposition to many dominant structures and ideologies—Brahminical religiosity and hierarchy, orthodox/prax Hindus and Muslims, ideologies that justify the discrimination of women and low castes—in short, pretty much any ideology or practice that divides human beings. But their nonconformity is not merely a reaction with little or no substance; Bauls create something different—"an anti-identity identity," to quote Openshaw 2002:244. Yet in terms of the overall context, that "anti-identity" remains necessarily and successfully diverse.

Jeanne Openshaw (2002) and Hugh Urban (1999) argue that the concept of *bāul* as a religious group is a recent construction, born amid the different fundamentalist and nationalist agendas that have condemned and praised this group for its practices and beliefs. I believe that if we look at the broader region of Bengal and include women in our study, we will observe that the fluidity and unboundedness of the term *bāul* persists despite tendencies to claim that Bauls form a distinct religious group. In fact, I suspect that this broader perspective of what *bāul* means is more akin to how the term was used before *bhadralok* became fascinated with Bauls. Even though I have used Baul as a noun, I often heard it used by those I knew as an adjective to describe their madness, their inability or unwillingness to conform, or a goal they had not yet reached (like Phulmala above).

The unboundedness of this term became most evident in my research in Sylhet, where clearly it does not imply a singular religious identity. Being a Baul or *bāul* in Sylhet suggests in rather broad terms nonconformity to normative society and orthodox Islam, particularly through emphasizing mystical approaches to worship and using music as a mode of religious expression. There is clearly some overlap here with Sufis, but those called Bauls are even more marginal and intentionally position themselves in opposition to norms. Two women in Sylhet singing the very same songs may not both call themselves Bauls, but the one who does makes particular claims about her marginality, usually also affirming a critique of societal norms. Furthermore, those claims may be very different from the claims made by women who identify themselves as Bauls in Birbhum or in Jhenaidah, where being a Baul is more connected to antisectarianism, egalitarianism, or sexo-yogic rituals. In whatever location, those called *bāul* are at the margins of society, ignoring some societal norms in their everyday lives while blatantly critiquing others.

Listening to Baul women in these diverse contexts not only necessitates an expansion of our scholarly understanding of what it means to be a Baul; it also shows that portraying oneself as a Baul is a public statement with real effects—positive and negative—on one's own position and status in society. Because Baul women are doubly marginalized, they frequently orient themselves toward normative society. The question for many of these women is how to live their lives as Bauls (in whatever way that means for them) given that the broader Bengali society has very different ideas about appropriate behaviors and beliefs. Women's participation as Bauls expands the concept not because there have not been women Bauls before (there have been plenty), but because Baul women have their particular concerns and agendas that get articulated through their practices of singing, raising families, taking renunciation, or wandering. Thus being Baul may include accepting being encumbered in a variety of ways. It may also include becoming single women renouncers within an otherwise couple-oriented tradition.

Attending to women's perspectives as they navigate expectations of them, Baul women emerge as actors in a "serious game" (Ortner 2006) of negotiating status, and in the process they reconfigure not only what it means to be Bauls but also what it means to be women in Bengal. However, it is critical that we understand how Baul women view their own agency, the limits of their agentive power, and what makes their lives meaningful. If we were to look only for the ways in which they challenge or resist norms, we would miss instances where norms are used to their benefit.

I began this book with an anecdote that illustrated the resistance of one woman against the structures that threatened to curtail her writing of songs, but I cautioned that not all women in this book are engaged in resisting societal structures, even ones they criticize. It seems that we should loosen the hold that the binary opposition of subservience/resistance has on our imagination, and not just to avoid the "romance of resistance" (Abu-Lughod 1990). Viewing all acts by women as either conforming to or subverting patriarchy may be valuable for its activist potential and for learning how to recognize subtle forms of individual power, but it is also overly simplistic, as it may miss other important projects that particular women may be invested in. There are multiple agendas held by single individuals and multiple motivations behind single actions.

Despite feminist temptations to conclude otherwise, evidence mounts to indicate that women who participate in such nonliberatory projects as the piety movement among mosque participants in Cairo (Mahmood 2005) and in women's Islamic schools in Pakistan (Ahmad 2009) or the Hindutva movement in India (Menon 2010) are not necessarily suffering from false consciousness by subscribing to women's subordination in the name of religion or nationalism—projects that may appear to be complicit with patriarchy—and may indeed be understood as (and may understand themselves to be) agents. Why, if someone chooses to be modest, veiled, or, for that matter, subservient, must that person be viewed as passive or deluded? The problems of this assumption are particularly clear when it becomes evident that women with aims, such as piety, may confront obstacles, like the authority of men and family, in order to realize their goals. The critical question[2] is if it is possible for those of us rooted in liberatory perspectives to recognize other goals besides equality and liberation.

Unlike the women in the mosque movement or the Hindu nationalist movement, however, the women in this book are engaged in a project of liberation, both personal and societal, and one that encompasses many of the humanist ideals feminists tend to admire. To the extent that Baul women embrace the Baul ethos of the value of all human beings, they are engaged in "culturally constituted projects that infuse life with meaning and purpose" (Ortner 2006:145). Baul women are not lone actors in this game; they are supported by the Baul community and by many of the sponsors who hire them. Baul songs, rituals, and ideology that emphasize the value of each human being are mutually reinforcing, and within this matrix women have ample rhetoric for arguing that they should also be valued—and they often do argue this. However, it is not a game that is centrally concerned with women's equality. Baul discourse clearly stresses the value of women, and indeed stating that Baul women have more mobility and voice than neighboring non-Bauls is important to Baul women's identity. But even when Baul women seem critical of normative views of women, many seem more invested in explicitly critiquing society's treatment of other categories of the disenfranchised.

Furthermore, this liberatory project does not run seamlessly throughout their lives; nor are their everyday lives infused with activism. They may celebrate their right to wander and perform and encourage others to do so, but they may also be invested in aspects of normative society for reasons that are not always straightforward or simple. In some cases, their actions appear to belie complicity with patriarchy. However, I do not believe that it would be correct to see some of their normative actions and statements as failings—as a *lack* of agency.

I find it useful to think of agency as the capacity to act. This definition does not mean that a person necessarily defies social structures, but that she can imagine alternatives even if and when she chooses to adhere to normative roles and behavior. In her study of Kalasha women in Pakistan, whose ethnic identity is based on the idea that Kalasha women are free, Wynne Maggi argues the following: "Freedom, then, lies not so much in actuality as in possibility, in choice. Women feel that they choose to be wives and mothers, choose whether to stay with their husbands and families or go. Most choose, of course, to stay, but the fact that this choice is theirs to make is an essential ethnic marker, something they feel differentiates them from other cultural groups" (2001:83), such as the neighboring Muslim women.

The women in these pages demonstrate their ability to face obstacles, think through options, and select among a pool of choices ways of acting and living in the world that might be meaningful to them. Baul claims that women are to be valued certainly contribute to Baul women's ability to imagine alternative gendered behavior, but these women demonstrate their resourcefulness in the many ways they draw on other ideals. Compared to neighboring non-Baul women, these women have considerable agency because of local understandings of Bauls as unfettered by societal constraints, perhaps because they are too mad to act otherwise. In fact, drawing on identities of Bauls or renouncers signals to others that they are liable to act in ways that do not conform to gendered norms for married women. But inhabiting norms for those who have the potential to choose otherwise is also agency and may even fulfill other goals and desires. This seems particularly clear in Muslim women's piety movements (Mahmood 2005 and Ahmad 2009) where modesty and veiling are choices made by women with the goal of submission to God but not to subjugate the self to patriarchal society. In these cases, piety may include obeying male kin, but it may also include defying them, especially if the men themselves are not particularly religious.

From the viewpoint of Baul women, probably the most important aim is to create a meaningful life, whether it is a life driven by spiritual longings, a life of freedom and independence, or a life with a roof over one's head. Crafting a meaningful life might sometimes find its expression in unencumbered actions, but I do not believe that most Baul women want to be completely unencumbered. Sometimes one's own desires are also the same as societal or familial expectations.[3] It may be tempting to conclude that "there is a natural disjuncture between a person's 'true' desires and those that are socially prescribed" (Mahmood 2005:149) when we look at women like Nur Jahan, who longs to wander freely and sing (but refrains by leading a married life), or Jaya, who longs to take renunciation in order to become a spiritual adept (yet resists because of community ties). But being respectable wives and mothers and living in a home, while inhibiting some desires, may fulfill others. Their aim of crafting a meaningful life is a project that is embedded in relationships and therefore is inextricably linked to the larger social structure that does not simply exert hegemonic control over their choices but can also enhance daily life in myriad ways. For instance, succumbing to societal pressure to reproduce may be articulated as inhibiting religious practice, but raising children may simultaneously be seen as producing considerable joy.

In addition to fulfilling other desires, adhering to some norms can also be an effective strategy for easing an otherwise nonconformist life. Susan Seizer, speaking of Tamil drama actresses, argues that "through their embodied practices, actresses comply with the powers that stigmatize them only in such a way that their perceived compliance manages to expand their possibilities for making their home in the world…somewhat more comfortable" (2005:327). Similarly, Baul women, whose Baul behavior and ideology threaten to stigmatize them, acquiesce to dominant norms to the extent that doing so may make their lives "somewhat more comfortable."

Furthermore, by fashioning themselves as good Bengali housewives and mothers or as renouncers, they also gain credibility. Jaya may go out of the home and village to perform publicly, thereby helping to support her family, but she draws on images of the ideal woman and wife when she does Lakshmi *pūjā* or gets up before dawn to clean and cook. Madhabi may lament her failed marriage or strategize about raising her daughter's status among her in-laws, but when she wanders she is a *sannyāsinī*. Both women draw on different models available to them in order to convince others that they are respectable women. If Baul women were to reveal everything they do or believe, however, they would quickly be dismissed as outsiders, *pāglīs*, or scandalous women, and no one would pay them much attention. Thus, signaling that they are modest and respectable housewives may also be part of their project of asserting the value women, even as they expand what that gendered category looks like.

With some respect and credibility, however, Baul women can in fact enact change, contributing to a serious game of shifting perceptions and options for both women and Bauls. In part they do this simply by acting the good Bengali woman and housewife. Baul women use a "strategy of expansion…[to] include themselves in the category 'good women,' potentially redefining the category" (Seizer 2005:329). By including themselves in the definition of good woman, Baul women expand that gendered role. Thus a strategy of hiding certain behaviors and beliefs while emphasizing others not only makes their lives more comfortable but also contributes to changes in those gendered expectations and norms. Some Baul women also draw on *sannyās* to gain credibility and justify their actions, and by doing so they insist upon the fluidity and applicability of that role as well. In addition, they assert that the public—including men, householders, anthropologists, ticket collectors, and sponsors—have a responsibility toward Baul women. Baul women not only reconfigure what it means to be Bauls and women in Bengal; they also try to influence the kinds of relationships others have with them.

But it is not only their embodied actions—which may be or may not be conscious—that may lead to a change in perceptions about what women can or cannot do. In fact, many of the women I met explicitly aim to change the society in which they live, transmitting their ideas through songs and conversations: Jaya talks to her neighbors about educating girls, and she encourages other women to gain street smarts so that they too can navigate the public; Kangalini sings about the rights of underprivileged groups; Rajani encourages women to follow a religious path rather than be imprisoned by patriarchy; Rina sings to audiences in order to encourage them to transform their views on social hierarchy and religious life; Siuli argues that her ability to perform onstage and to earn a living demonstrates that women's abilities are no different from men's. These are women who are very conscious of their place and role in society. They recognize their marginality, but they also utilize that position to critique normative society in often subtle but sometimes brazen ways.

Baul women's influence on others is evident at least in how many more women today identify themselves as Bauls. Despite all the legitimate concerns expressed by women in this book, the number of Baul women performers has increased. In Kolkata and Dhaka, several newspaper articles either focusing on or including Baul women have been published over the past decade. Sponsors are seeking Baul women for their events. Even the increasing number of women learning Baul songs just to earn a little money (i.e., with no interest in the religious or ideological angles) reveals that perceptions of women and of Bauls have been shifting. More work needs to be done to track these shifts as well as the influence that Baul women have had on them. But what should be clear is that Baul women have not only found a refuge in this path; many have also seized the social power that comes with being Bauls, *sannyāsinīs*, or good women in order to transcend and even transform the structures and norms that circumscribe their behavior. Baul women may not feel particularly carefree, but they utilize the tools of their encumbering in order to create new paths.

GLOSSARY

adhikār. Ability, competence; the rights to particular activities or responsibilities (*adhikārī*—one who is competent, qualified).

ādhyātmik. Inner or spiritual world.

āsar. All-night function, usually featuring musical or oral recitation of religious texts.

bairāgī. Vaishnava renouncer.

baishṇab. Vaishnava, or, one who worships Vishnu or one of his incarnations; in Bengal, Vishnu's incarnation as Krishna is worshipped most commonly along with his consort Radha.

bartamān. Path of direct knowledge; knowledge gained from direct experience instead of conjecture or hearsay.

bartamān-panthī. Follower of the path of *bartamān*; often considered Baul.

bāul-gān. Baul songs.

bāulinī. Baul woman.

bhakti. Devotion; a movement in Hinduism that began around the tenth century in southern India and spread throughout much of India and that emphasized a loving and often intimate relationship with God, usually regardless of one's caste or gender.

bhek. Formal rite of renunciation, usually Vaishnava or Baul.

bhek-dhārī. Someone who has taken a formal rite of renunciation; wearer of the clothes signifying *bhek*.

bīj. Literally means seed but often, especially in Baul usage, refers to semen.

Brahma/Brahman. Absolute truth; supreme being; essence of life. For Bauls, it usually also means semen or menstrual fluids (or an essence within these).

burqā. Worn by Muslim women, an overgarment and veil that covers the woman completely.

deha-tattva. Philosophy of the body.

dharma. Word with multiple meanings, including religion, expected behavior, virtuous behavior, disposition, character.

dīkshā. Initiation by a guru. Typically among Bauls and others in Bengal, *dīkshā* is the first initiation one takes when one receives a mantra from a guru. Bauls usually also take *śikshā* initiation, often by a different guru, in order to learn the esoteric meanings of Baul songs, philosophy, and ritual practices. Bauls may also be initiated a third time by taking *bhek*, a formal rite of renunciation. See also *bhek*; *śikshā*.

dotārā. Literally translates as two-stringed, but refers to a four-stringed lute.

ektārā. One-stringed rhythmic instrument commonly used by Bauls.

fakir. Typically means mendicant or renouncer; often used in reference to Muslim Bauls.

geruyā. Impermanent orange, ocher pink, or red dye applied to white cloth.

Hadith. (Arabic) Words and examples of the Prophet Muhammad.

hiṃsā. Discrimination, hatred, violence.

jāt/jāti. Word meaning "genus" or "birth" that can refer to any type of category. In common usage, it refers to the thousands of different castes throughout India and often is used also for one's religious affiliation. Differs from *varna* ("color"), which refers to the four traditional caste categories..

jāt baishṇab. Hereditary caste of Vaishnavas in Bengal.

jāti byabasā. Caste occupation.

kām. Lust, desire.

kartāl. Small cymbals.

kshamatā. Strength, power.

khilāphat. Caliphate; among Muslim Bauls, the term is used to refer to the institution of renunciation.

kīrtan. Form of Vaishnava devotional musical performance usually lasting all night.

lajjā. Shame, embarrassment, modesty; a term used to describe appropriate behavior particularly for women.

lājuk. Modest and shy.

lālan-giti. Songs by Lalan Shah, considered to be one of the most famous Baul composers and practitioners, though he never called himself a Baul.

lālan panthī. Follower in the lineage of Lalan Shah.

madhukarī. Begging for alms. Literally translated, *madhukarī* means gathering honey; the act of begging from door to door is poetically likened to a bee gathering honey from flower to flower. The bee (*madhukar*), like the wandering mendicant, is seen as taking a little nectar from many flowers, never a lot from one place.

majzub. Someone who has left worldly concerns due to having lost her or his sense; often interpreted as having ecstatic devotion or divine possession.

mālā. Garland or necklace.

mālābadal. Common Baul wedding ritual involving the exchange of garlands.

mālācandan. Literally, garland and sandalwood paste; a common Baul wedding ritual involving the exchange of garlands and the application of sandalwood paste on the partner's forehead and done with the guidance and blessings of a guru.

man. Mind/heart.

mānush. Human being.

Ma'rifat. (Arabic) Esoteric, mystical path associated with Sufis and Bauls and distinguished from the Shari'at (Muslim law), which is viewed as an exoteric path.

masjid. Mosque.

māzār. (Arabic) Muslim shrine dedicated to a saint.

māyā. Illusion; in Bengal, *māyā* also includes the attachments and affections one feels for others.

melā. Festival or fair.

murīd. (Arabic) Muslim term for disciple or devotee.

murśid. Muslim spiritual teacher or guide.

mūrti. Image of a deity in which it is usually believed the deity resides (for a time) so that devotees can worship her or him.

nāmāj. (*namāz* in Urdu/Hindi; from Persian) Muslim prayers, which traditionally are said five times each day.

nārī. Woman.

pāgal. Mad or crazy; someone who has lost bearing in the world, usually from being caught up in otherwordly feelings; divine madness.

pān. Common Indian treat made from a leaf related to pepper into which betel nut and various spices are wrapped.

pīr. Muslim title for spiritual teacher or saint (feminine form *pīrānī, pirāni-mā*).

prem. Love; unconditional love. In popular usage, it can also mean romantic love.

pūjā. Worship, typically of a deity or an image of a deity.

purdah (*pārda*). Literally "curtain"; a complex of practices, such as veiling, seclusion, and silence, in which women engage with the aim of displaying modesty and protecting their and their families' honor.

purush. Man.

rūp. Outer, physical form; beauty.

sādhak. Ritual practitioner (feminine form *sādhikā*).

sādhanā. In general, *sādhanā* means practice, though it often is used to mean ritual practice. When Bauls use the term, they usually mean esoteric rituals focused on the body that are done alone (some of which are also called *yogā*) or that involve specific sexual rituals done with a partner of the opposite sex (*yugal sādhanā*). *Sādhanā* can, however, also be used to describe musical practice.

sādhu. holy man (feminine form *sādhvi*).

sādhu-samāj. Society or community of *sādhu*s (holy men).

saṅginī. Female partner.

śakti. Literally "power" or "energy"; the active and creative power of the universe as well as the name for a goddess Understood as feminine.

samāj. Society or community.

sampradāy. Lineage; community or tradition.

sannyās. Renunciation of householder life for otherwordly pursuits.

sannyāsī. One who has taken formal rites of renunciation (*sannyās, tyāg,* or *bhek*) (feminine form *sannyāsinī*).

sevādāsī. Woman dedicated to serving a deity, temple, or other devotees. Although the term can carry the implication of prostitute, among Bauls and Vaishnavas it has a spiritual or ritual connotation (*sevā karā,* to serve, wait upon, or worship; can describe such actions as male or female hosts distributing food to guests).

Shari'at. (Arabic) Muslim law.

siddha. One who is perfected through spiritual practices; one who is realized.

śikshā. Learning, education. Among Bauls, this refers to the learning of esoteric Baul rituals and philosophy from a *śikshā* guru. *Śikshā* typically follows some time after *dīkshā,* a simple initiation in which one receives a mantra but generally learns little more from one's *dīkshā* guru. The *śikshā* guru is usually thought by Bauls to be the most important guru. See also *dīkshā.*

śilpī. Artist, performer. When Bauls are called *śilpī bāul,* the implication is that they are earning income through musical performances.

strī. Wife.

Sufism. Mystical form of Islam, which emphasizes the inner meanings of Muslim texts, mystical states to achieve closeness to God, and the importance of a guide (*pīr* or *mursid*) to gain knowledge; popular form of Islam in South Asia (Sufi; Muslim mystic).

svādhīnatā. Independence.

tilak. Sectarian marking made of sandalwood paste, clay, ashes, or other substance.

tulsī mālā. Garland made of carved wood from a sacred basil plant worn by Vaishnavas and some Bauls.

tyāgī. A renouncer; one who has relinquished wordly concerns (*tyāg* renunciation).

udāsi. Free or detached from worldly constraints and concerns; carefree.

ulta-pathik. One who travels the reverse path, that is, goes against conventional society.

ustād. Muslim teacher, primarily of music.

urs. Commemoration of the death of a Muslim saint.

Vaishnava. Worshipper of Vishnu or of one of his incarnations, such as Krishna. In Bengal, most Vaishnavas worship Krishna and his consort Radha and see Krishna as a supreme deity in his own right (that is, not as an incarnation of Vishnu).

yugal sādhanā. Sexo-yogic rituals performed by a male and female partner.

NOTES

Chapter 1

1. Although I use the term *Baul* throughout this book, I agree with Hugh Urban (1999) and Jeanne Openshaw (2002) that it is descriptively problematic in that it suggests a boundedness rather than the actual fluidity of beliefs and practices. Furthermore, in my experience, *bāul* is not always used as a noun to refer to a group of people (however unbounded), but also as an adjective describing behavior as well as a noun referring to a goal one would likely not claim one had reached, even if one is striving (as in: "How could I be a Baul? I have a family, home, responsibilities. . . . I have not yet become a Baul"). In this book, I use "Baul women" instead of *bāulinī*, the Bengali word for female Bauls, because of ease and because Bengalis I met tended to say *meye* or *mohila bāul* instead of *bāulinī*.

2. For the sake of simplicity, I use Bengali to refer to people from both West Bengal and Bangladesh. When I discuss those specifically from one region or the other, I specify Bangladeshis or Bengalis from West Bengal. Similarly, I use Bengal to indicate the entire Bengali-speaking region that today includes the Indian state of West Bengal and the country of Bangladesh.

3. Historical roots and origins of Bauls are highly contested among scholars, with some claiming Bauls were around as early as the fourteenth century. Part of the difficulty in determining any origin is that the term *bāul* has also been used as a descriptive label for someone considered crazy or divinely mad and does not always signify members of a religious group. Today the word *bāul* carries both connotations, though in current usage it usually refers to a religious group.

4. *Sahajiyā*, which comes from *sahaj* (easy or innate), is a Bengali term used primarily by others to reference people or a group of people who engage in certain unorthodox practices. Like Baul, Sahajiya is probably an umbrella term that does not reflect the actual diversity of beliefs and practices. People called Sahajiyas exist today, but the usefulness of the term, especially since it is not usually used for self-identification, seems questionable. To further complicate the matter, some people called Bauls are also called Sahajiyas. Openshaw (2002:199, 260) considers Sahajiya largely a scholarly category, but it seems that it is also a label orthodox Gauriya Vaishnavas use to name followers of particular unorthodox practices and beliefs.

5. See Openshaw 1997 for an interesting discussion on this topic.

6. Briefly, ritual practice (*sādhanā*) includes the sexual union of a male and female couple and involves yogic breath control and usually seminal retention.

7. By discourse I mean not only the ways in which people talk about ideology and expectations but also all the practices and unstated assumptions that reflect particular ways of thinking. In each community, there are likely multiple discourses reflected in practices, beliefs, statements, and ideas, and sometimes they struggle for dominance.

8. Recent work on *sannyāsinīs*, or women renouncers, has demonstrated that women are more likely to remain long-term in hermitages or other fixed locations at least partly for

reasons of safety, though more men also remain in place than previously assumed. See for instance Khandelwal 2004; Khandelwal, Hausner, and Gold 2006; and Hausner 2007.

9. Sarah Lamb (2001:28) argues that while a story is not a direct reflection of reality— of something that "really" happened—it is a lived reality: "[T]he very act of telling a story is itself an experience, a practice, a part of life.... The telling of stories is one of the practices by which people reflect, exercise agency, contest interpretations of things, make meanings, feel sorrow and hope, and live their lives."

10. *Bartamān-panthī* refers to those who see themselves as following the path of direct knowledge. That is, they claim to trust only knowledge that can be experienced with the senses and arrived at by their own judgment and not the conjectures of others (i.e., the orthodox).

11. Openshaw's dissertation has since been revised and published as a book, *Seeking Bāuls of Bengal* (2002).

12. *Jāt baishṇab*s are a hereditary group of Vaishnavas. It is likely that they were couples or individuals who at one point had taken a formal rite of renunciation but later had children. Because they had renounced association with their past caste, *baishṇab* serves as their and their families' caste identity.

13. Openshaw 2002 and Hanssen 2001 also touch briefly on some of these questions.

14. See Khandelwal 2004:141–142 and Narayan 1989 for a similar view of *sādhus*.

15. See Carol Salomon's excellent articles (1991, 1995) for more on Lalan Shah's life story, songs, and philosophy.

16. See Flueckiger 2006 for an important ethnographic study of what she calls "vernacular" Islam, the lived practices of Islam. She argues, "To study vernacular Islam [in places like South Asia]...is to identify sites of potential fluidity, flexibility, and innovation in a religious tradition that self-identifies as universal and is often perceived to be ideologically monolithic" (2). This idea of a universal and monolithic Islam (seen as rooted in the Middle East and accepted by many Sylhetis upon their return to Bangladesh) is in tension with Islamic practices elsewhere by Muslims who do not see their own practices as on the "periphery of some 'true (monolithic) Islam'" (12).

Chapter 2

1. When I attended Paus Mela in Santiniketan in 1998, many were talking and still upset about an event concerning Maki. She had come with her guru to perform onstage at the Mela, but a local Bengali with considerable power to influence many issues around the university and community protested that she was not really a Baul and could not be allowed to perform. As a result, she did not perform. When I asked Bauls whether or not they thought she was a Baul, they insisted that she was and that she should have performed with them. Cakrabartī (2001:167) refers to this event when discussing Maki and agues that she is the real deal.

2. In McDaniel's work on women Tantrics (2007), a group whose social positioning in Bengal bears some similarity with Bauls, women's status is considered, and McDaniel argues that domesticity and sexual activity lower the status of women. Although one cannot apply the findings about Tantric women to Baul women, the desexualization of women, particularly through renunciation, does appear to afford women more freedom and respect in public.

3. Openshaw's 2010 publication, *The Life and Philosophy of a Dissenting Bengali Baul Guru*, focuses on Rāj's autobiography and reports about his life from his followers.

4. After an analysis of literature on Bauls, in which she argues that the term *Baul* is problematic, Openshaw chooses to use the term *bartamān-panthī*, which she says was used most often by Rāj Khyāpā and his followers to describe themselves (and other "Bauls" as well). *Bartamān-panthī* means follower in the path of *bartamān*, or direct knowledge/experience, and is contrasted with those who follow conventional or orthodox religious views and practices, both Hindu and Muslim. Those in *bartamān* rely on their own direct experience, while those in *anumān* have faith in things that cannot be proven (e.g., deities, *mūrti*s, temple worship, religious texts, such as the Qur'an and the Vedas). *Bāul* is a term her informants often did not want to use to identify themselves, in part because of the sometimes derogatory connotations associated with the term, as discussed in this chapter. More recently, however, Openshaw has begun to use Baul in her work, after explaining the problems and limitations of that term (2010).

5. Such split images are common also in scholarly literature on women. See, for example, Kakar 1981 for a contrast between the good mother, who is nurturing and protective, and the bad mother who is lustful. Roy 1975 makes a similar split along lines of the maternal and sexual. See also Raheja and Gold 1994:30–38 for an important critique on such split images, which Gold argues are usually from male perspectives or based on interpretations of texts (also male written) and are not often reflected in the views of women.

6. Some Baul men, most often Muslim, wear an *ālkhāllā*, a longer *pānjābī* that may extend to the ground.

7. Much of the clothing is described by Bauls as decorative, though some will claim the significance of certain items. For instance, the patchwork jacket worn by some Bauls is said to represent their status as beggar, each piece of cloth received being sewn together into a jacket. Those Bauls who wear white as opposed to ocher-colored cloth explain that the white symbolizes the shroud one wears at death, reminding us that Bauls who have undertaken renunciation are dead to the social world.

8. Unbound hair for women frequently suggests deviance from societal norms in South Asia, where women, like their hair, should be restrained from being unruly. The goddess Kali, whose image is ubiquitous in West Bengal, is seen with long wavy hair and a host of other characteristics suggesting unchecked female power (and danger). Gananath Obeyesekere (1981) discusses the significance of hair among women ascetics in Sri Lanka, arguing that hair represents sexuality and power (*śakti*) and that the matted hair of his informants symbolized a rejection of mortal sexuality in favor of a divine relationship. Others (see for instance Leach 1958) suggest that hair is seen as a symbol of sexuality in other cultures as well.

9. In addition to Khandelwal 2004, see Narayan 1997, Hausner 2007, McDaniel 1989, O'Flaherty 1971, in which true and false gurus/saints are discussed. Distinctions made between sacred and secular madness is a similar process of evaluation (see McDaniel 1989, Frembgen 1998). Besides evaluations of authenticity, some differentiate between good and dangerous *sādhu*s, or saints, both of whom gained their spiritual or magical powers through austerities. The epic Dhola (Wadley 2004), for instance, features many dangerous yogis as well as women with magical powers. Khandelwal (2004:143–48) also notes distinctions made between real *sannyāsinī*s, who use their spiritual powers for the good of others, and dangerous ones, or "witches," who use powers for selfish reasons.

10. I also met an educated Bangladeshi man in Dhaka who was introduced to me as a Baul because of what was perceived as his carefree approach to life.

11. Parvathy Baul and Mimlu Sen are somewhat exceptions. Coming from elite backgrounds, they have embraced Baul life. Nonetheless, they still benefit from their privileged backgrounds and are able to observe some Baul behavior and circumstances with the eye of an outsider.

12. Wadley 1994 shows that there is a significant connection between purdah practices and class status so that purdah is more likely to be practiced among those who can afford to keep women within the home and can hire help to work in the fields, etc. In contrast, women in lower-class families are needed to work, often outside the home. Katy Gardner (1998) shows similar examples in her work among Sylheti Muslims. See Seizer 2005 for an interesting study of practices aimed at achieving feminine respectability among women drama performers, who also have to go out on the streets and meet the public eye. Also see Papanek and Minault 1982 for more on purdah practices in South Asia.

13. Khandelwal (2004:141–142) notes a similar view among "spiritual seekers and other observers [who attempt] to decide who is and who is not a genuine saint" that "the best sadhus are also hidden, either literally in that they live in some remote place, conventionally identified as a cave or jungle, or metaphorically in that they appear before us in some unrecognizable form: an ordinary beggar, an animal, or even a thief."

14. As I mentioned in chapter 1, this is one of the reasons why in conducting interviews I generally avoided the topic of *sādhanā*. Even when Bauls I knew spoke about *sādhanā*, I rarely pursued the topic unless I had been acquaintances with them long enough to believe they already knew and trusted my own intentions and interests (that is, that I was not searching for a Baul to initiate me into *sādhanā*).

Chapter 3

1. As Sarah Lamb (2001) states, once a woman is married, she belongs to her in-laws' family. Although she carries on relations with her natal family, she no longer belongs to them. Lamb further describes the status of widowed women, who, especially if they have no children, may end up belonging to no one if their in-laws do not want them. Kangalini claims that her in-laws loved her and that it was her husband's rejection of her that made her place in that home tenuous. Her status with them now is not that different from widows who are no longer welcome in the home of in-laws. For more on marriage and kinship in Bengal, see also Fruzzetti 1982; Inden and Nicholas 1977; Inden 1976.

2. The Hindu idea that a wife should worship her husband is encapsulated in the term *pativrata*, which literally translates as husband (*pati*) -vow (*vrata*). As such, a wife is expected to serve her husband as well as her in-laws throughout her life after marriage. Many of Kangalini's statements about the obligations a wife has to her husband are closely tied to Hindu ideals. While some of these ideals can be attributed to Kangalini's own upbringing in a Hindu home, many of them are shared by Muslim Bangladeshis, thus tapping into the larger and contentious identity question of whether Bangladeshis are more Bengali (and thus sharing practices and values with Hindu Bengalis) or more pan-Muslim. For more on the Hindu ideal and practices of *pativrata*, see Pearson 1996, Leslie 1989, and McGee 1987. For *pativrata* ideals and transgressions, see Harlan and Courtright 1995.

3. Radharani, or Radha, is considered the favorite consort of Krishna. She is one of a group of female cowherds (*gopīs*) who became enamored with Krishna. Among many Vaishnavas, Radha is worshipped alongside Krishna.

4. According to the Hindu worldview, Kali Yuga is the last of four Yugas, or eons, and is characterized by decay. After the Kali Yuga, the universe will be destroyed, and the cycle begins again. In popular discourse, Bengalis often mention Kali Yuga to explain all that is wrong with today's society.

5. An excellent critique of some tendencies in scholarship on women in South Asia can be found in Raheja and Gold 1994. For an important critique of feminist scholarship on third world women in general, see Mohanty 1991. Various recent works on folklore also help complicate stereotypes. See, for instance, Appadurai et al. 1991, Flueckiger 1996, Wadley 2004. See also Maggi 2001 for an example in Pakistan that does not fit stereotypes of women in South Asia, and see Menon 2010 and Ahmad 2009 for examples of pious and reformist women in the Hindutva movement in India and Islamic women's movement in Pakistan, respectively, who also complicate stereotypes.

6. According to the 2001 census of India, the literacy rate in the Birbhum district for women of all ages is 52 percent compared to 71 percent for men, with most of those numbers coming from rural areas. The 1991 data for West Bengal show that this difference has been narrowing among the younger generation (and improving overall), indicating that the education levels for girls is increasing: whereas rates for the general population in the state of West Bengal was 46.6 percent for women and 67.8 percent for men, among the 10–14 age group, girls showed a literacy rate of 63.5 percent while the rate for boys was 73.9 percent.

7. One who has committed the entire Qur'an to memory.

8. In a thought-provoking article on responses to literacy campaigns in rural Rajasthan, Ann Grodzins Gold (2002:97) points out that the education of girls "explicitly pits itself against family, home, and tradition" and that the causes of "gender discrimination lie in property rights, patrilineal descent, and patrilocal marriage" as well as a cultural emphasis on honor.

9. Arabic word meaning "favorites of God." Among Bauls, Auliya is sometimes used, often vaguely and without direct reference to an existing group, as another name for a Baul or a stage on the path of Bauls. Kangalini here appears to be referring to a Muslim who is recognized as having some authority.

10. See Gardner 1998 for a discussion on the influence of migrant workers on women and Islam in Sylhet.

11. See Feldman 1998 for a historical overview and analysis of the politicization of Islam in Bangladesh and its dialogue with women's participation in the workforce.

12. Orthodox Muslims (both outside and increasingly within South Asia) are often very critical of South Asian forms of Islam because of practices that are viewed as adulterated by Hinduism or as straying too far from Muslim law (Shari'at) and, thus, as un-Islamic. Sufism, or mystical Islam, is widely practiced in South Asia (see Eaton 1993 for an analysis of the spread of Islam into the Bengali region), and Sufism stresses Ma'rifat, which emphasizes mystical states and internal meanings of Muslim texts, over Shari'at, or literal readings of the Qur'an. Despite the conflicts that have occurred at various points in their coexistence, Muslims and Hindus in South Asia have traditionally intermingled and shared places of worship.

13. In Bangladesh, only men go to the *masjid* to pray, while women are expected to pray inside their homes. In 1998, when I interviewed Muslim women members of the *masjid* in

Syracuse, New York, they told me that they had a particularly hard time convincing Bangladeshi women that the *masjid* was open to women as well. In the Syracuse *masjid*, as well as those in many other cities and countries, women have a separate section for prayer outside the view of men.

14. The term *ṭupi-wallah* is slang for a Muslim who wears a skullcap. Along with *dāṛi-wallah*, or a beard-wearer, this term is often derogatorily used to refer to a conservative Muslim male.

15. For more on *śakti* or the Great Goddess, see Erndl 1993, Hawley and Wulff 1996, Wadley 1975, Kinsley 1986, Pintchman 1994, and Hiltebeitel and Erndl 2000.

16. See Wadley 1994 for an example of how men, especially Brahmin men, in a village in Uttar Pradesh (north India) rationalize the control of women and women's sexuality and how a similar logic of control underlies the subordinate position of lower castes. High caste men argue that women and low caste people lack understanding.

17. See Wadley 1994:41–42 for some similar stories about women's greater sexual power in a different context. The relative sexual powers of women is a pan-Indian concept and has been discussed by several scholars. G. Morris Carstairs (1967), for instance, states that his high caste interviewees in Rajasthan believed that semen is produced with great labor and resources and that each time a man spills his seed he loses some of his own strength.

18. See Openshaw 2002:219–223, and Das 1992 for discussions of the problematic and often contradictory aspects of the location of male and female principles in men and women and their roles in Baul ritual. Openshaw suggests that whereas the male and female principles may be more clearly differentiated in the man, it is likely that instead of seeing women as either embodying the same configurations as men or somehow their opposite, it may be more appropriate to conceptualize "vague, relatively undifferentiated and ultimately contradictory models of the female body." Thus the (undifferentiated) female may be seen as an adjunct to the (differentiated) male" (2002:222).

19. Bauls seem to disagree about whether gender is a biological or social construct, but regardless, divinity is to be found in all human beings.

20. The idea that all women are mothers (or potential mothers) is not unique to Bauls. In Bengal as well as other regions of India, it is common to liken women and girls to Devi, as demonstrated by the popular film by Satyajit Ray entitled *Devi*. Sometimes this identification with Devi, or the Goddess, manifests in the worship of girls or women, as seen in the *kanyā pujā*, in which young girls are said to be manifestations of the Goddess who is both virgin and mother (Erndl 1993) or in women who are said to be possessed by a deity, often a goddess (Hancock 1999). See also Samanta 1992 for an analysis of Bengali understandings of divine and human motherhood.

21. See also Samanta 1992 for a discussion on the importance of mothers in Bengal and its connection to the goddess figures.

22. Ann Grodzins Gold (Raheja and Gold 1994) discusses the literature on split image more thoroughly and has argued that such split images are not necessarily shared by women.

23. Sterilization.

24. The daughter of one of my early hosts in Santiniketan worked in a leprosy clinic, and one day while I spent several hours visiting her at the clinic I noticed that most women who came in for treatment were asked about their family, their plans concerning children,

and if they had had the "operation." More aggressive campaigns at educating and offering sterilization are common throughout South Asia.

25. This is also one reason given why Bauls bury their dead instead of cremate them.

Chapter 4

1. However, Kangalini probably has less material comfort to show for her successes. From my observations, Kangalini is not good at managing money. Part of the problem is that she supports a fairly large group of musicians and family members with her income from performances, and she often does not take much for a program. One afternoon while I was visiting her apartment in Dhaka, her husband was arguing with her about a program she had agreed her troupe would perform. The program was to take place in the north-western town of Rajshahi. He had calculated that after paying for their transportation to Rajshahi and food for everyone, they would do little more than break even. Kangalini, though she clearly felt bad that she had committed everyone to a fruitless program, argued that as Bauls they were bound to perform when someone asked them, whether or not they received remuneration for their performance. Although Kangalini had many people who were financially dependent on her, she did not view her music as purely business. My observations on this are in contrast to a large number of Bangladeshis I met in Dhaka who were sure that Kangalini, because of her fame, lived in luxury. The tiny apartment (basically one room and a kitchen area) I saw when I visited her was shared by about six people. Kangalini and her family had to move to a different place at least two times during the eight months I knew them because they could not afford to pay rent.

2. Many Bengali widows live out their final days in Brindaban (Vrindavan), an important Vaishnava site located in north India (Uttar Pradesh) where Krishna and Radha are believed to have played. While a few have formally taken initiation into a religious path, many others simply stay there hoping that pilgrims will contribute enough alms for them to live.

3. See Openshaw 1997, 2002 and Knight 2010 for more on Baul usage of Hindu and Muslim terms. See also Tony Stewart 2001 for an interesting discussion about the use of Hindu terms to convey Islamic concepts during the precolonial period when Islam began to spread into the region.

4. In chapter 2, I mentioned some upper-class women in Santiniketan and Calcutta who toyed with the Baul label. Although there were qualities about being Baul that they and many others among the Bengali elite value (like freedom from social constraints and responsibility), being a Baul is rarely something anyone of them would seriously consider her- or himself. Furthermore, Bauls generally come from the lower castes, and when a Brahmin, for instance, becomes a Baul, he or she often makes some break with that caste or caste rules because of Baul emphasis on egalitarianism.

5. The Bengali word *par* means outsider or not of one's own kin and is contrasted with *āpan*, meaning one's own. Although Madhabi uses the kinship terms *dādā* (brother) and *baudi* (brother's wife, or sister-in-law) when referring to the couple in whose house she has been living, she is also aware that they are actually not really her kin and therefore ultimately not responsible for her. In Bengal, as in other parts of South Asia, a woman is expected to live in the home with her husband and in-laws (unless her husband has established his own separate home, as is becoming increasingly common) after marriage.

She no longer belongs to her own natal family in the same way, though she does retain connections with them, and they may come and help her out in case of crisis, as was seen with Kangalini in the previous chapter. Madhabi's own circumstance is ambiguous and hence problematic as she must now depend on the good will of people not actually related to her. For more on Bengali kinship relations and terms, see Lamb 2000, Inden and Nicholas 1977, and Fruzzetti 1982.

6. Unless a cook is hired, as is done in many upper- and middle-class families, it is typically the housewife who cooks the food. Hired cooks, however, are often men.

7. One of their rooms contained posters of Radha and Krishna as well as the goddess Saraswati. Jaya had also painted *ālpanā* in the courtyard in decoration for the worship of Lakshmi, the goddess of household prosperity and well-being. Since my early impression of Bauls was that they did not worship deities, I concluded at that time that Jaya was probably not really a Baul.

8. See Gardner 1998 for a discussion of poor rural women in Sylhet, Bangladesh, who cannot afford to purchase a *burqā* or ride in covered rickshaws when going somewhere. It is those families with more economic means who are most likely to keep their women in purdah.

Chapter 5

1. The song titles given in Bengali are the same as the first line of the song, except where otherwise noted.

2. These two types of songs are based on my interpretation of the songs Rina selected to share with me and do not reflect Baul categories of *bāul-gān*.

3. *Hijra* refers to men who, as a result of having sacrificed their genitalia to a goddess, are powerful bestowers of fertility. Considered the third sex of South Asia, they are simultaneously revered, feared, and stigmatized. See Reddy 2005 for an ethnographic study of *hijras*.

4. Niranjan attributes this song to Haure Gosai. There is a version of this song with the *bhaṇitā* (signature line) of Kamala Das in Cakrabartī 2000 (1990):83–84.

Chapter 6

1. Madhabi often spoke using fragmented sentences, which was confusing at first and certainly affected my ability to understand her situation. In the following text, I have tried to retain some of the regional and personal character in Madhabi's speaking style, making only a few changes in tense, where appropriate, and filling in words, marked by the use of brackets, for clarification.

2. The expression that one's fortune, good or bad, is written on one's forehead is common among both Hindus and Muslims in South Asia (and among Muslims outside India where the expression is simply "it is written"). Among Hindus in South Asia, it is related to the belief in transmigration and the belief that when one is born, one comes into the world with a certain amount of qualities and fortunes related to the deeds, or *karma*, of previous lives. Thus previous *karma* reaped by an individual helps set the course for actions and circumstances in this life; it is written on the forehead and thus extremely difficult to change. Although it is common to dismiss one's unhappiness as being a matter of destiny and thus

out of one's control, another possible interpretation of Madhabi's statement is that she is suggesting that she has done everything right in her relationship with her husband but that it was not enough to change her fate.

3. Some Bauls claim that a place can be considered an ashram only if a *samādhi* is there.

4. See Burghart 1978 for a good discussion on why these northern sects would prefer to claim a lineage connection with the southern Vaishnava *sampradāy* than assert their own originality.

5. Peter van der Veer (1988:95–107), in his work on Ramanandis, gives a brief discussion of claimed connections between these northern and southern *sampradāy* and presents an interesting report on the controversy among the Ramanandis in the 1920s and 1930s as they debated their connection with the Sri-Vaishnavas, who marginally accepted a connection while dismissing the Ramanandis as inferior.

6. As Joseph O'Connell states, "If there is one message that sums up the meaning and purpose of Caitanya's *bhakti* movement in Bengal at the most popular level, it is that God Hari [Krishna] has mercifully descended as Caitanya to deliver from every manner of evil all of humankind (and perhaps other living beings), especially (those more unfortunate ones) women, Śūdras and sinners, if only they will respond to His grace" (1990:42).

7. S. K. De, however, suggests that Caitanya's *dīkṣā* guru Isvara Puri and *sannyās* guru Kesava Bharati, though both ascetics of the monistic Sankara order, followed a type of devotional Sankara *sannyās* tradition "which hardly stood in the way of [Caitanya's] practice of extreme forms of emotional Bhakti" (1942:12–16).

8. The Vaishnava *sampradāy*s who are part of the *bhakti* movement vary in the degree to which they follow the caste system both among themselves and with regard to recruitment. The Ramanandis, for instance, have open recruitment (which sometimes gets contested) though they observe caste rules within the sect.

9. See Openshaw 1998 for a discussion of how Bauls overturn hierarchy, challenging even the institution of the guru.

10. See De 1942:10–20 for a convincing argument as to why this link is unlikely.

11. *Bostam* is a colloquial pronunciation of the Bengali word for Vaishnava, or *baishṇab*, and sometimes carries derogatory connotations as seen in the often-heard pairing of *bostam-bostamī*, referring to a male and female who have taken renunciation but live together and engage in sexual relations.

12. See Hayes 1999 for a discussion on this antagonistic relationship between Gauriya Vaishnavas and Sahajiya Vaishnavas.

13. As O'Connell points out, "Often Vaisnavas asserted that any devout Vaisnava, regardless of jati, is superior to a Brahman without devotion to Krishna; sometimes they asserted that the virtues characterizing the ideal Brahman (e.g., knowledge, purity, non-violence, etc.) are to be found in a true Vaisnava, thus making a Vaisnava the same as a Brahman in all but birth, which could be considered secondary anyway" (1982:200). In an article asking whether the *bhakti* movement with its egalitarian religiosity can be seen as actually challenging and changing the dominant social structure, O'Connell argues that the Caitanya Vaishnavas, including the *jāt baishṇabs*, have delegitimized traditional Brahminical social structures in Bengal through a process of "desacralizing" its status "in deference to the ultimate sacrality of *bhakti*" (1990:60).

14. See Khandelwal 2004, Khandelwal et al. 2006, and Hausner 2007 for examples of how others, especially women, complicate traditional ideals of renunciation.

15. I am indebted to the insightful work of Jeanne Openshaw (1993, 2002) for some of the points I raise in this section, particularly the idea that renunciation is a "received" category, as discussed below. Although many other scholars have emphasized the importance of renunciation, my data and experience support the view that Bauls are largely ambivalent about renunciation.

16. Literally translated, *madhukarī* means gathering honey; the act of begging from door to door is poetically likened to a bee gathering honey from flower to flower. The bee (*madhukar*), like the wandering mendicant, is seen as taking a little nectar from many flowers but never a lot from one place.

17. Like many of the *bhadralok* and some Bauls I interviewed, Murase Satoru (1991), based on his fieldwork in the Birbhum area, argues that begging is a central characteristic of Baul renouncers. He admits that there is wide variety among those called Bauls—from householders to renouncers and many in between—but his thesis focuses on the centrality of begging and renunciation as defining characteristics of Bauls, whom he believes are, in general, critical of their status and options in Bengali society. Kristin Hanssen (2001) also emphasizes *madhukarī* as important to the identity and lifestyle of renunciant Vaishnava Bauls, though she stresses as well the injunction against having children implicit in renunciation, a point to which I return later.

18. Hanssen (2001:167–68) reports that the Vaishnava Bauls she knew might take more than one guru if they were displeased with one of them, thereby rejecting one guru's knowledge with the hope that another would provide them with what they seek. She also states that a disciple may no longer give donations to her or his previous guru, conferring those gifts instead to the new one, a situation which results in competition among some gurus.

19. Although many scholars and laypeople claim that Bauls who earn their living from performances are *silpī* Baul and not real Bauls (as discussed in chapter 2), these activities are not necessarily viewed as mutually exclusive by all Bauls. This is particularly the case when one remembers that many Bauls feel they have a message to spread throughout society, and what better place to do so than a stage? Some Bauls perform on a stage or engage in *madhukarī* at different points in their lives, and these activities can be seen along a continuum on their path rather than one or the other as negating their sincerity or commitment to their Baul path.

20. Hanssen (2001), when discussing the life stories of members of a Vaishnava Baul family, tells of a young woman who took renunciation several years before marriage. Later the young woman and her husband contemplated having their 13-year-old son take *sannyās* but were dissuaded by their guru.

21. See Openshaw 2002:134–139 for a similar conclusion; also, Murase 1991:62–121, which discusses renunciation as an alternative lifestyle and adaptive response to unpleasant social situations, providing real-life examples that show why people living in a stratified caste society might want to become Bauls.

22. This issue is addressed in a few chapters in *Is the Goddess a Feminist?* (2000), a book that is focused largely on the theology of the Goddess and its connection to everyday society. For instance, Menon and Shweder 2000 demonstrate that Oriyans (from eastern Indian state of Orissa, a region influenced by Tantra and the worship of the goddess Kali) view women and men as different and unequal and place high value on women's domestic work. The authors argue that Oriyan "gender relations are built on the logic of difference and solidarity rather than on equality and competition" (161). The work of these and other

authors (especially Mohanty 1991) challenge us to rethink Western ideas of feminism in order to acknowledge other perspectives on gender relations, including those held by South Asian feminists.

23. Methods of *sādhanā* are varied among Bauls, and it is misleading to generalize too much about them. For the sake of discussion in this book, *sādhanā* typically includes a stage of ritual practice with a sexual partner. By practicing with techniques of breath control and mantras, the male practitioner learns to retain semen instead of ejaculate. This is sometimes described as drawing the semen inward and upward toward the crown of the male practitioner's head, with the ultimate goal of uniting the male and female aspects. See Openshaw 2002:203-224 for a more detailed discussion.

24. Among Bauls, marriages are often marked by exchanging their garlands in the presence of a guru, and this can take place for second or third marriages as well, though it is less likely. More common is a couple simply deciding to be together and assuming a state of marriage. I suspect that this is the case with Kangalini, but any further interrogation would, I believe, have been fruitless and essentially inconsequential. What is important is that Kangalini changed her status from Hindu to Muslim and from single to married, and as a result she says she experienced much greater acceptance in the Muslim community that is Bangladesh.

25. Kangalini is referring to the dark color of her skin. In South Asia, dark skin color is considered less desirable, and a young woman with dark skin may have difficulties getting married and will sometimes receive ill treatment because of her complexion.

26. See Lamb 2000 for a close examination of *māyā* as a concept that some Bengalis utilize to describe the ties a person has to family and place. In her study, Lamb demonstrates that as women grow older and closer to death, they see themselves as struggling with the *māyā* that keeps them attached to their individual lives and homes.

27. Brindaban, or Vrindavan, believed to be the place where Krishna danced with Radha and the *gopīs*, is a pilgrimage site for many Vaishnavas. Many Bengali Vaishnava renouncers and widows live in Brindaban as well as Benares.

28. Literature on Hindu women frequently stresses the importance of a husband to secure the status of a woman, and a woman who has lost her husband, such as a widow, has also lost the valuable role of wife (and sometimes mother). Susan Wadley (1995) demonstrates how a widow's position depends on her relationship to other males, such as sons, father-in-law, brothers-in-law, and brothers, and her natal and affinal families make decisions about which of her roles in relation to those men will dominate. In Madhabi's case, her primary role after her husband left was as a mother to her only daughter, and her parents helped her fulfill that role by assisting in the daughter's marriage arrangements. It is this role which is still her concern, though since most of her responsibilities in that role have been met, she is also attempting to secure an independent position as a Baul singer. See also Lamb 2000 and 2001 for excellent studies of widows in West Bengal. Lamb (2001) found that when a widow has a child or children, it is her role as mother, not wife, that emerges most often in self-representations.

29. While this eagerness to pursue the path alone may lead some to question their Baul identity (see chapter 2), both Nur Jahan and Rajani find resonance with the label, which others also use in referring to them. Furthermore, their perspectives on being a wife and taking renunciation contribute not only to our present discussion of what it means for Baul women to take renunciation but also to similar discussions with Baul women in which they engaged at the times I interviewed them.

30. Munibor told a few stories about women trying to seduce Shah Jalal. One such story was about Raja Gaurgovinda's sister, who dressed in a white sari and golden jewelry and went to Shah Jalal's place in order to seduce him so that her brother could defeat him. She went to the hill where the *mazār* now is, and when Shah Jalal and his disciple came, she was waiting. Shah Jalal, realizing that she was there to harm him, said to his disciple that if she's a *jinn* (spirit made of fire, often considered evil), she'll fly away; if she's a human, she'll sink into the ground. She sunk all the way into the ground and disappeared. This place is still apparently on the hill, and the ground there is soft like quicksand. Munibor explained that this quicksand, located right next to the *mazār*, is one of the reasons women cannot go there.

31. The discussion in Wilce 1998 of Bangladeshis dismissing someone or rendering them powerless by calling them *pāgal* may provide some insight here. Although it does not appear that Nur Jahan or those who introduced me to her dismissed her religiosity, her reference to herself as *pāgal* in the past appears to serve as an excuse for behavior that may be perceived as unacceptable.

32. This woman, whom Nur Jahan calls her mother, used to visit her at the *mazārs*. Nur Jahan credits her with helping her clean up and become engaged with worldly affairs. As Nur Jahan had begun cleaning up, she said she was able to regain her ability to speak after many years (presumably she had no difficulties singing). It was then that her "mother" asked her what she wanted, to which she responded that she wanted to sing professionally. Nur Jahan says she became the first female singer in Sylhet and the third in Dhaka.

33. He said something two other times before this, but both times what he said was inaudible. Nur Jahan sent him away soon thereafter.

34. At the time of my fieldwork, I was not familiar with the concept of *majzub*. If it had been used at all by any of the people I had been interviewing, it is likely that they added, perhaps for my benefit, an additional word such as *pāgal*, *udāsi* (free from worldly concerns), or perhaps *marami* (mystic), all of which were very common additions to *bāul* in its descriptive sense.

Chapter 7

1. Teaching about Hinduism to undergraduates, I have found it convenient to fall back onto householder/renouncer and worldly/otherworldly distinctions to evoke the kinds of transformations involved when moving from the householder stage to renouncer. But as Khandelwal (2004) points out, those are not discrete categories. To be sure, there are tensions between some of those stages and realms, but they are not mutually exclusive—certainly not to the Bauls I met or to many *sannyāsinī*s encountered by those who work with them.

2. Mahmood has articulated the problem by contrasting the liberal activist project of emancipation, inherent in most feminist writing, with the analytical project aimed at comprehending agendas and practices on their own terms. What is problematic about the activist project is that it is rooted in a "language of assessment [that] is not neutral but depends upon notions of progressive and backward, superior and inferior, higher and lower—a set of oppositions frequently connected with a compelling desire to erase the second modifier even if it means implicitly forming alliances with coercive modes of power" (2005:198). The analytical project is a dismantling of a particular Western vision of liberation with the objective of trying to understand other goals and other lifeways.

3. Maggi 2001 and Mahmood 2005 present many examples that support this in their work.

BIBLIOGRAPHY

Abbas, Shemeem Burney 2002. The Female Voice in Sufi Ritual: Devotional Practices of Pakistan and India. Austin: University of Texas Press.

Abrahams, Roger D. 1992. Singing the Master: The Emergence of African American Cultures in the Plantation South. New York: Pantheon.

Abu-Lughod, Lila 1986. Veiled Sentiments: Honor and Poetry in a Bedouin Society. Berkeley: University of California Press.

———1990. The Romance of Resistance: Tracing Transformations of Power through Bedouin Women. American Ethnologist 17:41–55.

Ahearn, Laura M. 2001. Language and Agency. Annual Review of Anthropology 30:109–137.

Ahmad, Sadaf 2009. Transforming Faith: The Story of Al-Huda and Islamic Revivalism among Urban Pakistani Women. Syracuse, NY: Syracuse University Press.

Appadurai, Arjun 1986. Theory in Anthropology: Center and Periphery. Comparative Studies in Society and History 28(2):356–361.

———1990. Disjuncture and Difference in the Global Cultural Economy. Public Culture 2(2):1–24.

Appadurai, Arjun, Frank J. Korom, and Margaret Ann Mills, eds. 1991. Gender, Genre, and Power in South Asian Expressive Traditions. Philadelphia: University of Pennsylvania Press.

Baul, Parvathy 2005. Song of the Great Soul: An Introduction to the Baul Path. Thiruvananthapuram, Kerala, South India : Ekatara Baul Sangeetha Kalari.

Bauman, Richard 1986. Story, Performance, and Event: Contextual Studies of Oral Narratives. Cambridge: Cambridge University Press.

Bhaṭṭācārya, Upendranāth 1971 [1957]. Bānglār bāul o bāul gān [Bengali Bauls and Baul Songs]. Calcutta: Orient Book Co.

Bhattacharya, Jogendra Nath 1968 [1896]. Hindu Castes and Sects. Calcutta: S. Dey from Editions India.

Bradford, N. J. 1985. The Indian Renouncer: Structure and Transformation in the Lingayat Community. In Indian Religion. Richard Burghart and Audrey Cantlie, eds. Pp. 79–104. New York: St. Martin's.

Burghart, Richard 1978. The Founding of the Ramanandi Sect. Ethnohistory 25(2):121–139.

———1983. Renunciation in the Religious Traditions of South Asia. Man 18:635–653.

Butler, Judith 1997. Excitable Speech: A Politics of the Performative. New York: Routledge.

Cākī, Līnā 1995. Bāul saṅginī. In Bāul, Lālan, Rabīndranāth. Sarat Kumāra Mitra, ed. Pp. 81–90. Kalkātā: Loksaṃskṛti Gaveshanā Parishad.

———1997. Bāuler caraṇḍāsī. In Dhrubapad: Bāṃlār bāul phakir. Sudhīr Cakrabartī, ed. Pp. 176–188. Kṛṣṇanagara, Nadiyā, Paścim Baṅga.

———— 2001. Bāuler caraṇḍāsī. Kalkātā: Pustaka Bipaṇi.

Capwell, Charles 1974. The Esoteric Beliefs of the Bauls of Bengal. Journal of Asian Studies 32(2):255–264.

———— 1986. The Music of the Bauls of Bengal. Kent, Ohio: Kent State University Press.

Carstairs, G. Morris 1967. The Twice-Born: A Study of a Community of High-Caste Hindus. Bloomington: Indiana University Press.

Caudhurī, Ābul Āhsan 1997. Bāṃlādeśera bāulder cālacitra. *In* Dhrubapad: Bāṃlār bāul phakir. Sudhīr Cakrabartī, ed. Pp. 131–137. Kṛshṇanagara, Nadiyā, Paścim Baṅga.

Cakrabartī, Sudhīr 2000 [1990]. Bāṃlār dehatattva gān. Pustak Bipaṇi, Calcutta.

———— 2001. Bāul phakīr kathā. Kalkātā: Loksaṃskṛti o Ādibāsī Saṃskṛti Kendra, Tathya o Saṃskṛti Bibhāga.

Das, Rahul Peter 1992. Problematic Aspects of the Sexual Rituals of the Bauls of Bengal. Journal of the American Oriental Society 112(3):388–432.

Dasgupta, Shashibhusan 1962 [1946]. Obscure Religious Cults. Calcutta: Firma K. L. Mukhopadhyay, Publishers.

De, Sushil Kumar 1942. Early History of the Vaiṣṇava Faith and Movement in Bengal from Sanskrit and Bengali Sources. Calcutta: General Printers and Publishers.

Denton, Lynn Teskey 1991. Varieties of Hindu Female Asceticism. *In* Roles and Rituals for Hindu Women. Julia Leslie, ed. Pp. 211–231. London: Pinton.

Dimock, Edward 1966. The Place of the Hidden Moon. Chicago: University of Chicago Press.

———— 1987. The Bauls and the Islamic Tradition. *In* The Sants: Studies in a Devotional Tradition of India. Karine Schomer and W. H. McLeod, eds. Pp. 375–388. Delhi: Motila Banarsidass.

Dumont, Louis 1970. Homo Hierarchicus: The Caste System and Its Implications. London: Weidenfeld and Nicolson.

Duranti, Alessandro 1997. Linguistic Anthropology. Cambridge: Cambridge University Press.

Eaton, Richard M. 1993. The Rise of Islam and the Bengal Frontier, 1204–1760. Berkeley: University of California Press.

———— 2000. Essays on Islam and Indian History. New Delhi: Oxford University Press.

Egnor, Margaret T. 1989. Internal Iconicity in Paraiyer 'Crying Songs.' *In* Another Harmony: New Essays on the Folklore of India. Stuart H. Blackburn and A. K. Ramanujan, eds. Pp. 294–344. Berkeley: University of California Press.

Erndl, Kathleen M. 1993. Victory to the Mother: The Hindu Goddess of Northwest India in Myth, Ritual, and Symbol. New York: Oxford University Press.

Ernst, Carl W. 1999. Teachings of Sufism. Boston: Shambhala Publications.

Ewing, Katherine P. 1998. A *majzub* and His Mother: The Place of Sainthood in a Family's Emotional Memory. *In* Embodying Charisma: Modernity, Locality, and the Performance of Emotion in Sufi Cults. Pnina Werbner and Helene Basu, eds. Pp. 160–183. New York: Routledge.

Feldman, Shelley 1998. (Re)presenting Islam: Manipulating Gender, Shifting State Practices, and Class Frustrations in Bangladesh. *In* Appropriating Gender: Women's Activism and Politicized Religion in South Asia. Patricia Jeffery and Amrita Basu, eds. Pp. 33–52. New York and London: Routledge.

———— 2001. Exploring Theories of Patriarchy: A Perspective from Contemporary Bangladesh. Signs: Journal of Women in Culture and Society 26(4):1097–1127.

Flueckiger, Joyce Burkhalter 1996. Gender and Genre in the Folklore of Middle India. Ithaca, NY: Cornell University Press.

———1997. "There Are Only Two Castes: Men and Women": Negotiating Gender as a Female Healer in South Asian Islam. Oral Traditions 12(1):76–102.

———2006. In Amma's Healing Room: Gender and Vernacular Islam in South India. Bloomington: Indiana University Press.

Forbes, Geraldine 1982. From Purdah to Politics: The Social Feminism of the All-India Women's Organizations. *In* Separate Worlds: Studies of Purdah in South Asia. Hanna Papanek and Gail Minault, eds. Pp. 219–244. Delhi: Chanakya Publications.

Frembgen, Jurgen Wasim 1998. The *majzub* Mama Ji Sarkar: "A Friend of God Moves from One House to Another." *In* Embodying Charisma: Modernity, Locality, and the Performance of Emotion in Sufi Cults. Pnina Werbner and Helene Basu, eds. Pp. 140–159. New York: Routledge.

Fruzzetti, Lina 1982. The Gift of a Virgin: Women, Marriage, and Ritual in Bengali Society. New Brunswick, NJ: Rutgers University Press.

Gal, Susan 1991. Between Speech and Silence: The Problematics of Research on Language and Gender. *In* Gender at the Crossroads of Knowledge: Feminist Anthropology in the Postmodern Era. Micaela Di Leonardo, ed. Pp. 175–203. Berkeley: University of California Press.

Gardner, Katy 1998. Women and Islamic Revivalism in a Bangladeshi Community. *In* Appropriating Gender: Women's Activism and Politicized Religion in South Asia. Patricia Jeffery and Amrita Basu, eds. Pp. 203–220. New York: Routledge.

———1999. Women and the Islamic Revivalism in a Bangladeshi Community. *In* Resisting the Sacred and the Secular: Women's Activism and Politicised Religion in South Asia. Patricia Jeffery and Amrita Basu, eds. Pp. 203–220. New Delhi: Kali for Women.

Geiger, Susan 1986. *Review essay of* Women's Life Histories: Method and Content. Signs: Journal of Women in Culture and Society 11:334–351.

Ghosh, Pika 1995. Household Rituals and Women's Domains. *In* Cooking for the Gods: The Art of Home Ritual in Bengal. Pika Ghosh, ed. Pp. 20–25. Newark, NJ: Newark Museum.

Ghurye, G. S. 1953. Indian Sadhus. Bombay: Popular Book Depot.

Gilmore, David D. 1987. Introduction: The Shame of Dishonor. *In* Honor and Shame and the Unity of the Mediterranean. David D. Gilmore, ed. Pp. 2–21. Washington, DC: American Anthroplogical Association.

Gold, Ann Grodzins 1992. A Carnival of Parting: The Tales of King Bharthari and King Gopi Chand as Sung and Told by Madhu Natisar Nath of Ghatiyali, Rajasthan. Berkeley: University of California Press.

———2002. New Light in the House: Schooling Girls in Rural North India. *In* Everyday Life in South Asia. Diane P. Mines and Sarah Lamb, eds. Pp. 86–99. Bloomington: Indiana University Press.

Gottschalk, Peter 2001. Beyond Hindu and Muslim: Multiple Identity in Narratives from Village India. New Delhi: Oxford University Press.

Gupta, Akhil, and James Ferguson, eds. 1997a. Anthropological Locations: Boundaries and Grounds of a Field Science. Berkeley: University of California Press.

———1997b. Culture, Power, Place: Explorations in Critical Anthropology. Durham, NC: Duke University Press.

Hancock, Mary Elizabeth 1995. The Dilemmas of Domesticity: Possession and Devotional Experience among Urban Smarta Women. *In* From the Margins of Hindu Marriage: Essays on Gender, Religion, and Culture. Lindsey Harlan and Paul B. Courtright, eds. Pp. 60–91. New York: Oxford University Press.

———1999. Womanhood in the Making: Domestic Ritual and Public Culture in Urban South India. Boulder, CO: Westview.

Hanssen, Kristin 2001. Seeds in Motion: Thoughts, Feelings, and the Significance of Social Ties as Invoked by a Family of Vaishnava Mendicant Renouncers in Bengal. Ph.D. dissertation, Department of Social Anthropology, University of Olso.

———2006. The True River Ganges: Tara's Begging Practices. *In* Women's Renunciation in South Asia: Nuns, Yoginis, Saints, and Singers. Meena Khandelwal, Sondra L. Hausner, and Ann Grodzins Gold, eds. Pp. 95–123. New York: Palgrave Macmillan.

Harlan, Lindsey 1995. Abandoning Shame: Mīrā and the Margins of Marriage. *In* From the Margins of Hindu Marriage: Essays on Gender, Religion, and Culture. Lindsey Harlan and Paul B. Courtright, eds. Pp. 204–227. New York: Oxford University Press.

Harlan, Lindsey, and Paul B. Courtright, eds. 1995. From the Margins of Hindu Marriage: Essays on Gender, Religion, and Culture. New York: Oxford University Press.

Hausner, Sondra L. 2007. Wandering with Sadhus: Ascetics in the Hindu Himalayas. Bloomington: Indiana University Press.

Hawley, John Stratton, and Donna Marie Wulff 1986. The Divine Consort: Rādhā and the Goddesses of India. Boston: Beacon.

Hayes, Glen Alexander 1999. The Churning of Controversy: Vaisnava Sahajiya Appropriations of Gaudiya Vaisnavism. Journal of Vaisnava Studies 8(1):77–90.

Hiltebeitel, Alf, and Kathleen M. Erndl, eds. 2000. Is the Goddess a Feminist? The Politics of South Asian Goddesses. New York: New York University Press.

Inden, Ronald B., and Ralph W. Nicholas 1977. Kinship in Bengali Culture. Chicago: University of Chicago Press.

Inden, Ronald B. 1976. Marriage and Rank in Bengali Culture: a History of Caste and Clan in Middle Period Bengal. Berkeley: University of California Press.

Jeffery, Patricia and Roger Jeffery. 1994. Killing my Heart's Desire: Education and Female Autonomy in Rural North India. *In* Women as Subjects: South Asian Histories. Nita Kumar, ed. Pp. 125–171. Charlottesville, VA: University of Virgina Press.

Kakar, Sudhir 1981. The Inner World: A Psycho-analytic Study of Childhood and Society in India. Delhi: Oxford University Press.

Kaviraja Gosvami, Krisnadasa, Edward C. Dimock, and Tony K. Stewart, eds. 1999. Caitanya Caritāmṛta of Kṛṣṇadāsa Kavirāja: A Translation and Commentary. Cambridge, MA: Harvard University Press.

Kelting, M. Whitney 2001. Singing to the Jinas: Jain Laywomen, Mandal Singing, and Negotiations of Jain Devotion. New York: Oxford University Press.

Khandelwal, Meena 1996. Walking a Tightrope: Saintliness, Gender, and Power in an Ethnographic Encounter. Anthropology and Humanism 21(2):111–134.

———1997. Ungendered Atma, Masculine Virility, and Feminine Compassion: Ambiguities in Renunciant Discourses on Gender. Contributions to Indian Sociology 13(1):79–107.

———2004. Women in Ochre Robes: Gendering Hindu Renunciation. Albany: State University of New York Press.

Khandelwal, Meena, Sondra L. Hausner, and Ann Grodzins Gold, eds. 2006. Women's Renunciation in South Asia: Nuns, Yoginis, Saints, and Singers. New York: Palgrave Macmillan.

Kinsley, David 1986. Hindu Goddesses: Visions of the Divine Feminine in Hindu Religious Traditions. Berkeley: University of California Press.

Knight, Lisa I. 2006. Renouncing Expectations: Single Baul Women Renouncers and the Value of Being a Wife. *In* Women's Renunciation in South Asia: Nuns, Yoginis, Saints, and Singers. Meena Khandelwal, Sondra L. Hausner, and Ann Grodzins Gold, eds. Pp. 191–222. New York: Palgrave Macmillan.

————2010. Bāuls in Conversation: Cultivating Oppositional Ideology. International Journal of Hindu Studies 14(1):71–120.

Kondo, Dorinne K. 1990. Crafting Selves: Power, Gender, and Discourses of Identity in a Japanese Workplace. Chicago: University of Chicago Press.

Kotalova, Jitka 1993. Belonging to Others: Cultural Construction of Womanhood among Muslims in a Village in Bangladesh. Uppsala: Acta Universitatis Upsaliensis.

Lamb, Sarah 2000. White Saris and Sweet Mangoes: Aging, Gender, and Body in North India. Berkeley: University of California Press.

————2001. Being a Widow and Other Life Stories: The Interplay between Lives and Words. Anthropology and Humanism 26(1):16–34.

Lanser, Susan S. 1993. Burning Dinners: Feminist Subversions of Domesticity. *In* Feminist Messages: Coding in Women's Folk Culture. Joan Newlon Radner, ed. Pp. 36–53. Urbana: University of Illinois Press.

Leach, Edmund 1958. Magical Hair (Curl Bequest Essay 1957). Journal of the Royal Anthropological Institute 88(2):147–164.

Leslie, Julia 1989. The Perfect Wife: The Orthodox Hindu Woman according to the Stridharmapaddhati of Tryambakayajvan. Delhi: Oxford University Press.

————1991. Roles and Rituals for Hindu Women. Rutherford, NJ: Fairleigh Dickinson University Press.

Leslie, Julia, and Mary McGee, eds. 2000. Invented Identities: The Interplay of Gender, Religion, and Politics in India. New Delhi: Oxford University Press.

MacLeod, Arlene E. 1991. Accommodating Protest: Working Women, the New Veiling, and Change in Cairo. New York: Columbia University Press.

————1992. Hegemonic Relations and Gender Resistance: The New Veiling as Accommodating Protest in Cairo. Signs 17(3):533–57.

Maggi, Wynne 2001. Our Women Are Free: Gender and Ethnicity in the Hindukush. Ann Arbor: University of Michigan Press.

Mahmood, Saba 2005. Politics of Piety: The Islamic Revival and the Feminist Subject. Princeton, NJ: Princeton University Press.

Marcus, George E. 1995. Ethnography in/of the World System: The Emergence of Multi-Sited Ethnography. Annual Review of Anthropology 24:95–117.

Marcus, George E., and Michael M. J. Fischer 1989. Anthropology as Cultural Critique: An Experimental Moment in the Human Sciences. Chicago: University of Chicago Press.

McDaniel, June 1989. The Madness of the Saints: Ecstatic Religion in Bengal. Chicago: University of Chicago Press.

————1992. The Embodiment of God among the Bauls of Bengal. Journal of Feminist Studies in Religion 8(2):27–39.

———— 2003. Making Virtuous Daughters and Wives: An Introduction to Women's Brata Rituals in Bengli Folk Religion. Albany: State University of New York Press.

———— 2007. Does Tantric Ritual Empower Women? Renunciation and Domesticity among Female Bengali Tantrikas. Pp. 159–175. *In* Women's Lives, Women's Rituals in the Hindu Tradition. T. Pintchman, ed. Oxford and New York: Oxford University Press.

McGee, Mary 1987. Feasting and Fasting: Vrata Tradition and Its Significance for Hindu Women. Th.D. dissertation, Harvard University.

Menon, Kalyani Devaki 2010. Everyday Nationalism: Women of the Hindu Right in India. Philadelphia: University of Pennsylvania Press.

Menon, Usha and Richard A. Shweder 2000. Power in its Place: Is the Great Goddess of Hinduism a Feminist? *In* Is the Goddess a Feminist? The Politics of South Asian Goddesses. Alf Hiltebeitel and Kathleen M. Erndl, eds. Pp. 151–165. New York: New York University Press.

Metcalf, Peter 2001. Global "Disjuncture" and the "Sites" of Anthropology. Cultural Anthropology 16(2):165–182.

Minault, Gail 1982. Purdah Politics: The Role of Muslim Women in Indian Nationalism, 1911–1924. *In* Separate Worlds: Studies of Purdah in South Asia. Hanna Papanek and Gail Minault, eds. Delhi: Chanakya Publications.

Mines, Diane P., and Sarah Lamb 2002. Everyday Life in South Asia. Bloomington: Indiana University Press.

Mohanty, Chandra Talpade 1991. Under Western Eyes: Feminist Scholarship and Colonial Discourses. *In* Third World Women and the Politics of Feminism. Chandra Talpade Mohanty, Ann Russo, and Lourdes Torres, eds. Pp. 51-80. Bloomington: Indiana University Press.

Murase, Satoru 1991. Patchwork Jacket and Loincloth: An Ethnographic Study of the Bauls of Bengal. Ph.D. dissertation, Department of Anthropology, University of Illinois at Urbana–Champaign.

Myerhoff, Barbara 1979. Number Our Days. New York: Dutton.

———— 1982. Life History among the Elderly: Performance, Visibility, and Re-Membering. *In* A Crack in the Mirror: Reflexive Perspectives in Anthropology. Jay Ruby, ed. Pp. 99–117. Philadelphia: University of Pennsylvania Press.

Narayan, Kirin 1989. Storytellers, Saints, and Scoundrels: Folk Narrative in Hindu Religious Teaching. Philadelphia: University of Pennsylvania Press.

———— 1997. Mondays on the Dark Night of the Moon: Himalayan Foothill Folktales. New York: Oxford University Press.

Obeyesekere, Gananath 1981. Medusa's Hair: An Essay on Personal Symbols and Religious Experience. Chicago: University of Chicago Press.

O'Connell, Joseph T. 1982. Jāti-Vaiṣṇavas of Bengal: "Subcaste" (*Jāti*) without "Caste" (*Varṇa*). Journal of Asian and African Studies 17:189–207.

———— 1990. Do Bhakti Movements Change Hindu Social Structures? The Case of Caitanya's Vaiṣṇavas in Bengal. *In* Boeings and Bullock-Carts: Studies in Change and Continuity in Indian Civilization. B. L. Smith, ed. Pp. 39–63. Delhi: Chanakya Publications.

———— 1996–97. Does the Caitanya Vaiṣṇava Movement Reinforce or Resist Hindu Communal Politics? Journal of Vaiṣṇava Studies 5(1):197–215.

O'Flaherty, Wendy Doniger 1971. The Origin of Heresy in Hindu Mythology. History of Religions 10(4):271–333.

Ojha, Catherine 1981. Feminine Asceticism in Hinduism: Its Tradition and Present Condition. Man in India 61:254–285.

———1985. The Tradition of Female Gurus. Manushi 31(1):2–8.

———1988. Outside the Norms: Ascetics in Hindu Society. Economic and Political Weekly, April 30:WS 34–36.

Olwig, Karen Fog, and Kirsten Hastrup 1997. Siting Culture: The Anthropological Object. London: Routledge.

Omvedt, Gail 2008. The Bhakti Radicals and Untouchability. *In* Speaking Truth to Power: Religion, Caste, and the Subaltern Question in India. Manu Bhagavan and Anne Feldhaus, eds. Pp. 11–29. New Delhi: Oxford University Press.

Openshaw, Jeanne 1993. "Bāuls" of West Bengal: With Special Reference to Rāj Khyāpā and His Followers. Ph.D. dissertation, School of Oriental and African Studies, University of London.

———1997. The Web of Deceit: Challenges to Hindu and Muslim "Orthodoxies" by "Bāuls." Religion: An International Journal 27(4): 297–309.

———1998. "Killing" the Guru: Anti-hierarchical Tendencies of "Bāuls" of Bengal. Contributions to Indian Sociology 32(1):1–19.

———2002. Seeking Bāuls of Bengal. Cambridge: Cambridge University Press.

———2010. Writing the Self: The Life and Philosophy of a Dissenting Bengali Baul Guru. Oxford: Oxford University Press.

Ortner, Sherry B. 2006. Anthropology and Social Theory: Culture, Power, and the Acting Subject. Durham, NC: Duke University Press.

Papanek, Hanna, and Gail Minault, eds. 1982. Separate Worlds: Studies of Purdah in South Asia. Delhi: Chanakya Publications.

Pearson, Anne Mackenzie 1996. "Because It Gives me Peace of Mind": Ritual Fasts in the Religious Lives of Hindu Women. Albany: State University of New York Press.

Pemberton, Kelly 2004. Muslim Women Mystics and Female Spiritual Authority in South Asian Sufism. Journal of Ritual Studies 18(2):1–23.

———2006. Women *Pirs*, Saintly Succession, and Spiritual Guidance in South Asian Sufism. Muslim World 96 (1):61–87.

Pintchman, Tracy 1994. The Rise of the Goddess in the Hindu Tradition. Albany: State University of New York Press.

Pratt, Mary Louise 1986. Fieldwork in Common Places. *In* Writing Culture: The Poetics and Politics of Ethnography. James Clifford and George E. Marcus, eds. Pp. 27–50. Berkeley: University of California Press.

Radner, Joan N., and Susan S. Lanser 1993. Strategies of Coding in Women's Cultures. *In* Feminist Messages: Coding in Women's Folk Cultures. Joan Newlon Radner, ed. Pp. 1–29. Urbana: University of Illinois Press.

Radner, Joan Newlon, ed. 1993. Feminist Messages: Coding in Women's Folk Culture. Urbana: University of Illinois Press.

Raheja, Gloria Goodwin, and Ann Grodzins Gold 1994. Listen to the Heron's Words: Reimagining Gender and Kinship in North India. Berkeley: University of California Press.

Rahmān, Golām Eraśādur 1994. Netrakoṇār bāul gīti. Ḍhākā: Bāṃlā Ekāḍemī.

Ramanujan, R. K.1991. Toward a Counter-System: Women's Tales. *In* Gender, Genre, and Power in South Asian Expressive Traditions. Arjun Appadurai, Frank J. Korom, and Margaret A. Mills, eds. Pp. 33–55. Philadelphia: University of Pennsylvania Press.

Ray, Benoy Gopal 1965. Religious Movements in Modern Bengal. Santiniketan: Visva-Bharati Research Publications.

Ray, Manas 1994. The Bauls of Birbhum: A Study in Persistence and Change in Communication in Cultural Context. Calcutta: Firma KLM.

Reddy, Gayatri 2005. With Respect to Sex: Negotiating Hijra Identity in South India. Chicago: University of Chicago Press.

Richman, Paula 2008. Dalit Transformation, Narrative, and Verbal Art in the Tamil Novels of Bama. *In* Speaking Truth to Power: Religion, Caste, and the Subaltern Question in India. Manu Bhagavan and Anne Feldhaus, eds. Pp. 137–152. New Delhi: Oxford University Press.

Rosaldo, Michelle Z., and Louise Lamphere, eds. 1974. Woman, Culture, and Society. Stanford, CA: Stanford University Press.

Roy, Manisha 1975. Bengali Women. Chicago: University of Chicago Press.

Saheb, S. A. A. 1998. A "Festival of Flags": Hindu–Muslim Devotion and the Sacralising of Localism at the Shrine of Nagore-e-Sharif in Tamil Nadu. *In* Embodying Charisma: Modernity, Locality, and the Performance of Emotion in Sufi Cults. Pnina Werbner and Helene Basu, eds. Pp. 55–76. New York: Routledge.

Salomon, Carol 1979. A Contemporary Sahajiya Interpretation of the Bilvamangal–Cintamani Legend, as Sung by Sanatan Das Baul. *In* Patterns of Change in Modern Bengal. Richard Leonard Park, ed. Pp. 97–110. East Lansing: Asian Studies Center.

——— 1991. The Cosmogonic Riddles of Lalan Fakir. *In* Gender, Genre, and Power in South Asian Expressive Traditions. Arjun Appadurai, Frank J. Korom, and Margaret A. Mills, eds. Pp. 267–304. Philadelphia: University of Pennsylvania Press.

——— 1995. Baul Songs. *In* Religions of India in Practice. J. Donald S. Lopez, ed. Pp. 187–207. Princeton, NJ: Princeton University Press.

Samanta, Suchitra 1992. Maṅgalmayīmā, Sumaṅgalī, Maṅgal*Manṁgalmayīmā, Sumanṁgalī, Manṁgal*: Bengali Perceptions of the Divine Feminine, Motherhood, and "Auspiciousness." Contributions to Indian Sociology 26(1):51–75.

Sarkar, Rebati Mohan 1990. Bauls of Bengal: In the Quest of Man of the Heart. New Delhi: Gian Publishing House.

Sax, William S. 2002. Dancing the Self: Personhood and Performance in the Pāṇḍav Līlā of Garhwal. New York: Oxford University Press.

Schimmel, Annemarie 1997. My Soul Is a Woman: The Feminine in Islam. Susan H. Ray, trans. New York: Continuum Publishing Co.

Scott, James C. 1985. Weapons of the Weak: Everyday Forms of Peasant Resistance. New Haven, CT: Yale University Press.

——— 1990. Domination and the Arts of Resistance: Hidden Transcripts. New Haven, CT: Yale University Press.

Seizer, Susan 2000. Roadwork: Offstage with Special Drama Actresses in Tamilnadu, South India. Cultural Anthropology 15(2):217–259.

——— 2002. Offstage with Special Drama Actresses in Tamil Nadu, South India: Roadwork. *In* Everyday Life in South Asia. Diane P. Mines and Sarah Lamb, eds. Pp. 116–131. Bloomington: Indiana University Press.

——— 2005. Stigmas of the Tamil Stage: An Ethnography of Special Drama Artists in South India. Durham, NC: Duke University Press.

Sen, Mimlu 2010 [2009]. The Honey Gatherers: Travels with the Bauls: The Wandering Minstrels of Rural India. London: Rider.

Shaheed, Farida 1998. The Other Side of the Discourse: Women's Experiences of Identity, Religion, and Activism in Pakistan. *In* Appropriating Gender: Women's Activism and Politicized Religion in South Asia. Patricia Jeffery and Amrita Basu, eds. Pp. 143–164. New York: Routledge.

Sherinian, Zoe 2009. Changing Status in India's Marginal Music Communities. Religion Compass 3(4):608–619.

Smith, Margaret 1984 [1928]. Rābi'a the Mystic and Her Fellow-Saints in Islām. Cambridge: Cambridge University Press.

Sommer, Doris 1988. "Not Just a Personal Story": Women's *Testimonios* and the Plural Self. *In* Life/Lines: Theorizing Women's Autobiography. Bella Brodzki and Celeste Marguerite Schenck, eds. Pp. 107–131. Ithaca, NY: Cornell University Press.

Stewart, Tony K. 2001. In Search of Equivalence: Conceiving Muslim-Hindu Encounter through Translation Theory. In *History of Religions* 40(3):260–287.

Supriya, K. E. 1996. Confessionals, Testimonials: Women's Speech in/and Contexts of Violence. Hypatia 11(4):92–106.

Tagore, Rabindranath 1922. Creative Unity. New York: The Macmillan Company.

———1963 [1931]. The Religion of Man. London: George Allen and Unwin.Tripathi, B. D.

———1978. Sadhus of India: The Sociological View. Bombay: Popular Prakashan.

Turner, Victor W. 1969. The Ritual Process—Structure and Anti-structure. New York: Aldine.

Urban, Hugh B. 1999. The Politics of Madness: The Construction and Manipulation of the "Baul" Image in Modern Bengal. South Asia: Journal of South Asian Studies 22(1):13–46.

Vallely, Anne 2002. Guardians of the Transcendent: An Ethnography of a Jain Ascetic Community. Toronto: University of Toronto Press.

van der Veer, Peter 1988. Gods on Earth: The Management of Religious Experience and Identity in a North Indian Pilgrimage Centre. London: Athlone.

Vatuk, Sylvia 1982. Purdah Revisited: A Comparison of Hindu and Muslim Interpretations of the Cultural Meaning of Purdah in South Asia. *In* Separate Worlds: Studies of Purdah in South Asia. Hanna Papanek and Gail Minault, eds. Delhi: Chanakya Publications.

Visweswaran, Kamala 1994. Fictions of Feminist Ethnography. Minneapolis: University of Minnesota Press.

Wadley, Susan S. 1975. Shakti: Power in the Conceptual Structure of Karimpur Religion. Chicago: Department of Anthropology, University of Chicago.

———1976. Brothers, Husbands, and Sometimes Sons: Kinsmen in North Indian Ritual. Eastern Anthropologist 29(1):149–170.

———1992. The "Village Indira": A Brahman Widow and Political Action in Rural North India. *In* Balancing Acts: Women and the Process of Social Change. Patricia Lyons Johnson, ed. Pp. 65–87. Boulder, CO: Westview.

———1994. Struggling with Destiny in Karimpur, 1925–1984. Berkeley: University of California Press.

———1995. No Longer a Wife: Widows in Rural North India. *In* From the Margins of Hindu Marriage: Essays on Gender, Religion, and Culture. Lindsey Harlan and Paul B. Courtright, eds. Pp. 92–118. New York: Oxford University Press.

———2004. Raja Nal and the Goddess: The North Indian Epic Dhola in Performance. Bloomington: Indiana University Press.

————2008. In Search of the Hindu "Peasants'" Subjectivity. India Review 7(4):320–348.

Werbner, Pnina, and Helene Basu 1998 Embodying Charisma: Modernity, Locality, and Performance of Emotion in Sufi Cults. London: Routledge.

Wikan, Unni 1984. Shame and Honor: A Contestable Pair. Man, New Series 19(4):635–652.

Wilce, James M. 1998. Eloquence in Trouble: The Poetics and Politics of Complaint in Rural Bangladesh. New York: Oxford University Press.

Wilce, Jim 2002. Tunes Rising from the Soul and Other Narcissistic Prayers: Contested Realms in Bangladesh. *In* Everyday Life in South Asia. Diane P. Mines and Sarah Lamb, eds. Pp. 289–302. Bloomington: Indiana University Press.

Wulff, Donna M. 2008. "How Can a Wife Screech and Wail?" Respectability and Bengali Women Singers' Lives. *In* Speaking Truth to Power; Religion, Caste, and the Subaltern Question in India. Manu Bhagavan and Anne Feldhaus, eds. Pp. 107–120. New Delhi: Oxford University Press.

Wynne, Maggi 2001. Our Women Are Free: Gender and Ethnicity in the Hindukush. Ann Arbor: University of Michigan Press.

Yudice, George 1991. *Testimonio* and Postmodernism. Latin American Perspectives 18(70):15–31.

INDEX

CPSIA information can be obtained at www.ICGtesting.com
Printed in the USA
BVOW08s0548141215

430202BV00003B/9/P